PRAISE FOR *CHINA R$_x$*

"*China Rx* is a must-read for everyone who takes, makes, regulates, or sells a prescription drug or an over-the-counter medicine. It is a heroic and critical exploration into one of the greatest threats to both our national and health securities. China literally holds the health of much of the world in its business-driven hands. This is scarier than a Stephen King novel."

— Michael T. Osterholm, Regents Professor, University of Minnesota, and author of *Deadliest Enemy: Our War against Killer Germs*

"*China Rx* describes a major threat to the strategic position of the United States in the world, a matter affecting this country's health and its economic and social well-being. This book reveals how the loss of the manufacturing capability and control of the supply of critical medicines, and their component ingredients, endangers the medical future of the American public while also posing a serious threat to our economy as well. The authors prescribe what must be done to remedy this major deficiency in our nation's public health infrastructure."

— Edwin Meese III, seventy-fifth United States attorney general

"*China Rx* exposes the scary truth that a great number of prescription drugs and over-the-counter medicines in the United States have ingredients from China. There should be tougher import standards, a requirement for pharmaceutical companies to label a drug's origins, and a reversal of US dependence on China."

— Jim Guest, former president, Consumer Reports

"Everyone who has ever taken a pill needs to read this book. The American people won't be happy when they find out that many of the medicines they rely on are being made in China where regulations aren't enforced and/or documents are falsified. Homegrown industries where our members work are being decimated in a stealth attack on America's health security. Good family supporting jobs are being sacrificed for greed-driven corporate decisions. We need to bring good-paying jobs back home."

— Leo W. Gerard, international president, United Steelworkers

"Far too many Americans only see national security as a product of having strong armed forces, and while strong armed forces are an important part of a strong national security, it is just one of many components. Another equally important component of national security is the nation's supply chain. If a nation's supply chain of critical equipment is not secure, then one must ask just how secure the nation is. Rosemary Gibson and Janardan Prasad Singh do an outstanding job of guiding the reader through the inherent risk to the United States of becoming dependent on any one country, such as China, as a source for vital medicines, and the risks from weak enforcement of safety standards and quality control by foreign manufacturers."

— Maj. Gen. Larry J. Lust, US Army (ret.)

"*China Rx* is a compelling book that reveals America's troubling dependence on China for essential medicines and the pattern in US-China trade where intellectual property and value-added production are shifted to China to the detriment of US workers, businesses, national security, and the health of our citizens."

—Daniel Slane, commissioner,
US-China Economic and Security Review Commission

"The authors have done a great service by examining America's dependence on China for essential medicines and how it happened. *China Rx* is a wake-up call for the public and policy makers to bring drug manufacturing home, safeguard American jobs, and strengthen national security."

—Scott N. Paul, president, Alliance for American Manufacturing

"The authors tell how the institutions we trust have sold out to China and thrown American patients under the bus! As a quality professional, I am appalled that so many people care more about cost than the quality of our medicines. *China Rx* would make a great suspense thriller movie."

—Martin VanTrieste, former senior vice president for quality, Amgen

"*China Rx* opens our eyes to another key industry whose intellectual property and productive capacity are being transferred to China. The authors make a strong case that manufacturing our own vital medicines is a strategic asset and bringing it home is essential. The reshoring of this industry will bring good jobs home, help rebuild our prosperity, and strengthen our national security."

—Patrick A. Mulloy, former assistant secretary, US Department of Commerce
International Trade Administration

"*China Rx* makes an overwhelming case for the pharmaceutical industry to board the reshoring train. The United States is far too dependent on a country whose short-term interest is to grow rapidly at our expense and whose long-term interest will only be clear when it becomes the world's dominant economic and military power. Industries from apparel to transportation equipment are bringing manufacturing back home, and the pharmaceutical industry needs to do the same."

—Harry C. Moser, founder and president, Reshoring Initiative

CHINA Rx

CHINA R_X

EXPOSING THE RISKS
OF AMERICA'S DEPENDENCE
ON CHINA FOR MEDICINE

ROSEMARY GIBSON AND
JANARDAN PRASAD SINGH

Prometheus Books

59 John Glenn Drive
Amherst, New York 14228

Published 2018 by Prometheus Books

Cover design by Jacqueline Nasso Cooke
Cover image © Arun Benjamin Christensen/Shutterstock
Cover design © Prometheus Books

This book is based on information in the public domain and from expert opinion. The views expressed are the authors' observations. Patients with questions about their medication should talk with their doctor. This book is not intended to provide medical advice.

In an effort to acknowledge trademarked names of products and brands mentioned in this work, we have placed ®, SM, or ™ after the name in the first instance of its use in each chapter. Subsequent mentions of the name within a given chapter appear without the symbol. Any errors or omissions will be corrected in subsequent editions, provided that notification is sent to the publisher.

The internet addresses listed in the text were accurate at the time of publication. The inclusion of a website does not indicate an endorsement by the author(s) or by Prometheus Books, and Prometheus Books does not guarantee the accuracy of the information presented at these sites.

Inquiries should be addressed to
Prometheus Books
59 John Glenn Drive
Amherst, New York 14228
VOICE: 716–691–0133 • FAX: 716–691–0137
WWW.PROMETHEUSBOOKS.COM

22 21 20 19 18   5 4 3 2 1

Library of Congress Cataloging-in-Publication Data

Names: Gibson, Rosemary, 1956- author. | Singh, Janardan Prasad, 1960- author.
Title: China Rx : exposing the risks of America's dependence on China for medicine / Rosemary Gibson, Janardan Prasad Singh.
Other titles: Exposing the risks of America's dependence on China for medicine
Description: Amherst, New York : Prometheus Books, 2018. | Includes index.
Identifiers: LCCN 2017041442 (print) | LCCN 2017042236 (ebook) | ISBN 9781633883826 (ebook) | ISBN 9781633883819 (hardback)
Subjects: | MESH: Drug Industry—ethics | Pharmaceutical Preparations | Drug Contamination | Quality Control | Internationality | United States | China
Classification: LCC HD9665.5 (ebook) | LCC HD9665.5 (print) | NLM QV 736 AA1 | DDC 338.4/76151—dc23
LC record available at https://lccn.loc.gov/2017041442

Printed in the United States of America

To the one who made this book and so much else possible.

CONTENTS

Preface   9

Acknowledgments   13

PART I: THE DIFFERENCE A COUNTRY MAKES

Chapter 1: "They Took My Heart Away"   17

Chapter 2: What's in Your Medicine Cabinet?   27

Chapter 3: Washington Wakes Up   41

PART II: PIVOT EAST: HOW IT HAPPENED

Chapter 4: "These Drugs Can Reach Anyone
Including the President"   53

Chapter 5: The Vitamin C and Penicillin Cartels   69

Chapter 6: The China Trap   83

Chapter 7: The Great American Sellout   101

Chapter 8: Today's Gain, Tomorrow's Pain   117

CONTENTS

PART III: THE HIDDEN COST OF CHEAP DRUGS

Chapter 9: Are Drugs from China Safe?   137

Chapter 10: Made in China, Sue in America? Good Luck   161

Chapter 11: The Perfect Crime   173

Chapter 12: Where Does the Secretary of Defense
         Procure His Medicine?   189

Chapter 13: China Bashing? Take a Look at This   205

PART IV: BRING IT HOME

Chapter 14: A Ten-Step Plan to Bring It Home   221

Appendix: How to Find Out Where Your Medicines Are Made   231

Notes   235

Index   293

PREFACE

If you take a prescription drug, over-the-counter medicine, or vitamin, this book is for you. It reveals a dramatic shift in where the medicines in your kitchen cabinet or desk at work are made. The mainstream media has virtually ignored this shift, and their silence has kept you in the dark.

Antibiotics, chemotherapies, antidepressants, HIV/AIDS drugs, medicines for Alzheimer's and Parkinson's diseases, and birth control pills made in China are now sold in the United States. People taking them don't know it, and neither do the physicians who prescribe them.

China's biggest footprint, though, is making the key ingredients in prescription drugs and over-the-counter products. It is the dominant world supplier of the essential ingredients needed to make thousands of medicines found in American homes and used in hospital intensive care units and operating rooms.

Why is this a problem? Because we trust blindly, unquestioningly, the purity of the medicine we take. We place medicine in our mouths, inject it, or wear patches so it seeps into our bloodstreams. Our medicine becomes a part of us. A poorly made athletic shoe is not a matter of life or death. But a poorly made drug could be the difference between life and death for those who take it. With medicine, there is no room for error. And it better be available when we need it.

Worldwide dependence on a single country for life-saving medicines is breathtaking. "Without question, if China stopped exporting ingredients, within months the world's pharmacies would be pretty empty," says Guy Villax, chief executive officer of Hovione™, a Portuguese pharmaceutical company.[1] Surgeries would be canceled, cancer treatments halted, kidney dialysis rationed. Infections would spread.

China is the dominant global supplier of the essential ingredients to make penicillin. The United States doesn't make penicillin anymore. The last penicillin fermentation plant phased out production in 2004.[2] European and Indian plants have shuttered.[3]

When it comes to treating anthrax, "China is the largest exporter, head and shoulders above everybody else," of the building block to make ciprofloxacin, an anthrax antidote, says Bharat Mehta, cofounder of PharmaCompass.com, the largest open-access global pharmaceutical database.[4]

Medicines manufactured in Canada, Europe, India, and other countries are made with active ingredients from China, and the finished drugs make their way to the United States and elsewhere.[5]

If a global shortage occurs, countries will queue up and compete for available supplies. Countries without strong safety rules are more at risk of buying contaminated and ineffective medicines.

For an idea of how China might leverage our dependence, consider what happened in 2010 when China, the dominant global producer of rare earth metals, allegedly halted shipments to Japan. Toyota®, one of Japan's biggest carmakers, depends on rare earth metals to make its popular hybrid cars. China reportedly didn't end the embargo until Japan released the captain of a Chinese fishing boat that had collided with Japanese coast guard vessels in the East China Sea.[6]

The world can do without hybrid cars for a while, but in a public health emergency there is no time to wait for medicines.

Despite the national security risk our dependence on China represents, US pharmaceutical companies have advocated for making it easier for the Department of Veterans Affairs to buy drugs made in China. Even now, if an altercation in the South China Sea causes Americans to be wounded, military doctors may have to rely on medicines with essential ingredients made by the adversary.

China Rx is the story of America's reliance on China for essential drugs, how the country became dependent, the risks of dependence, and solutions to ensure self-sufficiency. We were inspired to write *China Rx* while in a Starbucks™ two blocks from the White House, reading an online story in an Indian newspaper about India's dependence on China for essential ingredients in antibiotics. India's national security advisor warned of the risk of a severe shortage if any tension arises between the two countries.

As we talked about whether America might also be dependent upon China, we saw a man sitting next to us popping a pill while sipping his coffee. We had seen him there before and knew he worked in the White House. We leaned over and asked him what he was taking. "An antibiotic for strep throat," he replied. "What would you think if that pill was made in China?" we asked. He shook his head in disbelief, mumbling, "Is it safe?" We wanted to find the answer.

We wrote this book because everyone affected by outsourcing decisions should be able to find out where his or her medicines come from, and if they are made to the highest standards.

This book scratches the surface of a multibillion-dollar marketplace remarkable for its lack of transparency. We were able to piece together information from federal government documents, industry press releases, media reports, and scientific articles. Many people we interviewed are employed in the industry or government, and others are retired. Some understandably wish to remain anonymous, so we use pseudonyms for them.

We wrote *China Rx* in the public interest, not for any special interest. It tells a human story of the impact of globalization and de facto deregulation of the safety and security of America's medicines. We hope the book, with its landmark investigative research, increases public awareness about where America's medicines come from and the risks.

China Rx raises more questions than it answers. We invite policy makers, public interest organizations, and journalists to build on this foundation and delve deeper into the vast array of topics that we have only touched upon.

PREFACE

When we mentioned to colleagues and friends that we were writing this book, one of the most frequent questions we heard was, "Why are we buying drugs from China? Can't we make them here?" Others responded with resignation, saying, "Well, everything else comes from there."

Many companies say they are trying to reduce their exposure to foreign sourcing but can't find products made in the United States.[7] We have been heartened by a small number of industry players who want to ensure the country has a basic level of manufacturing capacity to make essential medicines. Jobs will return, communities will be revitalized, doctors and the public will have greater confidence in medicines, and the nation's security will be strengthened.

We hope *China Rx* stimulates public policies and private initiatives to achieve these noble aims. It won't be easy, but with a spirit of optimism and determination, what seems impossible is possible. And it's the right thing to do.

Rosemary Gibson
Janardan Prasad Singh

ACKNOWLEDGMENTS

This book would not have been possible without Susan White, an editor of three Pulitzer Prize–winning stories who inspired us in more ways than we can say. Her keen journalistic eye for a good story and commitment to informing the public about critical issues of our time have been priceless. Together with Bob Laurence, Susan provided abundant enthusiasm and gracious hospitality that we will remember fondly for many years to come.

We are grateful to Charlisa Allen, MD, a courageous and remarkable woman, who allowed us to tell the human story of the hidden impact of globalization and deregulation on America's medicines. Kevin McNeil helped us wade through a nontransparent industry to tell a truth waiting to be told.

David Kessler, MD; Michael Wessel; Brigadier General John Adams; Scott Boos; Stephen Smith, MD; and Lucinda Maine, PhD, RPh, introduced us to leaders in the government and industry who shared their decades-long knowledge and experience with us. We are humbled by the professionalism and dedication of those who go to work every day to ensure people in the United States and around the world have medicines that are safe, every pill, every person, every day.

Roger Leonard, MD, carefully reviewed sections with medical terms and the uses of prescription drugs. Larry Jassie, MD, patiently read multiple drafts, as did Kevin Kavanagh, MD; Nisha Singh; Sarveshwari Singh; and Shriansh Singh.

We are indebted to Sandy Dijkstra and Elise Capron for believing in this book and finding the perfect home for it. They wisely encouraged us to put a human face on the risks of offshoring America's medicine making. We have no words to express our unerring gratitude to them.

ACKNOWLEDGMENTS

Steven L. Mitchell, editor in chief at Prometheus Books, grasped the significance and timeliness of the book, and we are immensely grateful to him. Jeffrey Curry and Hanna Etu perfected the manuscript with expert editing. Jake Bonar's creative ideas shined a publicity spotlight on *China Rx*. We are grateful to the entire Prometheus team for bringing the book to fruition.

PART I
THE DIFFERENCE A COUNTRY MAKES

CHAPTER 1

"THEY TOOK MY HEART AWAY"

After the Sonoran desert sun had set, Bob Allen, MD, walked into the emergency department at the Mayo Clinic Hospital™ in Phoenix, Arizona. It was Saturday, December 1, 2007.[1] Within twenty-four hours, the healthy forty-five-year-old Johns Hopkins–trained physician was facing a medical catastrophe.

It had rained that day, and the day before, nearly two inches total, copious amounts by desert standards. It was enough to quench the parched earth. Afternoon gusty winds accompanied the welcomed moisture plume.

The week before, Bob and his wife, Charlisa, easily conquered the rocky Echo Canyon Trail on Camelback Mountain, whose final quarter mile can be a climb on all fours straight up to the top overlooking Paradise Valley.[2] A silhouette of the granite summit at Pinnacle Peak, fifteen miles north, decorates the horizon.

As a doctor, Bob had the propensity to self-diagnose. He accurately figured out that his belly pain, which triggered the visit to Mayo, was caused by a bleeding peptic ulcer. Charlisa, also a physician, drove Bob to the hospital, joined by their two children, Jennifer, age eleven, and Joshua, age fourteen.

From the emergency department, Bob was admitted to the hospital in stable condition at 2:31 a.m. on December 2, according to the day and time stamped on the admission form, and was expected to be there for one to two days.[3] Doctors planned to scope him, shorthand for an endoscopy, a test that allows them to peer inside the stomach.

That night, Charlisa drove home so Jennifer and Joshua could go to bed, and planned to make the forty-minute return trip to the hospital the next day to bring Bob home.

At Mayo the next morning at 6:00 a.m., a nurse gave Bob his first dose of heparin, a common preventive measure for patients in the hospital to avoid the formation of clots in the blood vessels. Bob was connected to a heart monitor with a strap placed across his chest. The pulsating of his heart was captured by sensors attached to his skin, its movements whisked instantaneously to the monitor and appearing as multicolored squiggly lines on a computer screen. A nurse gave another dose of heparin at approximately 10:15 a.m.[4] At 10:29 a.m., the machine recorded the beginning of a cardiac event.[5] Five minutes later, Bob's heart was racing 152 beats a minute.[6]

At home in Paradise Valley, Charlisa was getting ready to pick him up and bring him home when the phone rang around 11:00 a.m. It was Bob, calmly telling her that he was having a heart attack. The monitor precisely documented its beginning at 10:29 a.m.[7] He told her he felt no pain in his chest or any other telltale signs.

"He was talking to me in a normal voice," Charlisa recalled.[8] That surprised her because many people having a heart attack wouldn't be able to make a phone call and speak so calmly.

Bob told Charlisa he was being moved to the cardiac catheterization lab so doctors could open up blockages in the arteries in his heart, and he wanted Charlisa to come to the hospital and bring the kids. Charlisa and the children got into the car and rushed to the hospital.

In the cath lab, doctors discovered multiple clots blocking the arteries in Bob's heart. They removed them so life-giving blood could flow.[9] He was administered two additional doses of heparin at 11:52 a.m. and 11:53 a.m.[10]

After arriving at the hospital, Charlisa was escorted to the cath lab by a nurse. As the door opened, she saw Bob lying on a gurney and a cardiologist and some nurses were standing nearby. His skin was ashen, and his body was covered with a gown and sheet. A skylight illuminated the unforgettable scene.

Before she could get to his side, she saw Bob grasp the edge of the gurney as he leaned over and vomited blood that splattered all over the floor.[11] "You need to get out of here," he told her, trying to protect her from the frightening turn of events.

Charlisa remembers walking out of the cath lab to where Jennifer and Joshua were waiting. After more hours went by, the cardiologist came to talk with Charlisa and the children.

"This is really unusual," Charlisa remembers the doctor saying.[12] "Your husband is in complete heart failure." As light streamed through the large arched window, giving the room a chapel-like feel, a stunned Charlisa remembers asking, "Are you sure you have the right person?" Bob's heart, kidneys, and other organs had shut down, leaving him and his wife to face a foe that shattered the boundaries of their medical training.

Bob was sedated and unconscious in the intensive care unit (ICU) where a mechanical ventilator breathed for him because his lungs could not. A machine purified his blood because his kidneys could not.

His heart had been irreparably damaged, and doctors said a heart transplant was the only way to save him. On December 6, doctors removed his damaged heart and gave him an artificial heart, a stopgap until a good match with a human donor could be found.[13] "They took my heart away," Bob said to his wife.

"It looked like a washing machine with a laptop sitting on it," Charlisa said of the box that housed a big machine that powered the artificial heart.[14] Bob was tethered to it by a three-foot cord.

On December 8, Charlisa wrote to family and friends about Bob's illness:

> Bob suffered a massive heart attack. His heart continued to deteriorate over the following days until an artificial heart was the only hope of survival. His artificial heart was placed on Thursday, December 6. The road was rocky, he had some bleeding, and had to return to surgery early Friday morning. He is now appearing stable, is off the ventilator, and appears to recognize me. His body will need to become stronger so

he may be listed for a heart transplant. . . . He will remain in the hospital until a heart is available due to his particular mechanical heart. . . . All good thoughts and prayers are so appreciated at this point.[15]

As days turned to weeks, Charlisa went to the hospital every day and returned home at night to be with the kids. Bob's parents stayed overnight with him. "Every night when I left the hospital, I didn't know if I would ever see him alive again," she said of the numbing uncertainty.[16] On December 18, Charlisa put on a brave face when she wrote,

Today was another day with good progress for Bob. . . . We are holding our breath for his kidney function to maintain. He was able to walk around the nurses' station with support today and yesterday. He is able to eat some soft foods now. He still receives tube feeding at night to keep up his nutritional status. His spirits are still good and I have shared all the wonderful cards and letters we have received. Thanks to everyone for all the prayers and support.[17]

CHRISTMAS IN THE ICU

The Allen family spent Christmas in the ICU. No Christmas trees were allowed, so a wooden Santa Claus would have to suffice. Bob could manage a gentle squeeze of a hand, a few words, "yes" or "no," and "I love you." On December 27, Charlisa wrote,

Bob continues on dialysis every day, but the doctor believes he should regain sufficient kidney function over time. . . . He was able to make it three times around the ICU today, and also do some squats and isometric exercises. He is still very motivated in spite of all the problems.[18]

As December turned to January, New Year's Day brought a welcome turning point. Doctors moved Bob out of the ICU to a regular room on four west, a unit in the hospital where others were waiting for a heart transplant. "This was a big step," Charlisa said.[19] She wrote,

> He continues to improve and is doing physical therapy twice a day. He has lost over thirty pounds, so the doctor told him he can eat anything he wants right now to try to gain weight. We are bringing him shakes, pudding, and high calorie snacks. . . . We are very encouraged by his progress.[20]

Conscious and speaking again, Bob shaved every morning, put on a clean shirt, and read the *Wall Street Journal*, yearning for a semblance of normality. Charlisa wrote, "Bob's appetite is finally returning. He ate an extra crispy meal from KFC[™] last night, and chicken and fried okra this evening. Thanks to all for your support."[21]

To withstand a heart and kidney transplant, doctors encouraged Bob to regain his strength. He began to stand up and take small steps. Soon, he was walking on the treadmill, still tethered to the washing machine–looking box. For the first time, the Allen family was optimistic as they waited for news of a good match for a heart and kidney transplant.

If he could just get a heart by Valentine's Day. That was Bob's wish. He called himself the Tin Man, the character in *The Wizard of Oz* who had no heart, when he realized his own heart had been cut from his chest and thrown in the trash with other biological waste. A new heart would make him human again.

EYE OF THE STORM

Fifteen hundred miles away, as winter tornadoes ripped across the Midwest in January 2008, doctors at Children's Hospital in thunderstorm-battered St. Louis were dealing with their own medical mystery.

Two children, hooked to machines that performed the functions their kidneys could not, had been given a dose of the same medicine on a Friday afternoon, and both suffered the same life-threatening reactions: racing hearts, swelling lips and tongues, blood pressure dropping dangerously low.

"What are the chances of that happening?" asked Dr. Alexis Elward, an infectious disease specialist at the hospital, reflecting on the incident nearly a decade later.[22] "This was way out of normal."

The hospital SWAT team sprang into action.[23] No other children in the hospital seemed to be affected, so the team lasered in on the dialysis clinic. They checked everything the children had come into contact with, including all their medicines, the machines purifying their blood, even the plastic tubing inside the machines.[24] They found nothing.

They contacted the city water department to ask if any boil-water alerts had been issued, in case bacteria were lurking in the hospital water supply. The answer was no.

Still without answers, they moved everything in the clinic to another room in the hospital. Children on dialysis typically need treatment three times a week, and the seven children scheduled for the next week had nowhere else to go. All the other clinics in St. Louis were full.

On Monday morning, the first patient of the day suffered the same frightening reactions, and the investigation took on new urgency. The team set up a command center in a conference room on the seventh floor. Tables were jammed with phones and laptops. As many as thirty people worked around the clock, tracking down leads and scribbling them on large sheets of paper plastered on the walls.[25]

Desperate for clues, the SWAT team broadcast an alert on Listservs read by doctors and nurses in children's hospitals around the country. Ten people responded, but none reported similar reactions. On Wednesday, another child had a reaction. Dr. Elward and colleagues reported the event to the US Food and Drug Administration (FDA), which sent a representative to the hospital to obtain samples of the heparin the hospital was using.[26] The Missouri Department of Health and Human Services and the federal Centers for Disease Control and Prevention (CDC) were contacted, too.[27] The CDC posted a message on a national Listserv that reached doctors and nurses in healthcare facilities, asking if they had seen patients with similar reactions. Soon, other dialysis centers and hospitals reported they each had at least one patient with similar reactions.[28]

All the children at Children's Hospital recovered after being injected with epinephrine, commonly known as adrenaline, which rapidly reverses swelling and raises dangerously low blood pressure. But reports coming in from other hospitals revealed some of the adults hadn't been so lucky.

On Friday, seven days after the first cases at St. Louis Children's Hospital, Dr. Elward and her colleagues were sitting in the command center when a call came from the CDC. Federal officials had discovered a pattern in the outbreak. The problem was traced to certain batches of heparin sold by Illinois-based Baxter Healthcare Corporation™.[29]

Heparin, a blood thinner, is used in kidney dialysis, surgery, and critical care to prevent blood clots that can trigger a heart attack or stroke. Twelve million seriously ill people need it every year, and Baxter controlled about 50 percent of the market.[30]

"We wondered what we were going to do if all of it was recalled," Dr. Elward said.[31] "We looked at each other, and the blood drained out of our faces."

Heparin is sold in different concentrations, and the more potent version the dialysis clinic used turned out to be the culprit.[32] Until a new supplier could be found, nurses used a lower concentration and no more children at St. Louis Children's Hospital suffered bad reactions.

On January 17, 2008, Baxter voluntarily recalled nine lots of heparin, each identified by a unique number, a kind of Social Security number assigned to each batch of a drug.[33] The recall was prompted by reports of people who suffered bad reactions in dialysis clinics and operating rooms.[34]

On February 11, the FDA held its first press conference on the toxic drug.[35] By this time, Baxter and the FDA had received reports of 350 injuries and four deaths.[36] With mounting harm, Baxter recalled remaining heparin and stopped making it.[37]

As the list of fatalities grew, Dr. Bob Allen lay in his hospital bed in Arizona where he was still kept alive by machines. While watching the evening news on television with Charlisa beside him, he heard a newscaster report that contaminated heparin had been found and it was being recalled.

"My God, I got a lot of heparin," Bob said, turning to his wife with a horrified look on his face. "Was it contaminated?"[38]

MADE IN CHINA

Along the New Jersey Turnpike at exit four, the trees are dwarfed by the Cherry Hill water tower that rises one hundred feet into the sky. The white behemoth greets motorists with a cheery "Welcome to Cherry Hill" painted on it, punctuated with two red ripe cherries.

In the suburban town of Cherry Hill, New Jersey, about ten miles from Philadelphia, Baxter manufactured the recalled heparin. It had been buying the active ingredient, which gives the drug its therapeutic value, from a Wisconsin company, Scientific Protein Laboratories™ (SPL). SPL produced the active ingredient in the United States until the mid-1990s, when it began buying it from China.[39]

In 2000, SPL built a plant in Changzhou west of Shanghai in a joint venture with a local firm.[40] Four years later, Baxter began buying the active ingredient from SPL's China plant.[41]

FDA officials traveled to China on February 20, 2008, to begin a week-long inspection of Changzhou SPL. The plant was located in a nondescript, two-story gated building with Chinese and American flags flying on poles at the entrance.[42]

Inspectors found conditions that violated US standards for making drugs.[43] As early as August 2006, the company bought raw material harvested from pigs from a supplier that Changzhou SPL itself had deemed unacceptable. The heparin ingredient was made in a dirty tank. The president of the local SPL plant refused to answer FDA inspectors' questions, and they were denied full access to the facility.[44]

Back home, scientists identified the contaminant, oversulfated chondroitin sulfate. In April 2008, the FDA reported that the link between the contaminant and the harmful reactions people experienced had been identified.[45] The scientific findings were published in the *New England Journal of Medicine*.[46]

Heparin making in China begins at slaughterhouses where piles of pig intestines are sold to factories and small workshops. Workers wearing bloodstained aprons and boots scooped pulp-like material from the intestines.[47] After boiling the slurry of entrails in large vats, it is processed into crude heparin. The crude heparin was sold to middlemen who, in turn, sold it to Chinese companies like Changzhou SPL that refined it into the active ingredient. Baxter Healthcare bought the active ingredient from Changzhou SPL and made the final product that was sold to hospitals and dialysis centers.

In 2006, a virulent respiratory-like virus, called blue-ear disease, decimated China's pig population.[48] As the price of pigs skyrocketed, companies scrambled to find a cheaper source of pig intestines. Some began getting them from primitive, unregulated workshops in poor rural areas of China where quality controls were nonexistent.

Enterprising minds figured out a way to make a cheap substitute that mimicked the real product, stretching a limited supply of the authentic product. The cheap knockoff, added somewhere during manufacturing, cost nine dollars a pound while the real product cost nine hundred dollars a pound, signaling the contamination was intentional and economically motivated.[49]

Dr. Janet Woodcock, director of the FDA's Center for Drug Evaluation and Research that oversaw the agency's response to the contamination, said that because the contaminant comprised one-third of some batches of heparin, "it does strain one's credulity to suggest that it might have been done accidentally."[50]

Federal officials determined that contaminated heparin had been shipped to eleven countries: Australia, Canada, China, Denmark, France, Italy, Japan, the Netherlands, New Zealand, Germany, and the United States.[51] The former FDA associate commissioner for policy and planning, William Hubbard, said Germany had several deaths.[52] The total number of people harmed globally has never been publicly reported.

Chinese officials denied that its companies were responsible. "The oversulfated chondroitin can . . . not be a suspected root cause of heparin adverse events as reported in the US media previously," said Jin Shaohong, deputy director general for China's National Institute for the Control of Pharmaceutical and Biological Products, at a news conference at the Chinese embassy in Washington.[53] He placed blame on the US manufacturer and wanted to inspect Baxter's Cherry Hill plant.

At 1:30 a.m. on February 27, the day after FDA officials finished inspecting Changzhou SPL, Charlisa Allen's phone rang.[54] It was Bob calling with good news. A match for a new heart and kidney was found. He told her to come quickly and to bring the kids.

Four hours later, as he was being wheeled into the operating room, he pulled her close and whispered, "One of the doctors told me I got the contaminated heparin. I didn't want you to worry, so I didn't tell you. If I don't make it, go after Baxter."[55]

CHAPTER 2

WHAT'S IN YOUR MEDICINE CABINET?

"It's made in China. I'm not supposed
to be telling you. I could get in trouble."

Sitting at a desktop computer in a small, windowless office in a well-known hospital, a pharmacist we'll call Barbara was on the phone with drug company giant Pfizer™ when a curious thing happened. "Where is the doxycycline made?" she asked, referring to the common antibiotic the hospital buys for conditions ranging from teenage acne to toxic anthrax. "Is it from the United States or coming from another country?"[1]

While on hold, she turned her head away from the receiver and said in a hushed voice, with an air of incredulity, "They were asking me if I was a member of the press. I've never had a drug company ask me that before."

After a minute or two, the call ended. Swiveling around in her chair, she was miffed. "They're not going to tell us." The company rep read from a prepared statement, saying that the company is global, its manufacturing is complex and includes numerous suppliers, and it does not provide information on their manufacturing locations because they are subject to change.

"I think it means they know people will be concerned based on where they may be getting it," she said.

Four months later, we called Pfizer and asked the same question: where is the doxycycline made that it sells? A customer service representative gave us the same answer. "I do not have a specific site for that product. . . . We are a global company so we have sites all over the world, and we source ingredients from all over the world."[2]

It's almost impossible to find out where prescription drugs are made. Millions of people are ingesting drugs made in China and don't know it. Hundreds of thousands of physicians are prescribing them, and they don't know it either. The medicines are packaged to look like an all-American product.

Information about where drugs are made is kept secret behind a Berlin-type wall. We looked for cracks in the wall and found them.

While browsing the internet, we stumbled upon a paper prepared in 2012 by an employee of Thomson Reuters™, a business intelligence company, that listed generic drugs including birth control pills, HIV/AIDS medicine, and medicines for Alzheimer's and Parkinson's diseases made in China and sold in America, and the names of US-based sales partners.[3]

The document shined a rare light on an opaque market, and it is the only publicly available information we could find that named generic drugs made in China and their distributors in the United States. Here are some of the generic drugs on the list:

BIRTH CONTROL PILLS

A birth control pill, Levonest™, is made in China by Novast Laboratories™.[4] It is sold in the United States under the name Northstar Rx™ located in Memphis, Tennessee.[5] Online pharmacy GoodRx® lists this generic drug made by this company for sale at big-box stores and retail pharmacies including Walgreens™, Walmart™, Rite-Aid™, Safeway^{SM}, CVS™, and Target™.[6] We verified the information about the country of origin on DailyMed, an authoritative website maintained by the National Library of Medicine located on the campus of the National Institutes of Health. It is the official source of information printed on the drug packaging. The FDA provides and updates the information, which is supplied by manufacturers.[7]

DailyMed usually has pictures of the drug package, and some images may show the name of the country where the product is made. For Levonest, the photo of the package says the pills are manufactured by Novast Laboratories in Nantong, China, for Northstar Rx in Memphis, Tennessee.[8]

HIV/AIDS

An HIV/AIDS drug, nevirapine, made by Zhejiang Huahai, is marketed by a privately held US firm Breckenridge Pharmaceutical Inc.™ that sells drugs to wholesalers, managed care companies, and retail drugstores.[9] Breckenridge issued a press release in 2012 to announce the marketing and distribution agreement.[10]

Nevirapine was the first generic drug made in China to receive FDA approval.[11] The *Wall Street Journal* predicted correctly that its approval was the likely "starting point of any timeline drawn years from now, when China's finished-generics industry is likely a force to reckon with."[12]

ALZHEIMER'S DISEASE

A drug for Alzheimer's disease, donepezil, the generic for the brand-name drug Aricept®, is made by Zhejiang Huahai Pharmaceuticals.[13] The drug is distributed by Solco™ in Cranbury, New Jersey.[14] Solco is the sales and marketing arm of Prinston Pharmaceutical™, a spin-off from Zhejiang Huahai.[15]

BIPOLAR DISORDER AND SCHIZOPHRENIA

A drug to treat bipolar disorder and schizophrenia, risperidone, the generic for brand-name Risperdal®, is made by Zhejiang Huahai and distributed by Solco.[16]

HIGH BLOOD PRESSURE

A generic, amlodipine besylate, for reducing high blood pressure and relieving chest pain, is made by China Resources Saike Pharmaceutical Company in Beijing for Secan Pharmaceuticals™ in Malvern, Pennsylvania.[17] According to the Secan Pharmaceuticals website, the company name was Beijing Pharma USA but changed its name to Secan Pharmaceuticals in 2007.[18] Thomson Reuters reported it is not uncommon for Chinese companies to use more Western-sounding names when selling generic drugs in the United States.[19]

A high blood pressure medicine, losartan potassium, is made by Zhejiang Huahai and distributed by Rising Pharmaceuticals™.[20]

Company press releases, consumer websites, and DailyMed are other sources of information about drugs made in China and sold in the United States.

CANCER

A drug to treat metastatic colon and rectal cancer, made in China by Jiangsu Hengrui Medicine Company, is marketed by Sagent Pharmaceuticals™, a company located in the Chicago suburbs, according to a press release.[21]

A chemotherapy drug to treat leukemia, lymphoma, and myeloma in children and adults, made in China by Jiangsu Hengrui Medicine Company, is sold in the United States by Swiss drugmaker Sandoz™.[22]

ANTIDEPRESSANTS

Solco is selling the generic for Wellbutrin®, an antidepressant, according to a press release issued by Prinston Pharmaceutical.[23]

EPILEPSY

An epilepsy medicine for seizures, levetiracetam, is made by Zhejiang Huahai Pharmaceuticals for Prinston Pharmaceuticals.[24]

ANTIBIOTICS

Doxycycline is being sold by Solco, according to a press release.[25] An antibiotic cream, clindamycin, is sold by Pfizer's generic subsidiary, Greenstone™. The drug is made in China, according to DailyMed.[26]

This list is hardly exhaustive, and while China makes a small number of generic drugs for sale in the United States, it is ramping up fast to make even more. Solco is one example, with thirty-four generic drugs pending approval from the FDA, according to the company's website.[27]

Eighty-nine percent of prescriptions filled in the United States are generic.[28] Consumers and doctors can choose among different manufacturers of a generic drug. When we searched DailyMed for companies that sell lisinopril for high blood pressure, for example, many options came up.[29]

As revealed in the following chapters, if China accelerates generic drug production and undercuts other sellers on price and drives them out of the market, Americans may eventually be unable to live without generics made in China.

For now, the United States is much more dependent on China for the active ingredients needed to make many generic and brand-name drugs, over-the-counter products, and vitamins.

WHAT'S INSIDE YOUR MEDICINES?

Inside every pill are active and inactive ingredients. The active ingredient creates the therapeutic effect. The inactive ones are dyes, preservatives, flavorings, and binders that form the tablet.

In regular strength Tylenol® tablets, the active ingredient is acetaminophen. Without it, pills would be as effective as a candy pill. The inactive ingredients are magnesium stearate, modified starch, powdered cellulose, pregelatinized starch, and sodium starch glycolate, according to Tylenol .com.[30]

China is the largest global supplier of the active ingredients and chemical building blocks needed to make many prescription drugs, over-the-counter products, and vitamins.[31]

For specific generic and brand-name drugs, it isn't easy to find where the active ingredients, also called bulk pharmaceuticals or bulk drugs, are made. Drugmakers say the information is proprietary and therefore a trade secret. Companies that manufacture them for generic and brand-name companies are typically required to sign nondisclosure agreements that prevent them from giving out the information to those like us who ask about the ingredients.

By scouring the pharmaceutical industry trade press and company press releases, we found drugs, sold by big-name pharma companies, made with active ingredients from China. Here are just a few:

The active ingredient in Imbruvica®, a medicine for treating lymphoma and leukemia marketed by Janssen™, a subsidiary of Johnson & Johnson™, is made in China.[32]

The active ingredient in a breast cancer and lung cancer drug, gemcitabine, sold by Hospira™, is made in China by Jiangsu Hansoh.[33]

The active ingredient in vancomycin, an antibiotic of last resort to treat infections that have become resistant to other antibiotics, sold by Hospira, is made in China by Zhejiang Medicines.[34]

THE BIG SHIFT

In the 1990s, the United States, Europe, and Japan manufactured 90 percent of the global supply of the key ingredients for the world's medicines and vitamins.[35] Now, China is the largest global supplier.

American dependence on China for the active ingredients in many medicines is so significant that a headline in a 2012 pharmaceutical industry newsletter, *FiercePharma*, blared, "Dangers Aside, Drugmakers Can't Live without Chinese Active Ingredients."[36] The accompanying article reported,

> When it comes to Chinese-made active pharmaceutical ingredients, Western drugmakers are between a rock and a hard place.... They know Chinese oversight of ingredient manufacturing is insufficient to snuff out substandard producers but that has not deterred companies from buying them anyway.[37]

Former federal official Ted Kirk acknowledged, "I think there are active ingredients out there that we basically only get from China, which is a little bit scary."[38]

The centralization of the global supply for essential ingredients for drugs in China makes it vulnerable to interruption, whether by mistake or design. If disruptions occur for an essential ingredient made in China, the United States will wait in line along with Europe, India, and other countries to obtain it. If a global public health crisis occurs, China will likely keep its domestically produced medicines at home and stockpile them to secure access for its citizens before seeing to the needs of other nations.

India makes generic drugs for the United States, but it, too, is dependent on China for key ingredients to make drugs such as penicillin, according to a Boston Consulting Group[SM] study.[39] Unlike the mainstream media in the United States, the Indian press doesn't hesitate to report the health and national security risks of dependence on China. A *Financial Express* headline blared, "Indian [active ingredient] Industry Faces Chinese Threat," because of its dependence on China.[40] The *Economic Times* published a story about the risks to national security, and the opening line was, "Imagine a situation where a soldier's medical kit is running out of essential drugs on a battle front."[41] A deterioration in India's relationship with China could trigger China to withhold supplies of vital components in essential medicines.

Indonesia is another country dependent on China, and the soaring prices of materials from there have increased the cost of drugs, the *Jakarta Post* reported.[42] The Indonesian government is having a harder time ensuring medicines are affordable.[43] Pressure from Indonesia's domestic pharmaceutical industry is mounting on the government to subsidize domestic manufacturing.[44]

WHERE DOES YOUR PAIN RELIEVER COME FROM?

Baby boomers may remember their mothers giving them orange-flavored St. Joseph® children's aspirin. Today the company sells low-dose adult aspirin in packaging reminiscent of yesteryear. Its label reads, "America's Aspirin" and "100 Years." It is US-made, according to the company website, but a customer service representative would not confirm that the white powdery key ingredient, acetylsalicylic acid, is made in the United States, saying the information is proprietary.[45]

In the 1980s, four US companies made the active ingredient in aspirin. Monsanto™ was the largest aspirin maker in the world and had a plant in St. Louis, Missouri. The other three companies were Dow Chemical™ in Midland, Michigan; Norwich-Eaton in Norwich, New York; and Sterling Drug in Trenton, New Jersey.[46]

The last aspirin manufacturer in the United States was French company Rhodia™. It bought the Monsanto plant but had to close it in 2002 when Chinese companies sold bulk aspirin in the United States at artificially low prices.[47]

In a last-ditch effort to save the plant, Rhodia brought an anti-dumping case to the US International Trade Commission and won.[48] The agency investigates the impact of dumped and subsidized imports on domestic industries and, in this case, ordered an anti-dumping tax on the Chinese firms. The remedy was too little, too late for Rhodia to keep the doors open.[49]

For another popular painkiller, acetaminophen (also known as paracetamol), China is the dominant global producer of the active ingredient, according to then FDA commissioner Dr. Margaret Hamburg.[50] More than six hundred over-the-counter and prescription medicines contain acetaminophen.[51] Rhodia owned the last acetaminophen factory in Europe, and the company ceased operations there in 2008.[52] *Bloomberg* captured the essence of the story in its headline, "Rhodia Shuts Europe's Last Paracetamol Plant as China Prevails."[53]

China made the 130-year-old chemical element at two-thirds the cost of its competitors. When it undercut Indian producers on price, the Indian government imposed anti-dumping duties on Chinese imports, the *Economic Times* reported.[54]

LABELING: BUILT-IN CONFUSION

Country-of-origin labeling requirements for prescription drugs are so confusing that even veterans in the industry are confused about where their medicines are made.

Two rules apply. According to US customs law, if your drug or its active ingredient was made in another country, customs law applies when it crosses the border into the United States. In that case, it must be labeled with the country of origin. The law defines country of origin as where the active ingredient is made.[55] If a blood pressure pill is made with an active ingredient from China, and the powders are pounded into pills in Ireland, the product must be labeled "Product of China."[56]

The FDA has its own rules that make it easier for companies to hide the country of origin. Once a drug is in the United States, the label has to include the name and place of the business of the manufacturer, packer, or distributor, according to lawyers who advise industry clients.[57] The place of business can be different from the country of origin as defined by the US customs agency. So a company in the United States that distributes a drug made in China can say that the United States is its principal place of business.[58]

"Right now, the labeling is so confusing," said industry veteran Craig Langdale, who has worked for more than thirty years in the industry.[59] "It might say the drug is manufactured for someone by someone else. You don't really know. I [use] Google[™] [to look up] the company . . . on its website to follow a trail, but even then it's not always apparent who made it."

If you pop a prescription drug after breakfast, it might be in one of those amber-colored plastic bottles with a childproof white cap, the ones you have to press down hard on and twist at the same time to open them. The label won't show the name of the company that made the drug, or where it was made, because the colored vials aren't the original bottles from the manufacturer. An industry employee told us that every drug he has ever taken has never had the name of the manufacturer on the label.

Congress had an opportunity to require drug companies to label their products. Senator Sherrod Brown, Democrat from Ohio, introduced a bill to require more transparent country-of-origin labeling on prescription and over-the-counter drug products.[60] The label would have to identify the country of manufacture of each active and inactive ingredient.

The Transparency in Drug Labeling Act was introduced in 2008 but didn't become law.[61] "Drug lobbyists got to the first draft of legislation and killed it, and it never reappeared," an industry insider told us.[62] "They realized what a firestorm it would create. If I'm a pharma company, I'm thinking it isn't good for my business for people to know."

BEYOND THE LABEL

Industry newsletters say 80 percent of the active ingredients in medicines come from China and India.[63] The number obfuscates America's deep dependence on China. Indian companies manufacture many active ingredients but may depend on China for the raw material.

Take the case of the acne and anthrax antidote, doxycycline. Let's say an American or European company makes the active ingredient and the finished drug. Guy Villax, chief executive officer of Hovione™, said, "To make doxycycline, you still have to get the fermentation starting material from China."[64]

Even for brand-name drugs, "[t]he building blocks of several of the new drugs that the FDA approves every year are not made in Western countries," Villax added.[65] "For generics, the dependence on China is even more serious. In terms of security, there's a big issue that nobody is acknowledging."

Another drug, ivermectin, is a highly valued medicine in Africa to treat river blindness, and it is being studied for its effectiveness in treating other neglected tropical diseases, Villax said. "All the production of the key starting material for ivermectin is today exclusively fermented in China. If China stopped exporting the active ingredient, it would take several years before fermentation of this compound could be started in the West," he added.[66]

When we asked what else China has control over, he replied, "More than half of the four thousand or so active ingredients needed to make a pharmacy depend on China."[67]

Dependence poses clear risks. Industry trade newsletter *Fierce-Pharma* reported the closure of a Novartis™ plant in Frankfurt, Germany, that made the chemical building block called 7-ACA, which is needed to make a large group of antibiotics called cephalosporins. They are antidotes for pneumonia, bronchitis, strep throat, staph infections, and other bacterial infections.

Chinese companies reportedly dumped the chemical building block on the global market, and prices collapsed.[68] Competitors were driven out of the market. The closure of the Frankfurt plant increased the risks of global dependence on China for the essential ingredient to make this group of antibiotics.[69]

Some Chinese producers of 7-ACA have had a troubled history, accused of using so-called "gutter oil" instead of more expensive soybean oil to make the chemical building block in the antibiotics.[70] Recycled cooking oil was fetched from restaurants' frying pans, grease traps, and sewage drains, the *South China Morning Post* reported.[71] One hundred tons of it was sold as part of a criminal racket spanning multiple provinces. Unnamed pharmaceutical companies were buying it.[72]

Within a year after Novartis ceased production of the chemical building block in Frankfurt, Luxembourg-based International Chemical Investors Group acquired the plant and maintained production in Europe.[73]

CONSUMERS DON'T TRUST DRUGS MADE IN CHINA

Drug manufacturers have good reason to keep the country of origin for drug ingredients secret. Only 6 percent of Americans are confident that medicines made in China are safe, according to a Hart Research/POS opinion poll conducted for the Pew Charitable Trusts in 2010.[74]

When Charlisa Allen learned that heparin was made with its key ingredient from China, she said, "Why are we making drugs there? Of all things drugs! Things that people need. Heparin is used every day in hospitals. Why in the world would we outsource a drug like that to China? They killed animals by putting melamine in pet food."[75]

Although manufacturers and distributors have managed to keep country of origin secret, they are getting ready for the backlash when customers eventually find out.

An online trade newsletter, *Outsourced Pharma*, said, "Pharmaceutical and biotechnology outsourcing is an unknown quantity to the global health care consumer. This will change and the biopharma industry ought to get in front of it."[76] Industry readers received advice about how to prevent a consumer backlash that included hiring public relations firms to convince Americans that their dependence on Chinese-made drugs isn't such a bad idea and is even beneficial.

The suggested gobbledygook spin for why outsourcing is good for America is "to bolster pipeline success and product supply on behalf of patients and consumers, access the newest science and technologies, reduce product costs, and raise patient safety."[77] Industry readers were encouraged to ensure that thousands of job cuts in the United States should not overtake the storyline to "better ensure a positive reception."[78]

The truth is that America's dependence on a single country for the active ingredients, raw materials, and chemical building blocks for so many essential medicines is a risk of epic proportions.

For now, secrecy swirls around where America's medicines are made. We asked a young customer service representative at a company selling a generic blood pressure medicine, losartan potassium, where the drug is made. She said, "It's made in China." Then, in a hushed voice, she added, "I'm not supposed to be telling you. I could get in trouble."[79]

CHAPTER 3

WASHINGTON WAKES UP

"There was a quantifiable, tangible body count."

An indolent Washington finally woke up after the heparin tragedy for one single reason: "There was a quantifiable, tangible body count," said John Taylor, a former FDA official who served as counselor to the agency's commissioner.[1]

In a packed hearing room on Capitol Hill on April 29, 2008, the chief executives of Baxter™ and Scientific Protein Laboratories™ (SPL) along with FDA officials were called to account for the tragedy.

It was a rare spectacle in Washington. Government agencies don't like to admit they can't solve a problem because it could embarrass their elected bosses in the White House and Congress. FDA officials were remarkably candid but walked a fine line. They couldn't speak ill of an industry that took calculated risks, nor could they be completely candid because the public's confidence in their medicines would be shredded.

The hearings revealed how a hamstrung FDA could not protect the public.

THE FDA DIDN'T KNOW WHO WAS MAKING AMERICA'S MEDICINES OR WHAT THEY WERE MAKING

"We need to get a grip on the basic inventory of firms," the FDA's Dr. Janet Woodcock, director of the Center for Drug Evaluation and Research, acknowledged to Congress. When asked how many manufacturing facilities around the world were making drug products for the United States, she replied, "It is most likely between three thousand and seven thousand, most likely on the lower end."[2]

A decade earlier, foreign companies were required to register with the FDA under a new federal law, the Food and Drug Administration Modernization Act of 1997. Nothing happened. Four years after the law was enacted, then representative John Dingell, a Democrat from Michigan, said at a congressional hearing on drug safety that there was still "no workable system for tracking who sends what and where to this country, and whether their manufacturing practices are acceptable."[3]

THE FDA LACKED THE MONEY TO INSPECT CHINESE PLANTS, OR SO THE FDA SAID

Even if the agency knew the names and addresses of the companies making drugs and ingredients for Americans, it couldn't inspect them. Congress apparently didn't give it the money.

When asked how much it would cost the FDA to inspect every manufacturing facility outside the United States with the same frequency it does domestically, Dr. Woodcock said an additional $335 million a year was needed, a paltry sum for Washington budget deal makers.[4] Woodcock conceded that under conditions at the time, some foreign facilities may never be inspected.

Why do FDA inspections matter? A chemist in the pharmaceutical industry, who hosts a blog for fellow scientists, offered this explanation:

> I don't love the regulations. But why do we do this? We do this for my daughters so when the doctor prescribes a pill, I drive to the pharmacy, give them the prescription, and I open the pill bottle, I don't question whether it was manufactured correctly. It's all done so people have confidence in the medicines we give to those who are sick.[5]

James Campbell, a former pharmaceutical executive, told us a different story about the agency's apparent resource constraints:

> In my experience, the FDA chose not to inspect plants in China. I had numerous conversations with FDA leaders to shift their resources from inspections in Europe to inspections in China. The FDA would say US legislation doesn't require inspections in China. I would respond saying, "So why do you inspect in Europe when you are not required by US law to inspect there? You could protect Americans better by redeploying your inspection resources from Europe to China, where the risk of substandard medicines is greater than in Europe because Chinese regulations and regulatory oversight are not as strong." Each time I would get back the same bureaucratic gobbledygook.[6]

INSPECTIONS OF DRUG PLANTS IN CHINA WERE OPTIONAL, ACCORDING TO FDA POLICY

FDA officials revealed during the hearings that the SPL plant in China had never been inspected because an FDA employee had mistakenly clicked on the wrong company name from a drop-down menu on the computer and inadvertently requested an inspection of a different plant. Both Baxter and SPL knew the FDA hadn't inspected it but sold products made in the plant anyway. Baxter was the only company buying the plant's heparin ingredient.[7]

Representative Bart Stupak, a Michigan Democrat, politely, but pointedly, lectured Baxter's then chief executive officer Robert Parkinson, and then SPL's chief executive officer David Strunce. "You are both companies that have been around for seventy-five years," Stupak said. "You know before you ship a drug or even produce a drug here in the United States, the plant has to be pre-approved by the FDA."[8]

Parkinson said in his testimony that his company received FDA approval to use the China plant as a supplier, and approval was not conditioned on an FDA inspection.[9] Parkinson was right. Inspections of drug-making plants in China were optional, according to FDA policy at the time, even though the agency knew factories located there were often problematic.[10] In another shocking revelation, David Nelson, an investigator for the House Energy and Commerce Committee, told Congress that the FDA official who made the decision to not inspect Changzhou SPL said if "he had the same information today that he had back then, he still wouldn't have sent out inspectors."[11]

BAXTER DIDN'T INSPECT ITS CHINESE SUPPLIER BEFORE BUYING FROM IT

If you have ever bought a house, you probably hired an inspector to make sure there were no hidden problems that cost a lot of money to fix.

Baxter was buying something much more important than a house but relied on inspections of the Chinese plant conducted by another pharmaceutical company, Wyeth™, that owned a subsidiary, ESI Lederle™.[12] In 2002, Baxter purchased ESI Lederle, which had been buying the heparin ingredient from the Chinese plant. In the deal, Baxter acquired the 330,000-square-foot Cherry Hill facility.[13]

The switch to the new supplier should have set off a warning at Baxter, said David Nelson.[14] Its new supplier was located in a country where manufacturers are known to often flout the rules, and where meaningful regulatory oversight didn't exist.

Baxter was not alone in failing to inspect its supplier.

At the time, many companies chose active ingredient suppliers in China without ever visiting the manufacturer and had no idea who was making the products they were buying.[15]

Companies were "misinformed about the identity of the manufacturing site of 39 percent of the drug substances they purchase from China," said Philippe Andre, who audited Chinese manufacturers at the request of European and American pharmaceutical companies.[16] Andre portrayed a dire situation. "Most ingredient plants supplying to patients in Europe are never inspected," he said in a presentation to European firms in 2011.[17] In one of the plants, rusted, multicolored industrial drums were found stacked on top of one another to hide a vast warehouse of substandard or falsely certified active ingredients.[18]

At another plant, Andre's employees had to force their way into a concealed workshop through its window. Elsewhere, a maker of ingredients for the common headache reliever, acetaminophen, refused to allow auditors into the plant.[19]

The manufacturing landscape in China was full of landmines, and some American and European companies walked right into them.

"Production of gigantic volumes of ingredients is taking place in no less than around three thousand manufacturing sites, many operating under very primitive conditions," wrote Dr. Chris Oldenhof in *Chemistry Today* in 2010. At the time Oldenhof was president of the Active Pharmaceutical Ingredients Committee (APIC), a European organization that advocates for high-quality drug ingredients.[20] "These sites are usually neither operating under any good manufacturing standard nor in compliance with any regulatory submissions to health authorities," Oldenhof added. "Therefore, the very important question arises what the final destination is for the massive volumes of illicit active pharmaceutical ingredients [APIs] from those 3,000 sites and where in the world patients are consuming medicines that contain them."

Many Western companies may have been unknowingly buying drug ingredients from shady manufacturers because their true origin was hidden within the Chinese supply networks. "Others may have been aware of things not being okay, but they may have been inclined to ignore this in view of the low prices," Oldenhof said.[21] He suspected that these ingredient manufacturers were also supplying the massive global trade in contaminated and counterfeit medicines, saying, "Indications have become stronger and stronger that these unsafe APIs are not only absorbed by the counterfeit medicines" but are also sold to legal supply chains in Western countries.

Guy Villax of Hovione™ put it more bluntly: "Nobody would imagine that in an industry like pharmaceuticals you have gangsters."[22]

Oldenhof estimated another sixteen hundred sites, licensed by the Chinese counterpart to the FDA, supplied the domestic Chinese market, and one hundred others operated at, or near, Western standards.[23]

WHEN COMPANIES INSPECTED SUPPLIERS, THEY WERE NOT AS RIGOROUS AS FDA INSPECTIONS

Baxter conducted its own inspection of the Chinese plant in September 2007, three months before Dr. Bob Allen walked into the Mayo Clinic Hospital™.[24] Why Baxter suddenly inspected its supplier is not publicly reported.

In a letter to the Chinese supplier, Baxter wrote that the plant complied with the highest manufacturing standards. The letter was sent more than a month after Baxter had recalled the contaminated drug. In an exchange between Representative Stupak and Mr. Parkinson, Stupak asked, "Why did the results of your two audits differ so much?" Parkinson replied, "We had an individual there for a day. . . . There is a correlation in my experience in the industry that the longer auditors, investigators spend in the facility the more things that they will find."[25]

Nelson, the House Energy and Commerce Committee staff investigator, offered his own answer to Representative Stupak's question. "Baxter had one person going there for one day. [The] FDA, which for a plant of this complexity, I'm told, usually takes a couple of weeks if it was here in the United States. It sent two inspectors for five days. If you want to measure how hard people were looking, time alone would suggest what the FDA was looking for and what Baxter was looking for," he said.[26]

Representative Charles Melancon, a Democrat from Louisiana, said during the hearings, "We've been told repeatedly by the drug industry that they police their own facilities in the supply chain."[27] Melancon asked

Nelson, "What kind of grade would you give Baxter in how it policed this facility?" Nelson replied, "Well, Baxter's was an incomplete, bordering on failure," later adding, "corporate due diligence cannot be relied upon."[28]

Baxter's Parkinson acknowledged that his company should have checked the plant before buying any heparin product from it.[29] He said his company tested every lot of it, but the contaminant could not be detected using standard testing procedures.

THE CHINESE FACTORY HAD LOWER STANDARDS THAN THE WISCONSIN PLANT

SPL's plant in Wisconsin was better equipped than the one in China, the chief executive officer David Strunce conceded to members of Congress.[30] A heparin expert was on-site full-time at the Wisconsin plant but not at the China facility.[31] The FDA inspected the Wisconsin plant every twelve to eighteen months and had never inspected the plant in China.

SPL's China plant didn't track and trace its suppliers back to the farms where pigs were raised, the slaughterhouses where the raw material came from, and all the workshops where crude heparin was made. The Wisconsin plant had a thorough tracking system.

"It almost seems like you're treating them differently, and it's the ones where you have the least amount of inspections . . . that have these problems," Representative Stupak said to Strunce during the hearing.[32] "Is that incentive to go develop drugs overseas because you don't have to put up with the FDA hassle and regulations?" Strunce didn't respond.

THE FDA DIDN'T HAVE THE AUTHORITY TO REQUIRE COMPANIES TO TEST HEPARIN FOR THE CONTAMINANT

The FDA developed a test to identify the contaminant in heparin and offered it to companies making the drug.[33] Six companies voluntarily agreed to test for the contaminant. An unknown number of other companies refused, yet they could continue importing the product. Dr. Woodcock told Congress that congressional requirements prevent the FDA from releasing the names of companies that chose not to comply.

When pressed about the safety of heparin entering the United States, FDA officials were quick to assure Congress that it was stopping and testing it at ports of entry. But the agency had only ninety-four port inspectors for more than three hundred ports, and a skeptical Congress questioned whether the FDA was certain it was catching all the heparin coming into the country.[34]

The agency was covering its bases, and the reason became clear when Woodcock interjected in a moment of candor, "I do not want to make patients in the United States feel afraid, all right?"[35] Dr. Woodcock assured Congress and the public that all supplies of the drug had been tested.

THE FDA LACKED THE AUTHORITY TO MANDATE A RECALL OF THE CONTAMINATED HEPARIN OR ANY OTHER UNSAFE DRUG

The FDA had to rely on drug companies to issue so-called voluntary recalls. Baxter voluntarily recalled its heparin. But many hospitals kept recalled heparin on their shelves, and here's why.

When employees from the California Board of Pharmacy, which regulates the distribution of prescription drugs in hospital pharmacies, visited more than five hundred hospitals in the state to make sure the recalled product had been removed, ninety-four still had it on the shelves nearly three months after Baxter's voluntary recall.[36] Pharmacists interpreted the voluntary designation to mean the situation was not urgent, so they kept the contaminated product on the shelves.

THE LIMITS OF FEDERAL OVERSIGHT

Dr. Janet Woodcock acknowledged that the FDA cannot alone ensure the quality and safety of America's medicines. Inspections and testing are necessary but not sufficient. "The FDA must have the tools to hold all of these parties accountable," she said. "We need to be able to find them, know who they are, and have the authority and resources to hold them accountable for quality."[37]

Representative Stupak asked FDA officials to identify the perpetrators. "Do you think the American people don't have a right to know which people produced contaminated heparin for shipment to the United States?" he asked Dr. Woodcock.[38] She replied that Congress limits the information the agency can release to the public. None of the perpetrators have been publicly identified.

Adding to the complexity of ensuring safe medicines has been a clash of culture surrounding drug making. Former FDA associate commissioner William Hubbard told Congress that drugs made overseas were not given the same special importance that the United States has given to drugs made domestically:

> In most countries, pharmaceutical products are subject to normal arbitrage, which means that drugs move about much as do electronics, apparel, auto parts, and thousands of other goods. Drugs are often purchased from suppliers who have little or no oversight by regulatory bodies. Key elements of safe drug production are ignored such as quality testing, expiration dating, and labeling. Producers have relatively easy access to the marketplace.... [T]he regulatory bodies, if they exist at all, are weak and ill-prepared to assure the safe production, distribution, and storage of drugs exported to the United States.[39]

THE BIGGEST RISK OF ALL

At the time of the contamination, China controlled half the world's supply of the active ingredient for heparin. FDA officials admitted during congressional testimony that they didn't ban all Chinese-made heparin because of fear of a shortage.[40] The federal government had the unenviable task of balancing the need to ensure that enough of the blood thinner was available, while preventing lethal copycats from slipping through the safety net and harming the American public.

During congressional hearings, Representative John Dingell, now retired from Congress, pressed the FDA's Dr. Woodcock for assurance that more people wouldn't be killed by contaminated heparin.

"We must also remember that this is an essential drug, and we can't simply stop the heparin supply," Woodcock said.[41] "We have to balance between access to heparin" and ensuring it is not contaminated.

In that brief exchange Woodcock revealed the biggest risk of all. The United States was so dependent on China for an essential medicinal ingredient that it had no choice but to keep buying it.

PART II

PIVOT EAST: HOW IT HAPPENED

CHAPTER 4

"THESE DRUGS CAN REACH ANYONE INCLUDING THE PRESIDENT"

*"[T]hese foreign drugs form a
string of ticking time bombs."*

A deadly blood thinner was a tragedy in the making for about two
decades. A 1996 internal FDA memo revealed the brutal truth.

"We literally have no control over bulk drugs that enter the United
States," it said.[1] It was an early wake-up call about the safety of the active
ingredients, known as bulk drugs, in America's medicines.

"Counterfeit or unapproved bulk drugs can unknowingly be received
by legitimate manufacturers and turned into tablets and capsules and sold
as legitimate drugs," the memo continued. "These drugs can reach anyone
including the President."[2]

More disturbing, though, is that some American companies knew
they were importing bad products. "Some members of the generic
industry and possibly some innovator firms are knowingly receiving
counterfeit and unapproved drugs," the memo continued.

Fred Fricke, a respected, self-effacing, and now retired FDA scientist, performed a valuable public service by writing the memo and calling
out the risks to America's medicines. Dr. David Kessler, FDA commissioner from 1990 to 1997, responded and declared the problem of unsafe
imported drugs a top priority.[3]

Soon after, Dr. Kessler left the agency and the problem did not receive
the same attention, according to Carl Nielsen, retired director of FDA

Import Operations. In testimony to Congress during the heparin hearings, Nielsen said he wasn't surprised that people died from imported heparin.[4]

Long before the 1996 memo was written, US-based companies were buying active ingredients to make America's medicines from unregulated factories in China and elsewhere. Pharmaceutical company executive Craig Langdale remembers when his company bought them from China in the 1980s. He explained to us what he witnessed:

> In the 1980s, the first company I worked for was small, and it bought active ingredients for antibiotics from China. I can remember getting some raw material that was just gray; it was contaminated with something. I was new in the industry, and we tested everything coming in and rejected some things. I never considered [that] those factories hadn't been inspected by the FDA.[5]

Around that time, large brand-name companies dominated drug manufacturing. They made the raw materials and finished tablets in-house, the industrial equivalent of home cooking. The quality of the ingredients and preparation could be tightly controlled.

Langdale remembers working at Upjohn in Kalamazoo, Michigan, in the late 1980s and early 1990s. "It was a close-knit community with a lot of pride in what they did," he said.[6] "All the operators I worked with, their parents and grandparents, worked at the factory. Everything was vertically integrated. They developed the products and raw materials, they manufactured the drugs, and they had their own sales force so everything was done internally."[7]

Why did some US companies import active ingredients from unregulated facilities in China? "Even back then, things were driven by money," Langdale said.[8] Soon, though, the big pharma companies would be driven by money, too.

FDA legal counsel appointed during the Bush administration "greatly, greatly restricted the use of warning letters and presumably, of import alerts," according to congressional investigator David Nelson, referring to actions the FDA takes when it has serious concerns about a product.[9] Import alerts ban designated products from coming into the country.

How many active ingredients bypassed US federal inspection and were used to make prescription drugs that doctors prescribed and patients consumed? The only information we could find is from more open and transparent European industry leaders.

"Large quantities of at least around forty very unsafe active pharmaceutical ingredients have been administered to patients in the EU for years," said Dr. Chris Oldenhof in 2008, when he was president of the European Active Pharmaceutical Ingredients Committee, or APIC, which is part of the European Chemical Industry Council.[10]

That year Dr. Oldenhof reported on the lack of regulatory oversight in Europe and shared an on-the-ground perspective from a French-Chinese trading company. Producers in China may submit false documents and refuse audits conducted by, or for, customers. If an audit or inspection is announced, the facility is in some cases immediately closed down to stop inspectors from entering a substandard manufacturing plant. Often there is no respect for European laws and regulations when these are not enforced by inspections. Competition based mostly on price, often with little regard for patient safety, was gradually destroying the European active ingredient industry.[11]

Thomas Lonngren, leader of the EU counterpart to the FDA, the European Medicines Agency, said at the time, "This is a new scenario for us as regulators on both sides of the Atlantic. Suddenly we discover that we have important manufacturing far away that we don't have any control of."[12]

THE CALL FOR CHEAPER DRUGS DRIVES MANUFACTURING TO CHINA

Generic drugs were made possible by federal law when the Drug Price Competition and Patent Term Restoration Act of 1984, known as the Hatch-Waxman Act, was passed. It had bipartisan support, and President Ronald Reagan was its chief proponent.

Here's how the law works. When a company develops a new drug and is granted a patent, it has an exclusive right to sell it and recoup the cost of discovery, testing it to prove it is safe and effective, and gaining approval from the FDA to sell it. Patent terms are set by federal law and are twenty years from the date when the patent application is filed in the United States.[13]

When the patent expires, other companies can apply to the FDA to make a generic version. With generics, the seller has to demonstrate that its drug is therapeutically equivalent to the brand-name product. As multiple companies sell a generic, competition drives down the cost and millions of people around the world benefit from life-saving, low-cost prescription drugs.

Let's take penicillin as an example. In the 1940s, it was a miracle drug and initially in short supply. Today, an online search to buy generic ampicillin, a penicillin antibiotic for pneumonia and bronchitis, among other ailments, reveals multiple companies including Mylan™, Teva Pharmaceutical Industries™, and Sandoz™ selling it.[14] When we looked for the cost of sixty capsules of ampicillin 500 mg, it was for sale in suburban New York for prices ranging from $12.55 to $17.84 at Walmart™, Costco^{SM}, Duane Reade™, Rite-Aid™, HealthWarehouse.com^{SM}, Stop & Shop™, CVS™, Walgreens™, Target™, and a local independent pharmacy.[15]

Cheaper drugs required a cheaper way to make them. China was a perfect place to buy active ingredients to make America's medicines because of its surfeit of chemists, cheap labor, and virtually nonexistent safety and environmental regulations.

And it was legal. "There was nothing in the regulations that precluded drug companies from manufacturing in a place like China," said Jack Mitchell, former director of the FDA Office of Special Investigations.[16]

WHEN MEDICINES BECOME COMMODITIES

Just as khaki pants sold in Costco and Walmart are commodities, generic drugs and the active ingredients to make them have become commodities.

As with any commodity, suppliers sell a similar product differentiated mainly by price. Price differences of a penny a tablet, or a dollar for a fifty-five-gallon drum of an active ingredient, can determine whether a manufacturer wins or loses a contract.

"If you are a buyer for CVS or Rite-Aid, let's say you can buy sixty pills for $2 from one company and $2.10 from another company," says Joe Graedon, cofounder of the People's Pharmacy®, which helps people make informed decisions about the pros and cons of prescription drugs and over-the-counter medicines.[17] "You'll buy from the company that sells them for $2 and save a dime, but at some point you have to ask how the company makes it for two bucks," he says. "You can't buy anything for that amount. How can you do that without cutting corners?"

Bottom-feeders. They can sell at a lower price and drive out companies that make medicines the right way. Noncompliance with US standards is a deliberate competitive strategy. As long as they aren't caught, they continue to win contracts. Lower prices discourage production in the United States and force worldwide sourcing, thereby risking poorer quality products.

When Europe's last factory that made the painkiller acetaminophen shut its doors because it could not compete with China, its owner sold the business to a French firm, Novacap™. Three years later, the FDA found metal particles in the product made in Novacap's plant in China, a high price to pay to save a few cents a pill.[18]

Unlike a poorly made shirt whose seams begin to fray after a few spins in the washing machine, the consumer can't tell if a pill is well-made by looking at it. Doctors and the public assume the federal government was enforcing drug safety standards for all medicines. But the FDA didn't have the authority to enforce the gold standard of drug manufacturing Americans had come to expect.

It costs more to inspect a manufacturing plant in another country. Travel costs are higher, and translators may need to be hired. The average cost of inspecting a facility in another country is $52,000 compared with $23,000 for an inspection in the United States.[19]

Most members of Congress and their staffs on Capitol Hill didn't know that the nation's medicines were made with products from unregulated factories in China and elsewhere. And yet, the White House and Congress were about to make a landmark decision.

PERMANENT NORMAL TRADE WITH CHINA OPENS THE FLOODGATES TO CHINESE DRUG IMPORTS

In 2000, the final year of President Bill Clinton's second term, after the Monica Lewinsky affair and his impeachment in the House of Representatives and Senate acquittal, the White House went into overdrive to pass legislation to give China permanent normal trade relations.

Congress had voted every year on whether to retain China's normal trade status and always voted to do so. The legislation being considered would make that status permanent and give China all the trade advantages other US trading partners have, including low tariffs on their products sold in the United States.[20]

In an impassioned plea at the Johns Hopkins School of Advanced International Studies that was remarkable for predicting the exact opposite of what actually happened, Clinton said,

> For the first time, our companies will be able to sell and distribute products in China made by workers here in America without being forced to relocate manufacturing to China, sell through the Chinese government, or transfer valuable technology—for the first time. We'll be able to export products without exporting jobs. Meanwhile, we'll get valuable new safeguards against any surges of imports from China.[21]

An overwhelming majority of the American people opposed opening the country to free trade with China.[22] A cross section of conservative Republicans, liberal Democrats, labor groups, consumer organizations, family farmers, and human rights activists believed American companies were merely looking for a cheaper place to manufacture their products for the US market and, in doing so, millions of Americans would lose their jobs.

Then congressman Bernie Sanders voted against the measure that would give up the leverage Congress wielded when it had to vote every year on whether to extend favorable trade status to China.[23] Veterans groups voiced concern that US companies would give away American-made technology.

The eclectic opponents were no match for the multimillion-dollar campaign launched and orchestrated by the China lobby comprised of companies eager to do business in China and their proponent in chief in the White House. The US-China Business Council and the Emergency Committee on American Trade were a tour de force with hundreds of corporate members in the pharmaceutical, auto, oil, insurance, retail, banking, and other industries.[24]

Former secretaries of state Henry Kissinger, Alexander Haig, and Cyrus Vance were among the chieftains of the China lobby. Opinion editorials, press releases, and television interviews featuring foreign policy "experts" saturated the media, failing to disclose the financial bounty some would reap from opening doors in China for US companies. Permanent normal trade relations would move China in the right direction, official US government talking points said.

Free trade proponents say consumers should be free to buy from whomever they choose and on terms they agree to with the seller. They benefit from lower prices by buying products from countries with lower labor costs, and can buy more material things and enjoy a higher standard of living. New jobs are created to replace those lost from imports, so the theory goes.

Behind the scenes, China pressured US companies to lobby on its behalf or face economic retribution.[25] It reportedly kept close tabs on the chief executives who lobbied Capitol Hill. Companies that rebuffed the Chinese government's expectations risked being barred from investing, manufacturing, and selling their products in the country.[26]

Three years after the US-China Trade Relations Act of 2000 was signed into law, the trade deficit with China climbed to a staggering $114 billion for the first eleven months of 2003, a factoid the mainstream media reported.[27] America had no trade deficit with any country for all of its first two hundred years.[28]

China could plan the construction of the biggest cargo ships the world has ever seen to carry the contents of America's hospital pharmacies, home medicine cabinets, and so much more.[29]

"DREAM ON"—AN UNPREPARED FDA

The FDA was unprepared for the flood of Chinese-made drugs and ingredients. "The foreign inspection system was not prepared to handle the challenge of the global market," said Jack Mitchell.[30] "The agency didn't have the resources in its labs or inspection personnel to do as many foreign inspections."

Agency officials had repeatedly sounded the alarm that the nation's drug supply was at risk. In 2001, Bernard Schwetz, then FDA acting principal deputy commissioner, told Congress, "[The] FDA must improve foreign inspection and physical inspection coverage and oversight of foreign producers to be able to maintain the safety of products . . . that we believe Americans expect and demand."[31]

The FDA was telling a different story to consumers. A 2002 article on its website assured the public of the safety of generic drugs. Firms making generic drugs must "undergo FDA inspection of the manufacturing facility to assure compliance," it said.[32] This was an aspiration it could not fulfill.

Former FDA official John Taylor said, "The FDA was doing the best it could, catch-as-catch-can, and it took a while for the regulatory system to catch up to the world."[33]

Drug company executives at home complained to the FDA about the uneven playing field. It was unfair that they were constantly inspected while businesses shifting production abroad to China were hardly ever inspected.

Warnings and complaints fell on deaf ears. Congress was operating in a regulatory world that ceased to exist.

The FDA was created in 1906 with the belief that America's medicines would be made in the United States. It had become expert at inspecting a domestic industry using field staff located in offices around the country. But drug making had changed while the FDA labored under old rules and limited budgets. With only a handful of inspectors checking plants in other countries, it lacked the authority and money to protect the American public.

Frustrated FDA officials told members of Congress that a tragedy was waiting to happen but couldn't get lawmakers' attention. "No one else cared a hell of a lot about it," said a former FDA official who wished to remain anonymous.[34]

Going public in an op-ed in the *Washington Post* in 2006, William Hubbard, former associate commissioner at the FDA, wrote, "Most raw materials for our drugs come from foreign producers that are rarely inspected. The rate of quality-control failures found in manufacturing facilities by FDA inspectors has soared. Think your pacemaker, heart valve . . . or morning vitamin was inspected? Dream on."[35]

Of the 714 plants in China making drug and active ingredients for the United States at the time, the agency inspected only about fifteen a year. At that rate, it would take nearly fifty years for FDA inspectors to visit all of them. Meanwhile, companies in the United States were inspected by the FDA about every two years, a dramatically uneven playing field.[36]

The Chinese plants the FDA did inspect had the highest rates of sanctions imposed from 2002 to 2007 for failing to comply with American standards.[37] In 2007, the first leader of China's national regulatory body, the State Food and Drug Administration, was executed for taking bribes to approve untested and fake medicines sold in China.[38] One of the drugs was blamed for at least ten deaths there.

After the death sentence was carried out, a spokesperson for the agency said with candor, "As a developing country, China's current food and drug safety situation is not very satisfactory because supervision of food and drug safety started late. Its foundation is weak so the supervision of food and drug safety is not easy."[39]

Remarkably, companies in the United States were offshoring the manufacturing of a product that can make the difference between life and death from a nation with the highest standards in the world to a place with basically no standards.

HOW DID THEY GET AWAY WITH IT FOR SO LONG?

How were the essential components of many American medicines allowed to be sold in the United States for more than two decades with little or no FDA oversight?

"Companies were not exactly advertising that they were getting ingredients overseas," said former FDA official John Taylor.[40]

Rather than strengthen oversight of drugs made in China, the FDA budget for 2007 included cuts to nearly all of its inspection programs, including foreign plants making drug products bound for the United States.[41] The amount of public funding Congress gave the agency that year—$2.5 billion—was about the same as the budget of the school district in Montgomery County, Maryland, where the FDA is headquartered.[42] To assure the safety of $1 trillion worth of food, drugs, and other products, the amount was a pittance. Taxpayers paid eight dollars a person a year, the cost of two lattes.

All the while, lawmakers had been piling on more responsibilities. From 1988 to 2007, the FDA had new functions to perform required by 137 specific federal laws, eighteen statutes of general applicability, and fourteen executive orders.[43] The number of federally funded employees in the agency plummeted from 9,167 in 1994 to 7,856 in 2007.[44] As the regulatory apparatus was being decimated, toxic products made in China flowed into the United States.

HERE IT COMES: CONTAMINATED TOOTHPASTE IN US HOSPITALS AND HOTELS

At pennies a tube, the price was right, but the product was not. In 2007, Florida Hospital Waterman in Tavares, Florida, and South Lake Hospital in Clermont, Florida, unknowingly provided Chinese-made toothpaste to patients that contained small amounts of a poisonous antifreeze ingredient, diethylene glycol, the *Orlando Sentinel* reported.[45] It came from giant pharmaceutical distributor McKesson™.[46] The contaminant was a cheap substitute. Former FDA associate commissioner Hubbard told Congress how the scheme worked:

> [P]harmaceutical grade glycerin is fairly pricey, and the antifreeze you can get down at the dollar store. So, you know, it tastes the same, it looks the same. It is just one will kill you, and one is perfectly safe.[47]

When Florida Hospital Waterman pulled the toothpaste from its shelves and replaced it with another brand, that one, too, was contaminated.[48] The number of hospitals that received contaminated toothpaste was not publicly reported. Other hospitals including four in Greenville, South Carolina, bought toothpaste made in China, although it was reportedly not contaminated.[49]

Some hotels unknowingly gave their guests toothpaste containing traces of the poison. Gilchrist & Soames™, an Indianapolis-based provider of toiletry products for hotels, tested the toothpaste and recalled it.[50]

Counterfeit Colgate® toothpaste was found in dollar discount stores in New York, New Jersey, Pennsylvania, and Maryland, according to an FDA alert to the public.[51] Psychiatric hospitals, prisons, and juvenile detention centers unknowingly bought the contaminated stuff. Around the world, mass poisonings occurred in Argentina, Bangladesh, Haiti, India, and Nigeria.[52]

Consumers were told to avoid using toothpaste labeled "Made in China." The agency said it wasn't aware of anyone being poisoned. The agency would only be aware of poisonings if the events were reported to it. But who would think toothpaste was the culprit making them sick?

THE SAME PLAYBOOK: MELAMINE AND A TOXIC BLOOD THINNER

The same year, 2007, dog and cat food products were recalled by the FDA after melamine, an industrial chemical used to make furniture, glue, and plastics, was discovered in an ingredient supplied by a Chinese firm to American companies selling pet food. In a financially motivated scheme, the perpetrators added the cheap chemical to wheat gluten to make it appear as if the pet food had higher protein content than it actually contained.[53]

About 150 brands of dry pet food sold by Costco, Del Monte^{SM}, Iams®, Petco™, PetSmart^{SM}, Procter & Gamble^{SM}, Target, Walmart, and others were affected. More than four thousand dogs and cats died, and up to fifty thousand more were sickened, after eating the contaminated pet food.[54]

The FDA was stonewalled. Senator Dick Durbin, a Democrat from Illinois, and Representative Rosa DeLauro, a Democrat from Connecticut, wrote a letter to the Chinese ambassador to the United States, Zhou Wenzhong, saying,

> The Agency has . . . made multiple requests to the Chinese Government to allow US inspectors to look at the facilities that are suspected to have produced the contaminated product. On April 4, 2007, the FDA sent its first letter to the Chinese Government asking for visas to allow inspectors to look at the facilities that are suspected to have produced the contaminated product. The request was not granted, and on

April 17, 2007, the FDA sent an additional letter emphasizing that it wished to be allowed to send its inspectors to China.[55]

When FDA officials arrived in China, one plant had been bulldozed and another was cordoned off. According to a former high-level government official knowledgeable about the events, the attitude of the Chinese government was that America should have controlled its media and members of Congress.[56] Problem solved.

The poison also entered the human food chain from animal feed given to chickens and hogs. On at least thirty farms in Indiana, chickens were fed with food made with melamine-contaminated wheat gluten from China.[57] By the time federal officials discovered the contamination, all the affected chickens had been sold and presumably consumed. An estimated three million Americans ate chicken that had been fed protein contaminated with it.

Hogs on farms in California, Kansas, New York, North Carolina, South Carolina, and Utah were thought to have been fed the contaminated product.[58] Public health officials said the risk to humans eating the meat was negligible. But if officials had known much earlier that the animals consumed the contaminant, affected hogs and chickens would have been banned from the food supply.

Federal prosecutors indicted two Chinese nationals living in China for sending more than eight hundred tons of the melamine-laced products to America.[59] Because China has no extradition treaty with the United States, federal officials could not arrest them. The chief executive officer of the US company that imported it, also a Chinese national, and its president, who lived in the United States, were indicted and pleaded guilty to two misdemeanors. The punishment? Fines and probation.[60]

The economically motivated contamination continued. In September 2008, the FDA received reports of melamine-contaminated infant formula in China sold by a leading dairy company there. Six babies died from kidney damage, and three hundred thousand other children were sickened. The punishment? The perpetrators were prosecuted in China and sentenced to death or life imprisonment.[61]

Back home, the FDA tested food ingredients from China made with milk and advised pharmaceutical companies to test products similarly derived from milk for possible contamination.[62] The agency didn't have any specific information that drugs were affected, but it listed twenty-seven components such as guar gum and lactose that should be tested. If any contamination was discovered in the drug supply, the information was not publicly reported.

These deadly scandals were not enough to deter companies from off-shoring to China the making of essential ingredients for America's medicines. As the melamine contamination erupted, enterprising minds were secretly plotting a copycat, financially driven plan to contaminate the active ingredient in a drug whose use in hospitals is as common as bandages.

THE FIX BEGINS

The FDA's Hubbard told Congress during a heparin hearing, "[T]hese foreign drugs form a string of ticking time bombs. Heparin's gone off and I think there are going to be more until we fix this problem."[63]

After months of negotiation with the Chinese government, US Secretary of Health and Human Services Michael Leavitt announced in Beijing on November 19, 2008, the opening of the first FDA office outside the United States. "We're opening up a new era, not just new offices," he said.[64] Later that month, two more offices were opened in Shanghai and Guangzhou.

Proximity to manufacturing plants in China would make it easier to track down rogue operators. For instance, when agency inspectors went to Shanghai No. 1 Biochemical & Pharmaceutical Company, which sold heparin for use in the United States, the facility apparently never made any heparin and was a so-called "show" factory.[65]

The company obtained the product from a "shadow" factory but placed its own name on aluminum drums shipped to the United States. It had been selling the product for several years with fake information about who made it and where it was made. The FDA wrote a letter to the company saying, in part,

> [The] FDA conducted the inspection of August 2008 to inspect your facility and review records relating to your ongoing manufacturing and testing operations.... There was no information at your site to show that you had ever produced any of this material shipped from your facility to the US.... Your firm used two other manufacturers to produce heparin sodium, failed to notify [the] FDA of this manufacturing arrangement, and affirmatively represented that no contract firms are involved in the manufacturing.[66]

Inspections were having an impact. In September 2009, the FDA placed nine Chinese companies and their drug products on import alert, which allowed FDA inspectors at ports of entry in the United States to stop these products from entering the country.[67]

By 2010, forty-six manufacturing plants in China were inspected, and the number climbed to eighty-eight the following year.[68]

A new law, the Food and Drug Administration Safety and Innovation Act (FDASIA) of 2012, gave the FDA needed authority and money. All drug product manufacturers around the world are required to register with the FDA every year, so federal officials know who is making America's medicines and what they are making.[69]

Companies pay an annual fee to cover the cost of inspections. All manufacturers, wherever they are located, are to be inspected as often as US-based companies.[70]

If a company refuses or interferes with an inspection, all of its products can be banned from the United States, confiscated, and destroyed.[71] Previously, products had to be returned to the manufacturer, and they might have shown up at another port, a strategy called port shopping where the sender bets that harried inspectors will overlook it.

"The FDA's new authority could help prevent the paramecium effect," said John DiLoreto, executive director of the Bulk Pharmaceuticals Task Force, referring to the movement of the single-cell organism that hits the wall, steps back, and goes elsewhere.[72] The task force is an industry trade group of US manufacturers of active ingredients, chemical building blocks to make them, and inactive ingredients, and it advocated for more inspections in China to level the playing field with US-based companies that were inspected about every two years.

Dr. Christopher Hickey, the FDA's first country director in the agency's office in China, said in 2014, "The majority of the drug inspections [the] FDA conducts in China focus on manufacturers of active pharmaceutical ingredients intended for use in generic drugs, and on sites that produce over-the-counter drugs."[73]

This was progress. But it was too late for people who received a lethal blood thinner and never knew what hit them.

CHAPTER 5

THE VITAMIN C AND PENICILLIN CARTELS

The Chinese government used US courts to upend market principles and permit Chinese cartels to control the supply and price of products they sell to Americans including medicine.

If you take a vitamin C pill with your morning coffee before dashing out the door to go to work, the vitamin's essence, ascorbic acid, probably came from China. Even if you don't take a pill, you're probably getting Chinese-made vitamin C in your breakfast cereal, soft drinks, or hamburger buns.

Most vitamin C comes from chemical factories, not from fresh-squeezed oranges handpicked in a sunny Florida grove. China controls more than 60 percent of the world market.[1] The only US-based maker of ascorbic acid we could find is in Belvidere, New Jersey, and is owned by Dutch company Royal DSM™.[2] The company's website says it is the only remaining Western manufacturer.[3]

We contacted grocery chain Trader Joe's™ to find out where the vitamin C it sells comes from, and a customer service representative said in an email that it is tested, processed, and packaged in the United States, but the ascorbic acid is from China.[4]

Whole Foods® told us that its 365™ brand of vitamin C contains ascorbic acid purchased like any other commodity on the global market and probably comes from China.[5] A customer service representative from Nature Made®, a brand sold in retail drugstores and grocery stores, said it also uses China-made ascorbic acid.[6]

Why tell the vitamin C story? It offers rare insight into the methods the Chinese government uses to control and manipulate the supply and price of a key ingredient in a product consumed by millions of Americans every day. If it can happen to vitamin C, is it happening to prescription drugs and their key ingredients?

HOW CHINA RAISED THE PRICE OF YOUR VITAMIN C

In the early 1990s, most ascorbic acid was made by European companies including F. Hoffmann–La Roche™, Merck™, and BASF AG™, and by a Japanese company, Takeda™. In the mid-1990s, Chinese companies entered the market, and soon more than twenty were making ascorbic acid.[7] By 2001, four major Chinese firms remained and they slashed prices by nearly half, but not for long.[8]

Unable to compete with the low prices, Western companies' share of the global market shrank to about 40 percent. The Chinese firms took advantage of their dominant market position by raising the price as much as 600 percent.[9] Food and beverage makers, vitamin companies, and pharmaceutical firms in the United States paid higher prices for products found in nearly every American home.

Two American companies, the Ranis Company™, a New Jersey vitamin distributor, and Animal Science Products™, a Texas livestock feed firm, alleged that the Chinese firms had formed an illegal cartel that colluded to restrict production and exports of vitamin C to the United States, creating a shortage and increasing prices.[10] They filed a class action lawsuit claiming violations of antitrust law in federal district court in Brooklyn, New York, in January 2005.[11]

Overwhelming evidence of collusion was presented at trial. Beginning in 2001, the companies agreed to create a shortage in the United States and elsewhere, and increase prices.[12] The Chinese companies were members of a trade association that organized meetings where the firms agreed to restrict production and set a minimum price, according to minutes from meetings that were submitted as evidence by lawyers for the American companies.

The cartel was working. The price of ascorbic acid nearly tripled in a year from December 2001 to December 2002.[13] Months later, demand for vitamin C, and its key ingredient, ascorbic acid, suddenly skyrocketed because of supply restrictions and the SARS (severe acute respiratory syndrome) epidemic that quickly spread around the world.

The companies admitted to price-fixing and acting under the direction of the Chinese government.[14] The Chinese Ministry of Commerce filed a brief with the court on behalf of the companies, and a ministry official testified on behalf of the companies, marking the first time a Chinese government official appeared before a US court.

After an eight-year legal battle, a New York jury found the companies guilty of conspiring to fix prices of ascorbic acid. North China Pharmaceutical Group Corporation (NCPC) and Hebei Welcome Pharmaceutical Company were ordered to pay $162 million in damages to the US firms.[15]

Collusion and price-fixing in the vitamin market are not new. In the 1990s, vitamin manufacturers in Europe and Japan created a global cartel that regularly exchanged price and sales data. In an antitrust case brought by the US Department of Justice, Swiss pharma giant F. Hoffmann–La Roche paid a record $500 million criminal fine for leading a conspiracy to raise and fix prices and allocate market shares for vitamin C and other vitamins sold in the United States.[16] The company's former director of global marketing for the vitamins division was sentenced to four months in prison.[17]

In the vitamin C case involving China, however, American companies and consumers received no help from the Justice Department. It did not file an antitrust complaint, nor did it prosecute any executives as it did in the 1990s. Cocounsel for the plaintiffs, William Isaacson, told Reuters that he was "bewildered" that the Department of Justice did not contact him about the case.[18] "I've never understood why they don't want to find out what's been happening," he said.[19]

When the American companies filed their antitrust case in federal court, they took on the power and resources of the Chinese government. North China Pharmaceutical Group Corporation is owned by the government.[20] It has investments in North China Pharmaceutical, Ltd., which is, in turn, a majority shareholder of Hebei Welcome Pharmaceutical Company.[21]

The Chinese government used its power and resources to hire American law firms to achieve its strategic industrial aims, not just win a case for a handful of domestic businesses.

The Chinese firms appealed the decision.

They argued that they were penalized by the lower court for complying with their nation's laws that require them to set prices and production targets. The US court "attacked the credibility of the Chinese government," they alleged, and interfered with China's sovereignty.[22] The jury's decision was "a massive extension of US federal judicial power into the affairs of a sovereign nation and matters of foreign affairs," according to their brief filed with the court.[23]

The Chinese Ministry of Commerce filed its own brief in support of the Chinese firms, claiming that because "Chinese law required them to coordinate in setting minimum export prices and maximum export quantities of vitamin C," the companies are immune from US antitrust liability.[24]

The Chinese government sent a diplomatic note to the State Department urging the US government to file a brief in the court of appeals and support China's view that the lower court's decision should be overturned.[25]

SAY GOOD-BYE TO AMERICA'S FREE MARKET

In September 2016, the US Court of Appeals vacated the lower court's judgment that the Chinese companies violated US antitrust law.[26]

The court ruled that the Chinese firms "were required by Chinese law to set prices and reduce quantities of vitamin C sold abroad and doing so posed a true conflict between China's regulatory scheme and US anti-trust laws."[27]

Given this conflict, the court concluded that China's "interests outweigh whatever antitrust enforcement interests the United States may have in this case as a matter of law."[28] The court said its decision was based on international comity, a principle of maintaining amicable working relationships between countries, a form of good neighborliness.

The court said it abstained from adjudicating the merits of the US companies' claims and noted the executive branch is the best venue for handling foreign policy and bilateral negotiations.

The vitamin C case illustrates how the Chinese government used US courts to upend market principles and permit Chinese cartels to control the supply and price of products they sell to Americans, including medicines.

Free trade acolytes, who ardently supported giving China unfettered access to the US market, are nowhere to be found when defense of the country's market-based economy is needed. The silence is deafening.

In an inescapable irony, as the Chinese government claimed its domestic companies are required to fix prices and control exports to the United States, it was reportedly investigating US-based and other drug companies for antitrust violations in the sale of drugs in China. According to *China Daily*, in May 2016 the government's price regulator, the National Development and Reform Commission, summoned Pfizer™ and unnamed other companies to hand over information to determine whether they violated competition regulations.[29]

THE PENICILLIN CARTEL

Using a playbook similar to the vitamin C cartel, a handful of companies in China became the dominant global producers of the essential chemical building blocks to make penicillin.

The story begins in the 1940s when the United States, and the world, entered the penicillin era. The first person to be successfully treated with penicillin was a thirty-three-year-old woman who suffered a miscarriage and was dying of sepsis, a severe complication from an infection, at Yale–New Haven Hospital in Connecticut.[30]

After obtaining a small vial of the medicine from pharmaceutical firm Merck & Company in Rahway, New Jersey, her doctor, Dr. Charles M. Grossman, administered the first dose on March 12, 1942.[31] After a weekend of treatment, she arose from near death, ate a hearty breakfast on Monday morning, and lived until age ninety, dying of unrelated causes.

One-half of the total supply of penicillin in the United States was used for this patient.[32] In a triumph of science, industry, and medicine, penicillin was mass produced in time for the D-day landing on Normandy Beach in France in 1944. Pfizer supplied 90 percent of the penicillin that went ashore with Allied forces that day.[33] Untold numbers of American soldiers survived the ravages of infected wounds as a result of being administered penicillin.

Fast-forward thirty years to the scenic seaside town Groton, Connecticut, situated on the Thames River and overlooking Long Island Sound. Dr. Lucinda Maine, chief executive of the American Association of Colleges of Pharmacy, remembers waking up to smells wafting from Pfizer's penicillin fermentation plant on Eastern Point Road a mile away.

"Some days it smelled like peanut butter," she says.[34] "We lived in a house at the corner of Tyler and Shore Avenues, and my sister and I slept in the garret. When the breeze was blowing offshore toward the Sound, we could smell the antibiotics being made."

John Scott, the owner of Bailey Insurance Agency in town, remembers going to Eastern Point Beach in the summer for swimming lessons when he was growing up. "The place used to have a funk to it as you drove by, and we used to joke that we should inhale so we might feel better," he says.[35]

In 1990, Pfizer's Groton plant was making enough penicillin to supply one-third of America's needs.[36] By 2008, Pfizer had shuttered all of its drug manufacturing there.[37] Now, pharmacists fill prescriptions for penicillin with essential ingredients made in China.

The Chinese government began to invest in penicillin ingredient production in the 1980s. By 2001, companies in China had built massive production capability on a scale unanticipated in the United States and Europe.

When you put a round, white pill in your mouth to beat a bout of strep throat, it can be hard to imagine that such antibiotic making is messy business. "It's dirty industrial work, and historically it has gravitated to countries with less regulation," said former government official Ted Kirk.[38] "A lot of manufacturing is in China for environmental reasons," he said because of its weak rules that tolerate massive amounts of air and water pollution.

Using a familiar playbook, Chinese companies dumped penicillin ingredients on the global market at very low prices from 2004 to 2006, according to the European Fine Chemicals Group, the industry trade association for drug ingredient makers in Europe.[39] Western manufacturers couldn't compete and were forced out of business. The trade group called the loss of business a "landslide."[40] When Chinese companies attained a dominant share of the global market, a spectacular price increase followed in 2007.[41]

When European firms tried to sell their penicillin ingredients in China, the Chinese government imposed high trade barriers, charged astronomical fees for product testing, and held foreign firms to a higher standard than domestic ones.[42] According to an analysis by European producers, China's strategy was to increase the cost for foreign competitors to sell in the Chinese market, and push "foreign competitors out of the Chinese and global markets by selling below manufacturing cost for years at a stretch with help from the government."[43]

The impact of China's penicillin cartel reverberated across the Atlantic. In 2004, Bristol-Myers Squibb™ announced it was closing its factory in East Syracuse, New York, the last plant in the United States to make the raw material for penicillin and other antibiotics.[44]

China undercut India's manufacturers on price, causing its plants that make penicillin raw material to shutter.[45] Now, Indian pharmaceutical companies are acutely dependent on China for the chemical building blocks to make penicillin.[46]

SUNDAY MORNING BACON AND THE CHINESE HEPARIN OLIGOPOLY

If you look forward to sizzling bacon on Sunday mornings, or a baked ham on New Year's Day, it probably came from the world's largest pork producer, Smithfield Foods™. The Virginia company is known for its ham, sausage, and bacon sold under Armour®, Eckrich®, and Gwaltney® labels.[47]

"We're the largest bacon processor in the country," said Smithfield's then chief executive officer Larry Pope in a 2010 interview with the *Virginian-Pilot* newspaper.[48] "We are the largest ham company in the country," he added. And if you relish a sausage and an egg biscuit from McDonald's™, you're eating sausage from Smithfield. Said Pope, "I just had a sausage and egg biscuit from McDonald's. That was our sausage and egg biscuit."[49]

Today, bacon, ham, and sausage sold in the United States may come from a company that is a surrogate of the Chinese Communist Party. Here's how it happened.

In 2013, a Chinese company struck a goldmine in the controversial purchase of the venerable American firm. China's largest meat-processing business, Shuanghui International, bought Smithfield. The sale of Smithfield was the largest acquisition of an American firm by a Chinese company. Goldman Sachs^{SM} owns a 5 percent share of Shuanghui.[50]

Daniel Slane, a member of the US-China Economic and Security Review Commission, said at a January 2017 commission hearing,

Shuanghui appears to be a private company but the senior manage-ment is appointed by the Chinese Community Party. When Shuan-ghui approached Smithfield, it took the Bank of China twenty-four hours to approve a $4 billion loan. The Bank of China is not really a bank, but an arm of the Chinese treasury.[51]

At the time of the sale, Smithfield was the source of the raw material to make 25 percent of the heparin used in the United States, according to a government official who spoke on condition of anonymity.[52] The Smithfield purchase increased US dependence on China for heparin. It takes one pig to make one vial of heparin, a former FDA official told us.

Before the sale, Republican members of the House Committee on Energy and Commerce wrote a letter to Smithfield's CEO Larry Pope and asked for information about the company's heparin opera-tions, including any Chinese customers.[53] They were concerned that the Chinese owner would export the raw material from Smithfield's pigs to China and increase the risk of a heparin shortage in the United States. The lawmakers wrote,

> It is our understanding that Smithfield Foods, in addition to being the largest producer of pork in the United States, is also a major supplier of crude heparin used in the manufacturing of heparin in the United States. We are concerned over how the Shuanghui acquisition would impact Smithfield Foods heparin operations. The Committee's investi-gation indicates that the US heparin supply is stressed, and could well be in shortage. . . . Smithfield Foods under Shuanghui control may be pressured to export its crude heparin product to China instead of sup-plying US companies.[54]

The committee asked Smithfield to provide details of its heparin oper-ations, including the size of its production and a list of heparin customers, including any Chinese customers. They also asked for the names of the key executives at Smithfield Foods involved in processing pig intestines and crude heparin, and details of key managers at any Smithfield facility involved in manufacturing crude heparin. We contacted the Committee on Energy and Commerce to obtain a copy of Smithfield's response to the letter but were told that the information is not disclosed to the public.

Now that Smithfield is a wholly owned subsidiary of a Chinese company, Congress has no leverage to question where a product from America's heartland ends up.

America is dependent on China for one-half the heparin it uses, according to the FDA's Dr. Janet Woodcock in 2014, and the agency is concerned about a shortage of the blood thinner.[55] Four Chinese companies control 70 percent of China's global exports of heparin.[56] These conditions create the potential for economically motivated adulteration, says the FDA.[57]

DID THE HEPARIN TRAGEDY MAKE A CHINESE COMPANY VERY RICH?

Following the discovery in 2008 of the deadly heparin contamination with a fake knockoff, the genuine product became highly profitable. Within three years, the price quadrupled from about $3,000 a kilogram to nearly $12,000.[58]

A Chinese company, Shenzhen Hepalink, whose manufacturing facilities met FDA standards and were not implicated in the contamination, reportedly benefitted financially. Two years after the contamination was discovered, Hepalink's founders were reported to be the richest people in China after an initial public offering on the Shenzhen stock exchange. Their stake was valued at about $7.3 billion. Goldman Sachs reaped a $1 billion return that year on a $4.9 million investment it made in the company in 2007, the same year that reports of contamination surfaced.[59]

Hepalink expanded its control over global production in 2013 when it bought Scientific Protein Laboratories™, the Wisconsin company whose plant in China supplied the contaminated active ingredient to

Baxter™. Shenzhen Hepalink now owns plants in Waunakee, Wisconsin, and Sioux City, Iowa.[60]

CHINESE CARTELS AND DRUG SHORTAGES: IS THERE A LINK?

Before 2000, drug shortages in the United States were rare. Beginning that year, unprecedented shortages of essential drugs started to appear. Within a decade, more than two hundred drugs were simultaneously scarce, including antibiotics, chemotherapy for cancer treatment, and anesthesia for surgery.[61] Shortages of antibiotics and the loss of US self-sufficiency would probably shock the pioneers who propelled the nation, and the world, into the antibiotic era.

The FDA diligently tracks all shortages and provides general explanations ranging from a shortage of raw materials, quality problems at a plant, or equipment breakdowns. But it doesn't tell the names of the manufacturers with problems and the precise reasons, making it impossible for doctors and the public to know why they can't get the drugs they need or why the price suddenly goes up.

One of the reasons active ingredient shortages occur is because manufacturing becomes unprofitable as procurement departments squeeze manufacturers. Meanwhile, regulators are enforcing high-quality standards. Bharat Mehta at PharmaCompass says,

> Purchasing managers are constantly being evaluated based on cost savings rather than supply chain sustainability. You have to cut corners somewhere. When really low prices prevail, manufacturers aren't making enough money to invest in improving their manufacturing facilities. If they aren't reinvesting, quality standards will not improve. Without high-quality manufacturing, you are creating conditions for drug supply shortages. The shortages promote opportunism and crazy price hikes rather than sustainable delivery of medicine. This is a big issue, but unfortunately no one cares about pharmaceutical manufac-

turing. The pharmaceutical industry needs long-term thinking, but the capitalist model isn't designed to do that. It's a recipe for disaster.[62]

A Chinese government edict to shut down polluting antibiotic manufacturing plants triggered a tripling of the price of key ingredients needed to make some antibiotics in 2010, Thomson Reuters™ reported.[63]

The following year, the Chinese government forced penicillin ingredient producer Harbin Pharmaceutical Group to cut back manufacturing because its factory was a top polluter.[64] The company website says it is one of the biggest producers of penicillin and other antibiotics in China.[65]

Three months later, in September 2011, the Australian Broadcasting Corporation (ABC) reported a global shortage and rationing of penicillin in Australia.[66] The cause of the shortage was not stated. A physician interviewed for the story speculated that a supplier problem was the cause, but this was not confirmed.

NOT ALL DRUG CARTELS ARE TREATED EQUALLY

A colleague who lives in New England, Helen Hollingsworth, sent us an email about how her husband had difficulty finding the antibiotic doxycycline in 2013 that was prescribed for Lyme disease:

> We've been paying $20 for 120 tablets of doxycycline at Walmart[™]'s pharmacy. I went to refill it last night and they told me it was now $399. They said, "Short supply, high demand." I have been checking with other pharmacies today and they all said the same thing. We're OK for now, we're going to drive 3.5 hours tomorrow (each way) to get a script filled in New Hampshire where they still had some in stock at the old price. But what about all the other patients? It's outrageous that they can do that.[67]

Two months before we received this email, the FDA reported a shortage of doxycycline.[68] China is a dominant global producer of the chemical building block to make the active ingredient. The American Society of Health-System Pharmacists, which also tracks drug shortages, cited increased demand and manufacturing issues as the reasons.

Prescription drug price-fixing might be the reason our colleague saw the price of doxycycline skyrocket. In December 2016, the Department of Justice charged two former executives of Heritage Pharmaceuticals™, a generic company based in Eatontown, New Jersey, with fixing the prices of doxycycline and the diabetes drug glyburide.[69]

The alleged doxycycline price-fixing occurred from April 2013 until December 2015, and the alleged glyburide price manipulation occurred from April 2014 until at least December 2015, the Justice Department said in a press release.[70] The charges are the result of a federal antitrust investigation into price-fixing, bid rigging, and other anticompetitive conduct in the generic pharmaceutical industry. The investigation is ongoing and may yield more charges.

Not all cartels are treated equally. While the US justice system goes after an alleged domestic prescription drug cartel, it allows companies in China to freely operate a vitamin C cartel in the United States.

Are Chinese companies that sell active ingredients, over-the-counter products, or prescription drugs operating cartels in the United States? Are any drug shortages and price increases caused by Chinese government edicts or cartels? A transparent investigation conducted in the public interest is needed.

As China ramps up manufacturing of a growing number of generic drugs for sale in the United States, its drug cartels can roam free from impunity, limit supply, and raise prices for America's hospitals, pharmacies, and consumers. Will Washington sit on the sidelines and let it happen?

CHAPTER 6

THE CHINA TRAP

*As China manufactures the old drugs and steals
the intellectual property for new ones, what is left?*

When Rich Kramss woke up one morning at home in Connecticut where he had been planning to retire, the chemist in his forties, with a heavy heart, decided to put the house up for sale.[1] He was one of about a thousand scientists researching new drugs to treat cancer and other diseases when he lost his job at drugmaker Bayer™, which shuttered its 113-acre research facility located off Interstate 95 in West Haven, Connecticut, in 2007.[2]

After cashing out his 401k, Rich fixed up the house so it would sell quickly before the local real estate market, glutted with other homes, tanked. Crisscrossing the country, he took nearly any job he could muster, some lasting as little as five months. "I've taken contract jobs to keep the wolves away from the door," he says.[3] The pay wasn't good, 30 percent less than what he earned at Bayer.

More than eighty-six thousand chemists were laid off in the US pharmaceutical industry from 2010 to 2013, according to *Chemical and Engineering News*, a weekly publication of the American Chemical Society.[4] "The situation today is a tragedy of national proportions," said Madeleine Jacobs, then executive director and chief executive officer of the society.[5] "It's devastating to individual lives, and it's devastating to this country."

BRAIN DRAIN

A long-time recruiter for the pharmaceutical industry lamented in a blog that top pharmaceutical companies laid off many high-ranking scientists and outsourced the research to contract research organizations (CROs) especially in China where wages are much lower.[6]

"These chemists are being tossed aside often at the peak of their careers," the recruiter wrote. "These were top chemists from prestigious universities with experience at the top pharmaceutical companies. . . . There is just no place to absorb all these scientists."[7]

The pain is palpable. Laid-off workers took to social media to vent their reactions to job cuts. Employees at drugmaker Novartis™ are just one example. On CafePharma, an online industry message board, employees thrashed layoffs after a company announcement on December 22, 2014, at 4:00 p.m. in a conference call. A post titled, "Merry Christmas your [sic] fired!" generated an outpouring.[8] "There is no reason they had to call a last-minute conference call during Chanukah and two days before Christmas and destroy the holidays for over one hundred families," an employee wrote. "Now, instead of working today, I need to figure out which Christmas gifts to return."[9]

Like Rich Kramss, many scientists have resorted to temporary jobs or fixed-term contracts with lower wages and no benefits. Job security and career development are at risk, a trend with no end in sight as the world they have known vanishes.

"I SEEM TO HAVE LOST PURPOSE"

A chemist in the pharmaceutical manufacturing industry has a website called Chemjobber that has helped chemists find jobs in a tough market.[10] The website hosted the Layoff Project that collected the oral histories of chemists affected by changes in the pharmaceutical and chemical industries. One of them was a researcher at a major pharmaceutical company for thirty years, and her job was slated to go to China. "I seem to have lost purpose," she wrote to her fellow scientists.[11]

As the industry was bleeding jobs in the United States, a pharma trade newsletter opined in 2011 that it was the "fashion" for drug companies to announce job cuts at home and expansions in China "in almost the same breath."[12]

Among the companies pivoting east was Johnson & Johnson™, based in New Brunswick, New Jersey, which announced 4,800 job cuts in 2007 and another eight thousand layoffs in the United States and globally two years later.[13] Meanwhile, it was preparing for the opening of its research and development center in Shanghai in 2009.

Six years later, its chief executive officer, Alex Gorsky, told the *Wall Street Journal*,

> We see this as a way to move from bringing great products to China to actually discovering and developing things in China. . . . [U]ltimately what we would love to do is then be able to take those from markets like China and take them to other markets around the world.[14]

Drugmaker Merck™ announced up to five thousand job cuts in the United States in August 2011. Four months later, the company tagged Beijing as the site of its $1.5 billion Asia research and development headquarters slated to employ six hundred scientists.[15] An online industry newsletter, *in-Pharma Technologist.com*, noted gloomily, "The investment in R&D Asia is in stark contrast with Merck activities elsewhere in recent years," citing the closure of eight labs in 2010 in the United States, Europe, and Canada.[16]

Viagra-maker Pfizer™ announced the closure of its Ann Arbor, Michigan, research and development site in 2007 where the blockbuster cholesterol-lowering Lipitor® was created, affecting 2,100 people and hundreds of support service workers.[17] Two years later, research labs were shuttered in Princeton, New Jersey; New York; and North Carolina.[18]

In 2011, more than two thousand Pfizer researchers were laid off as part of a $2 billion retrenchment in research. Eleven hundred layoffs were at the company's biggest research site located in Groton, Connecticut, nearly a quarter of the positions there.[19]

Pfizer has a long history in Groton that began in 1946 when it bought a World War II shipyard, the Groton Victory Yard.[20] Penicillin was one of the first products made at the Groton plant on a massive scale for America and the global market.[21]

One of the casualties of the 2011 layoffs was Groton's antibiotic research program, which was reportedly moving to Shanghai, the local newspaper, the *Day*, said.[22] The shift was "the first wholesale move of a major US pharmaceutical research unit to China," according to the local newspaper.[23]

Pharmaceutical industry consultant David Shlaes is concerned about the loss of scientists from layoffs. "If you think about it, it's like a guaranteed brain drain" at a time when the threat of life-threatening superbugs resistant to many existing drugs is escalating and new drugs are needed.[24] While new antibiotics are coming, he says, "The depth of the pipeline now is very shallow, and given the rapidity with which bacteria become resistant, we're not keeping up."

Pharmaceutical companies have shied away from investing in new antibiotics because it's not a profitable business. For a drug like Lipitor, a person may take it for years, guaranteeing a large, steady customer base. Antibiotics are prescribed for a short time to kill bacteria causing an infection and don't generate long-term customers.

Eight months after Pfizer's decision was reported, the company announced it was delaying the offshoring of the antibiotic research facility.[25]

Meanwhile, at Pfizer's China Research and Development Center in Shanghai that opened in 2005, the company says it is "developing the skills and talents of local scientists, biostatisticians, medical professionals, pharmacists, and others" and collaborating with leading universities and scientific institutes.[26]

"China is increasingly seen as a source for innovative health care research," said Martin Mackay, then president of Pfizer global research and development, in a press release in 2009.[27] In an interview with *China Business Weekly*, Mackay said, "So far, we're not scaling back our R&D budget, which allows us to work on diabetes, cardiovascular disease, infectious disease, and the like."[28] In addition to funding its own research center, Pfizer has funded basic research in drug discovery at the Shanghai Institutes for Biological Sciences.[29]

US-based pharmaceutical companies are creating their own future competitors, as shown by a Pfizer statement about its goals in China. Pfizer says its aim is to

> help accelerate China's transition to an innovative economy by cata-lyzing the upgrade of local R&D capabilities, systems, technologies/IP, and culture to address unmet medical needs, and create a world-class biopharmaceutical R&D ecosystem for China.[30]

END OF AN ERA

For decades, American scientists could count on the pharmaceutical industry for good-paying jobs. A retired Pfizer clinical researcher whom we'll call Steve Krieger remembers when he first arrived at the company's research facility in Groton at the tail end of the glory years. His new job was in the Building 118 complex, Pfizer's 750,000-square-foot research headquarters. It was a time when jobs were secure and the campus was alive with good minds. "When I first got there, I had to pinch myself," he said.[31] "It was like a research institute, and I was surrounded by all of these highly motivated, super bright people. It was incredible."

In 2013, Pfizer announced it was planning to demolish Building 118, which was actually comprised of six buildings. "I couldn't believe they took down that whole complex," the retired clinical researcher said. He wanted to remain anonymous because he receives retirement benefits from the company.

Blockbuster drugs with expiring patents prompted layoffs. Pfizer's cholesterol-lowering Lipitor, the all-time best-selling drug, felt the heat. From a revenue peak of $13 billion, Lipitor sales reportedly slumped to about $7 billion in 2010, according to an estimate.[32] The following year, Lipitor was on the patent chopping block. In the first nine months of 2012, revenue plummeted a whopping $5.5 billion.[33] Across the industry, patent expirations triggered $200 billion in losses from 2012 to 2015.[34] The industry's woes were a salve for Americans' wallets, quickly cleaned out by high-priced brand-name drugs.

A weak pipeline of new blockbuster drugs added to financial pressure on the industry. As layoffs were beginning in earnest in 2006, only nine of eighteen new treatments introduced in the United States came from the research labs of the big pharma companies, said a PricewaterhouseCoopers^{SM} report.[35]

Once upon a time a prevailing belief was that more money and scientists will deliver new blockbusters. Innovation didn't materialize at a pace investors demanded, and pharma companies pared basic research and looked to academia to drive discovery.

THE UNDERTOW IN SMALL-TOWN AMERICA

The view of Long Island Sound from Groton is spectacular. In the summer, panoramic views of Fishers Island and sailboats skimming on the water stretch along the horizon. Shennecossett Road hugs the coast and is home to the University of Connecticut Avery Point maritime studies campus that overlooks the shimmering water.

Along the shore, the Block Island Express can be spotted, the 160-foot catamaran ferry from New London that docks at Old Harbor on Block Island. Looking west, the Cross Sound Ferry leaves New London for Orient Point on the tip of Long Island's North Fork.

Going inland from the shore, Shennecossett Road becomes Eastern Point Road, which heads north, passing Beach Pond Road and the golf course. Soon, the bucolic scenery morphs into industrial complexes, with Pfizer's Groton campus less than two miles from the coast.

The scenic beauty belies an economic undertow upending the town as Pfizer layoffs hit hard. "Small town America is no longer what it once was," wrote a former Pfizer employee who worked in Building 118 and whose job was offshored, in a comment to the *Day* about the demolition.[36] "Happy people loved their jobs and were an integral part of the community. Now those who work here live with the daily stress of losing their jobs."[37]

State representative John Scott, owner of Bailey Insurance Agency in town, says, "These are people who were making $50–$100 or more per hour. They're not buying from local stores or contractors or insurance agencies like mine, and it's created a real hole in our economy."[38]

When laid-off employees tried to sell their houses at the same time, there weren't enough buyers, so they were dumped on the market for a fraction of their value, according to Scott. "Those of us with houses of comparable quality are sitting on homes worth one-third what they used to be," he says, and it's been an economic disaster for eastern Connecticut.

Groton real estate agent Lian Obrey sees the impact on the housing market. "Most people are doing a short sale; they're leaving the area because of what we're going through," she says.[39] "None of it's happy. I said to someone the other night, 'I want a happy listing.'"

Obrey knows a lot of people who once worked at Pfizer. "I remember a former employee who had a really good job, and I could just tell what the person was going through after losing it," she said. "When you see people like that, they're a little broken; it's heart-wrenching."

At Spare Time Bowling Alley, manager Tony Simpson says Pfizer funded bowling leagues for employees but not anymore. "The Pfizer league had thirty-two teams with five people on a team, and they'd come every Wednesday night," he said.[40] "You see some people for thirty-five weeks a year, and you get to know their story, and we've seen people lose their jobs. I don't think anyone from Pfizer bowls anymore." Times are really tough in Groton now, he says. "The biggest thing I've seen here in the past few years is an increase in drugs, an increase in heroin with people being out of work. There was a big heroin seizure yesterday at a car dealership used as a front."[41]

Scientists who can hang on are caught in a maelstrom. "I ran into a friend at the post office," said another Pfizer retiree.[42] "We had the same boss, and he used to work as a researcher. Now he's working as a contractor for Pfizer four days a week. They lay you off, and then they can't find anyone who can do what you did, so they rehire you as a contractor."

A talented physician with a PhD and board certification in his medical specialty was not immune to the turmoil. "The company decided to move him across the country," Steve Krieger said.[43] "He was there for a short while, and then he had to go find another job when the company decided to no longer do research in that therapeutic area at the facility where he had been working. It's a perfect example of taking a bright person with years of experience, moving him, and he gets screwed. Those things would never have happened in the old days, and they are not unique to Pfizer."

China's lower labor costs are a big draw for companies looking to pare expenses. "A bench chemist costs $250,000 in the United States when workspace, health insurance, retirement, parking, and other benefits, along with the cost of complying with Occupational Safety and Health Administration (OSHA) and Environmental Protection Agency (EPA) rules are included," said Peter Saxon, a chemical engineer who helps manufacturers prepare for FDA inspections and who has studied the difference in labor costs.[44] "In China, it's no more than $50,000," he said.

"LINK OUR FATE TO THEIR FATE"

The pivot east by pharmaceutical companies coincided with the contaminated heparin scandal that tarnished the reputation of China's drug industry. The lack of trust among Chinese consumers in medicines made by domestic companies created a vacuum that Western multinational pharmaceutical companies were more than willing to fill.

Consumer demand for high-quality medicines in China is at an all-time high and growing. By 2020, there will be 280 million affluent consumers in China, outpacing the entire 261 million US population over age eighteen, according to a Boston Consulting Group[SM] (BCG) analysis.[45]

The affluent in China have annual household disposable incomes of at least $20,000, according to BCG's report. While this amount will not make a household affluent in the United States, the figure is based on relative income and purchasing power in China.

To meet the growing demand in China for quality medicines, China is becoming a manufacturing powerhouse. It won't want to buy drugs made in America.

China's 12th Five-Year Plan for National Economic and Social Development for 2011–2015 called for the creation of one or two large-scale, national-level pharmaceutical companies with internationally renowned brands with revenues of $15 billion each, and twenty major companies with annual sales of $1.5 billion each.[46]

The country's grandest and most recent campaign to boost its domestic pharmaceutical and other industries, Made in China 2025, is a blueprint for turning the country into a global high-end manufacturing powerhouse in time for the hundredth anniversary of the founding of the People's Republic of China in 2049.[47]

To help meet the ambitious goal, General Electric™ is building prefabricated drug factories and shipped its first one from Germany to China in 2015, *Bloomberg* reported.[48] Workers on-site assemble the factory-built modules in a scaled-up version of cobbling together toy building blocks.

The price is right, about 45 percent less than building a traditional manufacturing plant, no small amount when traditional factories can cost up to $500 million.[49]

When it comes to research, China's equally ambitious goal is to discover homegrown brand-name products to compete globally by 2025. The plan is to evolve from "Made in China" to "Designed in China."[50] China aims to become a rival to the United States as a place of drug discovery and high-end innovation.

A large talent pool awaits. Eighty thousand graduates of PhD programs in the sciences from Western universities have returned to their home country.[51] More than two million Chinese students in science, technology, engineering, and math (STEM) fields graduate every year, five times the number in the United States.[52]

China is using US and other Western companies to help its domestic firms succeed, acknowledging a "go-it-alone" strategy won't work.[53] The quickest and most direct route to success for China has been to establish joint ventures or other tie-ups with multinational companies.[54]

Pfizer, the world's largest drugmaker by sales, entered into a joint venture with a government-owned pharma company named Hisun, which has a controlling stake.[55] The Chinese news media reported that the deal will help Hisun make key ingredients and generic drugs.

Not all joint ventures succeed. Merck dissolved a joint venture with a Chinese company for undisclosed reasons about four years after it was announced with substantial fanfare.[56] Pfizer sold its stake in Hisun five years after the joint venture was formed.[57]

Thomson Reuters assessed the deals this way: "We expect that if these joint ventures are successful, the agreements could be extended to regulated markets in the future."[58] In other words, the ventures are a gateway for Chinese drugmakers to obtain a growing share of the nearly $400 billion spent in the United States annually on pharmaceuticals.

The deals inextricably bind Western countries to China as the source of their medicines. The chairman of research and development for British pharma company GlaxoSmithKline™ (GSK), Moncef Slaoui, told the *Financial Times* in 2007, "For us, China is not about outsourcing and cheap labor. . . . We will link our fate to their fate. . . . Within five to ten years we will be moving from 'made in China' to 'discovered in China.'"[59]

For the Chinese government, the holy grail is for domestic companies to discover drugs, make them, and sell them in the United States. Chinese consumer confidence in their country's domestic drug industry will rise inexorably.[60]

ALL THAT GLITTERS

In return for gaining access to sell drugs in China, Western companies are paying a high price. They have built manufacturing and research facilities in China, transferred intellectual property, and trained Chinese workers to do the jobs Americans performed for generations. Chinese companies obtain know-how and access to global markets.

A US Chamber of Commerce report bluntly acknowledges that American companies across industries are forced to "anguish over balancing today's profits with tomorrow's survival."[61] China's industrial policies compel Western companies to transfer technology in return for the privilege of selling drugs in China. "But the problem now goes far beyond the China market, as multinationals expect to see their own technology coming back at them globally in the hands of Chinese competitors," the US Chamber of Commerce report noted.[62]

Western drugmakers are already being cut out of big deals. With Beijing's blessing, domestic companies will make more of the drugs for the Chinese people. Hospitals are the largest market for drugs in China, and government procurement favors domestic companies.[63]

"Competition has increased as local manufacturers geared up production levels and are being favored in regional bidding," says Lars Rebien Sorensen, chief executive officer of Danish drugmaker Novo Nordisk™.[64]

It is one of the world's largest insulin makers and the first international company to establish modern insulin making in China, and the company is reportedly losing market share to local Chinese competitors.

Global management consulting firm Bain & Company^{SM} painted a "doomsday" scenario for Western pharmaceutical companies in China, and projected that their current business model will be unsustainable in five to seven years.[65] A *Bloomberg* headline added to the gloom, blasting, "China's Drug-Price Cuts Are Hitting Big Pharma Where It Hurts."[66] China squeezed 50 percent price cuts from big pharma on expensive imported drugs for cancer and other conditions.[67] A *Wall Street Journal* headline blared, "Drug Companies Face Pressure despite China Price Pledge," and the article bemoaned how China has "long kept a tight rein on drug prices."[68]

The American Chamber of Commerce in China, or AmCham China, paints a bleak picture. Annual foreign pharmaceutical sales growth in China fell from 20 percent in 2013 to only 5 percent in 2015, causing some Western drug firms to "reevaluate their initial enthusiasm about the Chinese market."[69]

A similarly sober assessment was made in the US Chamber of Commerce report about American businesses in China generally: "The belief by foreign companies that large financial investments, the sharing of expertise, and significant technology transfers would lead to an ever-opening China market is being replaced by boardroom banter that win-win in China means China wins twice."[70]

But with China's $167 billion market for pharmaceuticals in 2020, the game is too big for Western companies to sit on the sidelines.[71]

GRAND THEFT PHARMA

The research-intensive pharmaceutical industry is investing in research and development in a country with the worst reputation in the world for purloining intellectual property. The US Chamber of Commerce report declared that China's strategy to appropriate Western technology constitutes "theft on a scale the world has never seen before."[72]

A 2013 survey of US companies in China in a range of industries conducted by AmCham China found that 72 percent of respondents said China's enforcement of intellectual property rights was either ineffective or totally ineffective, a dramatic leap from 58 percent in 2011.[73]

Employees are a weak link. A case in point is a research scientist who worked in the Bridgewater, New Jersey, headquarters of the French pharmaceutical firm Sanofi™ and stole trade secrets for compounds that could be used in future drugs. A Chinese national, the employee downloaded information including the chemical structures from company computers to a thumb drive and personal email accounts. The compounds were put up for sale by a subsidiary of a Chinese chemical company located in the United States that was half-owned by the Sanofi employee. The employee was sentenced to eighteen months in federal prison and ordered to pay $131,000 in restitution.[74]

In another case, an employee of a Chinese pharmaceutical company, WuXi Pharma Tech, stole patented medical compounds owned by Merck, while they were being tested in China, and sold them on the internet. Merck was outsourcing research and development to the company. The compounds were being studied for possible new treatments for diabetes and hepatitis C.

The former employee was convicted in a Shanghai court and received a far lighter sentence than that meted out in the US court in the Sanofi case: eighteen months' probation and $7,000 in restitution. The slap on the wrist manifests China's support for piracy of US intellectual property if it helps a Chinese company gain technological superiority.[75]

In 2013, the pharmaceutical company Eli Lilly™ obtained an injunction in a case involving trade secret theft against its former chief research chemist in its subsidiary in China. Eight months after being hired and signing a confidentiality agreement, the employee allegedly downloaded twenty-one confidential documents from the company's server and refused to delete any of them, choosing to resign instead.[76] The company alleged trade secret misappropriation under the Anti-Unfair Competition Law. A Shanghai court issued an injunction that prohibited the employee from using the information or giving it to someone. No fine or imprisonment was ordered.[77]

In another case, two former employees of Eli Lilly in Indianapolis were indicted in federal court in August 2013 for allegedly stealing patented trade secrets and emailing them to a competing company in China, Jiangsu Hengrui Medicine.[78] The trade secrets reportedly involved drugs being developed to treat cancer, diabetes, and heart disease. The company claimed the information was the culmination of ten years of research that cost $55 million to discover, the *IndyStar* reported. About a year later, the federal prosecutor dropped the charges without giving a reason.[79]

CHINA'S RACE FOR THE CURE

China's race for a cure for cancer reportedly includes cyber espionage and hacking US healthcare companies that provide cancer treatment. In 2013, a China-based group targeted three firms, says FireEye™, a cybersecurity group.[80] Theft of cancer treatment protocols is thought to be part of the government's plan to accelerate acquisition of knowledge to respond to the epidemic of cancer, which has surpassed cardiovascular disease as the leading cause of death in Beijing.[81]

FireEye also reported that "suspected nation-state threat groups" target pharmaceutical companies. In the case of one company, vast amounts of intellectual property were compromised by two China-based advanced persistent threat (APT) groups affecting more than a hundred systems.[82] Digital back doors were installed to maintain ongoing access to the company's network.

One of the APT groups stole IP and business data from the victim, including information on bio cultures, products, cost reports, and other details pertaining to the company's operations abroad.[83]

The attackers are not random tech geeks. "APT attackers receive direction and support from an established nation state," FireEye says. "[They] pursue their objectives over an extended period of time, typically months or years. They adapt to organizations' efforts to eradicate them . . . and they frequently return to the same victim multiple times."[84]

Research and product information are appropriated by Chinese companies to meet government targets for industry growth without the cost and bother of doing the research. Stealing specifications for manufacturing facilities speeds up acquisition of production know-how. Cost and price reports, and details on a company's sales in other countries, are used to undercut US companies on price around the globe.

US academic medical centers conducting biomedical research are hacked by China. A chief executive officer of a large teaching hospital said that his organization experiences millions of attempted intrusions per day.[85] One of the targets is believed to be government-funded research conducted at the university. The center's payroll was hacked, and a small number of employees' pay was stolen.

Seventy-seven percent of American companies responding to the 2016 annual survey on China's business climate conducted by AmCham China said it is less welcoming to foreign businesses.[86] Research-intensive industries are especially feeling the pinch.

Robert D. Atkinson, president of the Information Technology and Innovation Foundation, summed up China's strategy during testimony in January 2017 before the US-China Economic and Security Review Commission:

The forced technology transfers and the intellectual property theft—I think it is very clear . . . that China is simply not a normal country in the sense of playing by the rules and being market-driven. . . . So I think we should be under no illusion that this is a long-term strategy for them to catch up and surpass us, and ultimately to either destroy our companies' market share or just put them out of business.[87]

LURED INTO THE TRAP

Will Western pharmaceutical companies thrive in the long term in China? Drained of intellectual property, undercut on price, and exhausted from legal battles, will American companies be eventually pushed out, replaced by Chinese firms?

The industry's big gamble on China has far-reaching consequences for Americans' health security. Surely China is watching how Western pharmaceutical companies charge exorbitant prices in the United States and get away with it. Members of Congress will be powerless to obtain information on a Chinese-government-owned company's price-setting practices.

When doctors, hospitals, and consumers realize that China is the only country that produces an essential drug developed with American know-how, and whose price is out of reach for most Americans, the impact of the "pivot east" strategy will be stark. K Street lobbyists and public relations companies hired by China will press Medicare to pay for the drug at a price demanded by China.

Decisions about access to life-saving drugs could become inherently political. Medical need and humanitarian considerations may play no part in China's decision on whether to stock America's pharmacies and home medicine cabinets.

Meanwhile, the FDA is transferring its intellectual capital to China. In a speech at Peking University in November 2014, then head of the FDA, Dr. Margaret Hamburg, said the university received support from the FDA and multinational pharmaceutical companies to establish a master's degree program to train future leaders in that country's pharmaceutical industry and regulatory agency.[88]

Hundreds of thousands of American workers spent decades imagining, creating, building, and continuously improving state-of-the art research, development, and manufacturing. American ingenuity created a highly productive and disciplined culture that spawned a golden era in the making of medicines to relieve suffering and treat disease. All of this is being given away for a short window of revenue to appease shareholders.

This is the China trap. China thinks long term. America thinks short term. China plays chess. America plays checkers.

With a slip of the grip, an industrial sector is at risk. As the manufacturing base at home hollows out, human talent withers. If scientists are beset by constant worry about landing the next short-term contract, the prospects for profound discovery will not be auspicious.

As China manufactures the old drugs and steals the intellectual property for new ones, what is left?

CHAPTER 7

THE GREAT AMERICAN SELLOUT

No industry is off-limits when it comes
to surrendering production to China.

As we were writing this book, we found ourselves wondering how the public's health and safety enters into decisions about offshoring medicine making. How are trade-offs made between safety and globalization, and who decides?

In the not-very-transparent pharmaceutical industry, the balancing act takes place out of public view. So, we found a story about a different industry with more transparency that is on track to be offshored to China and where public health and safety matter. It shows that public concern about safety is not a priority when decisions are made by the industry and government to buy "Made in China."

The country that promised a chicken in every pot is eating nuggets, pot pies, or other chicken delights made with chickens processed in China. That's not all. Chicken raised in China is on track to be imported, sold in America's grocery stores, and served on Americans' dinner plates at home and in restaurants.

Chicken and medicines have a lot in common, aside from chicken soup being a time-honored remedy to soothe annoying symptoms of the common cold and flu. People have strong opinions about what they put in their mouths. They want to know that someone is checking to ensure it's safe. No one wants to consume substandard drugs or food.

Many consumers want to know where their food comes from. Chicken sold in the meat or frozen food sections of the grocery store is not usually labeled with the country of origin. Many prescription drugs are not labeled either.

As generic drugs have become commodities, as has food, the American appetite for the less expensive drives production to low-cost countries. But there's more to it than economics. It's also about politics. Elected politicians in Washington and corporate interests have been working hand in hand to open up a homegrown, highly efficient industry to imports from China.

THE CHICKEN STORY

The story of how the federal government agreed to import chicken from China began in 2004 when China asked the US government for approval to sell chicken to American consumers.[1]

Federal law requires that countries' requests be honored, so food safety experts from the US Department of Agriculture (USDA) traveled to China to inspect its poultry plants. The department regulates meat, poultry, and egg production, while the FDA oversees the rest of the food supply.

The timing could not have been worse, or so it would seem. A widespread outbreak of avian flu infected Chinese poultry in sixteen provinces in 2004 and continued through 2005. Nine million poultry were culled.[2]

Unfazed by the highly pathogenic avian flu, China wanted its chicken on America's dinner plates. Rarely does the Washington bureaucracy move with lightning speed. In this case, it did.

Two years after China's request, the USDA ruled that China's chicken inspection system provided a level of protection that met US standards. There was one caveat. Because of outbreaks of the infectious H5N1 strain of avian flu in Chinese poultry, chicken raised and slaughtered in China could not be exported to the United States. The chickens had to be raised in the United States or other approved countries and sent to China for processing.[3] Workers in China would pound it into nuggets and tenders, and ship them to the United States, ready to pop in America's microwaves.

The timing was impeccable. On April 18, 2006, the USDA transmitted the final regulation to the White House Office of Management and Budget (OMB) for review.[4]

Within a day, OMB, the erstwhile graveyard for proposed regulations that lack the grease of powerful special interests, approved the USDA's new rule just in time for a visit from China's president to the White House.[5] On April 20, 2006, President George W. Bush met with then Chinese president Hu Jintao, and it was announced that China was added to the list of approved countries that could export processed chicken to America.[6]

Congresswoman Rosa DeLauro, a Democrat from Connecticut, opposed the decision, saying it was

> an outrage that the United States is going to open our border to imports of poultry from China, a country that lacks the fundamental safety functions in its processing plants, has questionable export practices, and a country where a deadly animal disease and possible pandemic is running rampant.[7]

Pushing back on the White House, Congress blocked federal money from being used to inspect chicken plants in China.[8] Without inspections, chicken could not be imported into the United States. The congressional funding ban continued into 2009.

BAD TIMING

Once again, the timing could hardly be worse to consider importing chicken from China. The deadly melamine and heparin contaminations were wreaking global havoc, and the FDA was trying to get inside Chinese drug-manufacturing plants and inspect them.

Family farmers and consumer groups wrote a letter to President Obama opposing Chinese imports, saying China does not enforce food safety standards, and worse, it hides major foodborne illness outbreaks. The letter said the Chinese government went to great lengths "to prevent news of illnesses and deaths caused by the food adulteration from being made public because it would have conflicted with the staging of the Beijing Olympics in August 2008."[9]

The letter included a litany of 467 food items from China in the preceding four months that were contaminated and unsafe, ranging from seafood to candy, that the FDA had banned from entry into the United States. Agency inspectors found illegal animal/veterinary drugs, unsafe food and color additives, filth, salmonella contamination, toxic pesticide residues, and poisonous products unsuited for human consumption.[10]

Using Freedom of Information Act requests, food safety organizations obtained a copy of the USDA inspection reports of Chinese chicken processing plants. The department's auditors identified major deficiencies during their initial visit to China. In five of the seven food establishments they examined, food safety breaches were identified. In two of the facilities, federal officials identified sanitary issues that were so terrible that they would have recommended the products be banned from the United States.[11]

Even with its troubling food safety record, China challenged the congressional ban on funding for inspections of Chinese chicken establishments at the World Trade Organization (WTO), saying the ban was "discriminative."[12]

CHINA LAUNCHES ITS CAMPAIGN

Two months later in the summer of 2009, China launched a fierce campaign to stop buying American-raised chicken as part of its "buy Chinese" program.[13]

After another two months, China launched an investigation into claims that the United States was dumping chicken in China at below-market prices. American chicken producers said the Chinese government's move was retaliation for the United States refusing to allow chicken from China into its market. Another irritant may have been new tariffs on motor vehicle tires from China imposed by the Obama administration around the same time.[14]

Succumbing to pressure, Congress voted to soften the ban on funding inspections if certain conditions were met. Congress instructed the secretary of agriculture to audit China's poultry safety system and conduct on-site inspections of processing plants before any chicken could come to the United States.[15] The USDA was also required to increase the number of reinspections at US ports of entry and make audit and inspection reports available to the public. The Chinese government bristled, saying in a letter to the secretary that it did not need to provide any additional information on its food safety laws.[16]

As the United States began to open the door to Chinese chicken, China did not withdraw its case from the WTO, which eventually ruled that the US ban on inspection funding ran afoul of international trade rules.[17]

China was getting what it wanted, but that wasn't enough. It slapped duties of more than 100 percent on some US-raised chicken.[18]

The US government challenged the duties at the WTO, and in 2013 the trade body ruled that the duties were unjustified.[19] However, it was a Pyrrhic victory. Companies had spent millions of dollars on legal fees.[20] American chicken farmers felt the pain as sales plummeted more than 80 percent and caused a loss of about $1 billion in sales.[21] Real damage had been inflicted. China didn't bend. Three years later, the US Trade Representative announced it was requesting the WTO to take action against China for failing to eliminate the duties.[22]

The Washington bureaucracy moved forward on China's request to sell its chicken. In March 2013, inspectors traveled to China and the

USDA affirmed again that China's safety inspection system was equivalent to the US system.[23]

The USDA wrote to the Chinese government saying China has the "ability to provide consistent government oversight" in accordance with US laws and regulations, and the People's Republic of China could take the next step and certify a list of poultry establishments as meeting US standards.[24]

More than a year later, on November 5, 2014, the day after the US midterm elections, the USDA announced four poultry processing plants in China were eligible to export processed chicken to the United States.[25]

China could not sell any chicken raised and slaughtered in China because its safety system didn't meet US standards.[26] But it could process chicken from the United States and export it back.

Tony Corbo, senior lobbyist at the nonprofit Food and Water Watch, who has advocated for stopping the import of chicken from China, said, "How do you know we would be getting our poultry back? We might be getting their stuff instead."[27]

Jonathan Buttram, a forty-year chicken farmer and former president of the Alabama Contract Poultry Growers Association, predicted what would happen with chicken:

> US companies will import Chinese chicken meat, bring it into the port, ship it into their plants, mix it with US-processed chicken, and ship it to the grocery stores, and no one will know the difference. It's cheaper for them, but they'll sell it at the same price and pocket the difference.[28]

The pattern is similar to prescription drugs. US-based companies import active ingredients from China, use them to make pills and tablets, and ship them to hospitals and pharmacies. No one knows the difference. It's cheaper for the companies; they'll sell it at the same price and pocket the difference.

CHANGE.ORG PETITION

A Change.org petition to ban chicken from China in supermarkets and the National School Lunch Program garnered more than 328,180 signatures.[29] Representative DeLauro introduced the Safe Chicken and Meat for Children Act, a bipartisan bill banning Chinese-produced or Chinese-processed meat and chicken from the school lunch program and other federal nutrition programs.[30] Representative DeLauro said, "Given China's demonstrably poor food safety record, it is unacceptable to take any unnecessary risks with the health of American school children—our most vulnerable population with respect to foodborne illnesses and sensitivity to potentially dangerous chemicals."[31]

CHINA BANS US FARM-RAISED CHICKEN

China was not satisfied. It didn't want to merely process US-raised chickens. It wanted to sell chickens it raises to American consumers. This was China's intent all along, said Tony Corbo.[32] "By approving imports of processed chicken, the US was offering a halfway gesture," he added.

As China relentlessly pressured the federal government for access to the US market, it slammed the doors on American-raised chickens. Minor cases of avian flu were used as an excuse to block the sale of American-raised chickens in China. In Kent County, Delaware, bird flu with a low risk of serious illness was found on a farm in 2004. Chinese authorities suspended imports of all poultry from across the United States for a period of time.[33]

In 2007, China banned poultry from Virginia after a low-risk bird flu was reported on a single farm in the gently rolling hills of the Shenandoah Valley.[34] Virginia had been selling up to $15 million worth of poultry products to China.[35]

After waiting a long time for China to reopen its doors, Virginia poultry industry officials spoke of collaboration with the Chinese government. Chinese officials had come to inspect Virginia farms and agreed to buy wingtips and chicken feet, delicacies at home. Polite talk belies China's intention to buy as little of anything made in America. After an unjustified seven-year ban, a ship carrying US-raised chicken parts left the Port of Virginia in Norfolk in June 2014.[36] The progress didn't last long.

In January 2015, China took another swipe and banned all poultry products from the United States because of highly pathogenic avian flu cases found in wild birds and backyard chickens on the West Coast, even though the US Department of Agriculture determined the virus was not detected in commercial poultry.[37] The ban persisted even after the World Organization for Animal Health determined that the United States was free of the highly pathogenic flu as of April 2016.[38]

The US-China Economic and Security Review Commission said China has persistently banned US meat products following isolated outbreaks.[39] Although it is usual for a country to stop imports from certain affected regions of an exporting country if there is an outbreak, China's bans have often exceeded any reasonable bounds.

DIVIDE AND CONQUER

Even as China shut the door on American chicken farmers, the US government continued to help China at the behest of American agribusinesses operating in China that want to send Chinese-raised chicken to America.[40] Cargill China™ and OSI Group^{SM} spent millions of dollars to build poultry breeding facilities and processing plants in China. "US companies hire thousands of employees and, in some cases, finance training at their facilities in the United States," the US-China Economic and Security Review Commission noted.[41] They expect to become a "future export platform to US consumers," according to the commission.[42]

But when the Chinese government certified local companies to export to the United States, it excluded US agribusinesses from the list, according to USDA correspondence with China.[43] "The Chinese government picked the companies that can export chicken to the US," said Tony Corbo, "and the companies selected were Chinese, not American."[44]

Nearly forty organizations, mostly food and agriculture groups, advocated for Chinese-processed chicken to be sold in the United States. The National Chicken Council, the American Meat Institute, the Grocery Manufacturers Association, and the US Chamber of Commerce were among the proponents.[45]

The beef industry was an especially ardent supporter of importing chicken. The Chinese government had banned American beef for more than a decade, beginning on Christmas Day in 2003, because of the discovery of mad cow disease.[46] Beef producers longed for China to remove its ban.

Chinese officials offered a deal, pitting one special interest against another. China would allow US beef into the country if the United States would buy China's chicken.[47] The beef industry took the bait and lobbied for chicken imports, even if it meant American chicken farmers were put out of business.

China maintained its official ban on US beef while buying from Australia, Uruguay, New Zealand, and Canada.[48] An industry blog captured the reality: "Chinese Beef Market Surging: US Locked Out."[49] While officially locked out, large amounts of US-raised beef were smuggled into China from Hong Kong, according to the *South China Morning Post*.[50]

US CHICKEN COMPANIES GRILLED IN CHINA

While American poultry farmers struggled at home with the loss of huge sales to China, American companies in China were taking a big hit in the Chinese state-run media. They faced a monumental challenge to create and sustain islands of safe, high-quality food production in a cultural sea of scandals and lax enforcement.

The US-China Economic and Security Review Commission acknowledged that state-run media campaigns were ensnarling US brands in food scandals:

> US companies have not been granted fair market access in China. A pervasive problem is regulatory uncertainty, in the form of state-run media campaigns targeting foreign brands, stricter oversight than for domestic companies, and corrupt practices by officials at the local level.[51]

In July 2014, an undercover video of a processing plant aired on local Chinese television showing workers using expired chicken and beef products sold to McDonald's™, Papa John's™, Burger King®, Starbucks™, KFC™, and Pizza Hut™ in China.[52] The plant was operated by Shanghai Husi Food, a subsidiary of Illinois-based OSI.

OSI had been a long-time supplier of McDonald's in China. When it shut down the processing plant in the aftermath of a social media uproar, Big Mac® hamburgers and other menu items were scarce. The following year, McDonald's announced it was closing many restaurants in China because of a big slump in sales. OSI said the scandal cost its company nearly $1 billion.[53]

Fried chicken king KFC was recovering from an earlier slam in the so-called "instant chicken" scandal. State-run China Central Television (CCTV) reported that local chicken producers supplied chicken to KFC that had been fed eighteen types of antibiotics and hormones to make them grow faster, hence the name "instant chicken."[54]

In another bombardment, Chinese social media spread false rumors that KFC chicken is genetically modified to have six wings and eight legs.[55] KFC sued three companies for allegedly tarnishing its image. After the company experienced explosive growth in China a decade ago, it is no longer the easy, lucrative market it once was.

Around the same time as the undercover video surfaced, the Chinese media reported that thirty thousand tons of chicken feet were found to have been soaked in hydrogen peroxide. The immense scope of the scandal, with thirty-five national sales networks purveying the putrid product, reveals the challenge China faces.[56]

In July 2015, *China Daily* reported that chicken wings, beef, and pork that had been frozen for up to forty years had been smuggled into China by gangs in a massive operation that spanned fourteen provinces. It was sold at restaurants and by street vendors. Valued at $483 million, it was named "zombie meat" by the local media.[57] Smuggling is fueled by growing demand for meat in increasingly prosperous China.

A LAST-MINUTE SURPRISE FROM THE OBAMA ADMINISTRATION

In early 2017, we called the USDA Meat and Poultry hotline for an update on whether any processed chicken from China had been imported. A young representative said, "It has not been made legal yet, and we have no updated rule allowing that into our country."[58] After we mentioned information on the USDA website, she put us on hold and later confirmed that processed chicken from China is allowed to be sold in the United States, but she wasn't sure if any is being sold in supermarkets.

We contacted Tony Corbo from Food and Water Watch who said, "Every month I file a Freedom of Information Act request to the USDA to see if we have received any imports, and as of January 2017, we haven't received any."[59]

Then Corbo told us about a remarkable last-minute move by the Obama administration. It agreed to move forward on approving chicken raised and slaughtered in China. USDA inspectors had gone to China to conduct another inspection and concluded China's slaughter system meets US standards.[60] Corbo said, "When the Obama administration left office, as part of its regulatory agenda, it was going to propose a rule to allow China to ship its own poultry to the United States."[61]

The USDA was under enormous pressure to resolve the beef ban,

Corbo said, and the decision to go ahead with chicken was tied up with China's unwillingness to take US beef.

In a quid pro quo, the Chinese government sweetened the deal by including Cargill facilities in China on a draft list of companies slated to export chicken raised in China to the United States.[62] "China told the USDA that if you allow us to ship our poultry to the United States, we'll make sure that some of the Cargill plants will be designated to export," Corbo said.[63]

China estimated that Cargill will send sixty-four million pounds of cooked chicken breasts to the United States over five years. Two domestic Chinese companies will send fifty-five million pounds of chicken quarter legs and 140,000 pounds of cooked chicken breasts.[64]

For Americans who enjoy eating duck meat, two Chinese domestic plants will send four million pounds of duck quarter legs, sixteen million pounds of cooked duck breasts, and fifteen million pounds of boneless roast duck.[65]

SUPERBUGS WITH YOUR BARBECUED CHICKEN?

Shortly after the Obama administration gave the USDA the go-ahead to move forward on importing chicken raised in China, an international team of researchers found that more than 87 percent of the chicken meat sold in supermarkets in a province in China was contaminated by bacteria resistant to antibiotics, including a so-called "last-resort" antibiotic administered after all others have failed.[66]

The bacteria were traced all the way back to commercial chicken farms where 97 percent of the samples taken were contaminated with superbugs, said the *South China Morning Post*, which reported the story.[67] Superbugs were found in slaughterhouses, too. The pervasive presence of superbugs suggests widespread environmental contamination.

"THE BEGINNING OF OFFSHORING"

Alabama chicken farmer Jonathan Buttram predicted what was going to happen to American chicken farmers:

> The big companies want to raise it for nothing there and bring it here. China will be sure to dump it at below-market prices. It [chicken] is already so cheap it is hard to think how it can be done cheaper, but there must be a way.[68]

Buttram was right. The Cargill plant slated to send chicken to the United States was described by Food and Water Watch's Corbo this way: "One is brand-spanking new, and it can handle 250 chickens a minute. That's the line speed. In the United States, it's 140." When we asked the importance of the line speed, Corbo said, "This is the beginning of off-shoring our chicken processing."[69] The plant can process chicken much faster, making it more efficient and, of course, cheaper.

Chicken from China will take jobs away from American farmers, and many of them work under soul-crushing terms of employment. Most chickens in the United States are raised by independent farmers who sign contracts with giant agribusinesses such as Tyson Foods™ and Perdue®. The majority of farmers who depend on the business for their livelihood have incomes near or below the poverty line, according to the National Contract Poultry Growers Association and the US Department of Agriculture.[70]

With poverty-level incomes, they are expected to take on and pay down hundreds of thousands of dollars in debt to build, equip, maintain, and operate chicken houses with the latest technology that companies require.[71]

A North Carolina chicken grower who despaired over enormous debt was the subject of a John Oliver segment on HBO. A fellow farmer described what happened: "This past Monday morning, one of these . . .

growers went out, drove down a country road, about to lose his home, took a gun, and ended his life. This is personal. It is real for growers."[72]

Every couple of years, more than a hundred farmers can have their contracts terminated when processing facilities shut down. The companies usually have a monopoly in a geographic area, so when that happens, the farmers have no one else to contract with to raise chickens and service their debt. Once farmers sign up, they are stuck.

These are the people who will be out of a job because of competition from Chinese farmers who earn even less.

WHAT DID AMERICA GAIN?

What did America gain from more than a decade of wrangling? US chicken producers lost their market in China. Sales of US chicken to China plummeted from a peak of $722 million in 2008 to virtually nil in 2015.[73] Taxpayer money was spent advocating for US interests at the WTO, but China ignored international trade rules. Meanwhile, USDA employees traveled to China at taxpayer expense to inspect the poultry safety system to support that country's bid to sell its chicken to the United States.

The chicken trade war is a textbook example of China's strategy. China knows that America, divided by its special interests, can't win. Exploiting these divisions, China is adept at pitting special interests against one another. China baited the American beef industry to lobby against American chicken farmers by pressing for China to be permitted to sell its chicken in the United States.

The strategy draws from an ancient Chinese saying: "Encourage your enemy to expend his energy in futile quests while you conserve your strength. When he is exhausted and confused, you attack with energy and purpose."[74]

In May 2017, the Trump administration reached agreement with China to promote market access for American beef. As of this writing,

China has yet to import any beef. But cooked chicken processed in China began to reach American consumers. The chicken has to be raised and slaughtered in the US, Canada, or Chile. Next up, is Chinese-raised chicken coming into the United States? Stay tuned.

GLOBALIZATION OF REGULATION AND THE RACE TO THE BOTTOM

No industry is off-limits when it comes to surrendering production to China. That's a lesson from the chicken story.

Consumers will have to trust the Chinese government to assure chicken from there is safe. In the United States, federal inspectors are on-site in every plant, but they won't be present in plants in China. They will conduct annual audits and inspect batches when they cross the border into the United States, but that's all they can do.

The chicken story has been in public view because the public interest group Food and Water Watch has forced transparency in government decisions. In contrast, industry and government decisions about importing drugs and over-the-counter products from China are made behind a Berlin Wall–type barrier.

When deals like this are made for chicken, what deals are made with prescription drug regulation? What compromises do professionals in the FDA, who are committed to the public's health, feel compelled to make when the agency's commissioner receives a phone call from a member of Congress, the White House, a company, or surrogate for the Chinese government? Is the FDA pressured to give a clean bill of health to a manufacturing plant in China because an import ban would cause a drug shortage?

The chicken story portends a possible change that may occur with America's medicines down the road. In 2012, Congress permitted the FDA to recognize drug inspections conducted by foreign regulatory bodies. The agency must first determine that another country's inspection system meets US federal requirements.[75]

Five years later, the FDA announced it will recognize inspections of manufacturing facilities conducted by regulatory authorities in the European Union (EU).[76] Manufacturers there will avoid duplicative inspections, and the FDA will use the EU inspection reports, allowing it to concentrate on high-risk countries. A little-recognized provision in the agreement opens the door for the FDA to recognize EU inspections in countries outside Europe, such as China, to substitute for the FDA's own inspections.

It is not unreasonable to predict that the China lobby will eventually pressure Washington to determine that China's inspection system for its domestic drug-manufacturing plants meets US standards, similar to how the USDA was compelled to determine that China's chicken inspection system meets US federal requirements.

If that happens, the United States is on the precipice of losing control over assuring the safety of its medicines. The prospect of such an epic surrender is worth pondering.

CHAPTER 8

TODAY'S GAIN, TOMORROW'S PAIN

*"The best way to beat the enemy is
probably to go to their homeland."*

Sailing into placid English waters on a gray winter day in January 2015, a brand-new cargo ship, the largest in the world at the time, made its maiden voyage from Shanghai to Felixstowe, a port in the south of England.[1] A photo of the behemoth in the *Daily Telegraph*, a national newspaper in Britain, showed stacks of giant blue, green, brown, and red shipping containers and "China Shipping Lines" emblazoned in large letters on the side of the ship. If all the crates were stacked on top of each other end to end, they would reach 382,000 feet high in the sky, more than thirteen times higher than Mount Everest.[2]

Food, clothing, electrical goods, and furniture destined for Main Street shops were among the contents of the behemoth that was "so big it could supply everyone in the country with something."[3] The local media reported the pride of English know-how to build a new port to accommodate the big ship that was longer than four football fields.

Absent were photos of unemployed skilled workers, shuttered factories, and decrepit communities, shadows of once vibrant cities and towns where people once knew how to make things that a country and its citizens use in their everyday lives.

Why describe a photo of a cargo ship unloading in Britain and not the United States? A story and photo of a giant ship marked with "China Shipping Lines," with mountains of cargo from China entering a US port destined for American homes, would be axed from the front pages of US newspapers and CNN headline news to avoid igniting discontent among Americans fed up that so many products in their kitchens, living rooms, dining rooms, bedrooms, and closets, and now medicine cabinets are made in China.

About a year later, the *Wall Street Journal* reported on the largest container ship to dock at a US port, the 1,300-foot-long *Benjamin Franklin* owned by a French shipping line.[4] An accompanying photo shows the ship with "Benjamin Franklin, London" stamped on the bow, calling at the Port of Los Angeles. US ports aren't prepared to handle the cargo from the megaships during peak periods of loading and unloading, the story reported. The reader learns only that the ship came from Asia and returned there after stopping in Oakland.

The local ABC News affiliate in San Francisco reported the arrival of the same ship as it made its way north to the Port of Oakland. The story title was "Largest Container Ship to Ever Visit US Arrives in Bay Area."[5] A photo shows the ship barely making its way under the Golden Gate Bridge, with just twenty feet to spare. The Port of Oakland invested millions of dollars to accommodate gigantic ships. The last sentence in the story reads, "The megaship is expected to set sail for China on Sunday." No mention is made of where it came from, or what may have been in its eighteen thousand shipping containers.

The Associated Press (AP) account of the megaship was the only one we found that reported more details. The photo caption says the ship was built in China and set sail from there.[6] NBC News.com reported the AP story online.

A quick Google™ search of the *Benjamin Franklin* cargo ship led us to the website of the shipping company that proudly announced two weeks before the maiden voyage that the ship would be deployed on the Pearl River Express, connecting the main China ports including Xiamen, Nansha, and Yantian, with US West Coast ports.[7]

Back in Britain, three months after the Felixstowe port welcomed the first big ship docked there, CNN Money reported an even larger cargo ship, big enough to carry 1.15 million washing machines, entered Felixstowe.[8] The headline read, "This Ship Is Too Big for Any American Port." At least for now.

WHAT'S IN THE MEGA CARGO SHIPS DOCKING AT US PORTS?

The US trade deficit with China in pharmaceuticals was nearly $3 billion in 2013, according to Dr. Margaret Hamburg, then FDA commissioner, in a speech at Peking University in 2014. The United States imported nearly $4 billion in pharmaceutical products that year, mostly ingredients, and exported $1.22 billion.[9] Surely the Chinese audience was delighted that the United States has a trade deficit in drug products. We could find no media reports of a federal official telling a US audience about the US trade deficit with China in pharmaceuticals.

The cargo ships sailing from China to the United States are bringing loads of medical products. We combed through trade information from the US Department of Commerce, which uses broad categories of products and does not name specific drugs such as blood pressure pills or antidepressants. The top three imports from China listed in the trade data are the key ingredients for heparin, vitamin C, and vitamin E. The United States spent nearly $4.5 billion on them from 2007 to 2014, according to the trade data.[10] A billion dollars of diagnostic contrast agents used to perform X-rays and CT scans were the next largest import.

The ubiquity of China-made prescription drug products, vitamins, and over-the-counter items is revealed in a small slice of trade data showing what arrives in the United States on the big ships:[11]

vitamins A, B, and D
antibiotics tetracycline, streptomycin, and erythromycin
ibuprofen, the painkiller
hydrocortisone, a common steroid

contraceptives
the hormones estrogen and progestogen
digoxin, a heart medicine
toothpaste
caffeine
citric acid
hand sanitizers
bandages, sutures, and first-aid kits

TURNING POINT

As we were writing this chapter, we realized that the US-China Trade Relations Act of 2000 was a catalyst for importing medicinal products from China.

Within four years of the law's passage, Baxter™ began to buy heparin from China. China's vitamin C and penicillin cartels were wreaking havoc on American producers, and the last penicillin fermentation plant in the United States was shuttered. Cheap aspirin made in China flooded the American market, driving out Rhodia™, the last US-based maker (see chapter 2). The factories that made many of America's medicines closed their doors with very little public awareness, except perhaps for an article in a local newspaper reporting their demise.

Just as a trip to Walmart™, Target™, or Bed Bath & Beyond^{SM} is like shopping in a Chinese warehouse, so, too, is stopping by the pharmacy in a big-box store or Pathmark^{SM} or Safeway^{SM} supermarket to pick up a prescription. Distribution centers owned by companies that sell billions of dollars of medical products to hospitals and retail pharmacies are becoming more like the big-box stores, stocked with made-in-China items.

HOW EBOLA HELPED CHINA'S ECONOMY

With the first diagnosed case of Ebola in the United States and the death of its victim, Thomas Duncan, at Texas Health Presbyterian Hospital in Dallas, fear rippled in every hospital across the country. As demand for protective suits and masks surged, workers at a factory in Shandong province in China toiled day and night to churn out six thousand suits a day for its New York–based owner, Lakeland Industries™.[12] A photo in *China Daily* showed a woman sitting at a sewing machine, surrounded by heaps of yellow cloth, making the protective clothing.

The US Department of Veterans Affairs bought its Ebola protective gear from China because federal procurement decisions are made on the basis of lowest price, according to a physician in the department who spoke to us on the condition of anonymity. When we tried to confirm this information with department procurement officials, they did not want to speak with us because of concern that it could add to the negative publicity the VA had been weathering about veterans' access to care.

Aside from protective gear, China is the largest overseas supplier of components to make infusion pumps, which are commonly used in hospitals and other healthcare facilities to administer chemotherapy drugs, pain medicines, insulin, and antibiotics.[13] China is also the top supplier of components to make catheters that drain fluids from the body.

When we asked the chief executive of a healthcare system on the East Coast if he knew that so much of the equipment and supplies in his hospitals were made in China, he was not aware. He was surprised that his costs have not declined. Patients don't see lower hospital bills either.

WHERE IS YOUR KNEE IMPLANT COMING FROM?

The United States had a $900 million trade deficit with China in medical devices in 2012, according to an online industry report in *FierceMedical-*

Devices.[14] This is the latest figure we were able to find in publicly available sources. Chinese companies sold $3.5 billion in products to the United States but bought only $2.6 billion.[15] When we called the medical device trade association for an updated figure, we were told that the information is not available for specific countries.[16] Medical devices include products ranging from simple tongue depressors to sophisticated hip and knee joint replacements, pacemakers, and diagnostic imaging equipment such as CT scanners.

MRIs MADE IN CHINA, APPROVED FOR SALE IN THE UNITED STATES

The giant cargo ships from China are carrying containers filled to the brim with medical devices and equipment destined for America's hospitals, but what's in them is hard to know because publicly available information is protected like gold in Fort Knox. The companies selling them don't seem to want their customers to know.

Here's a sample of products made in China that the FDA approved for sale in the United States:

Magnetic resonance imaging equipment (MRIs)[17]
Dental implants to replace missing teeth[18]
Screw systems used in spine surgery[19]
Balloon catheters used to open up clogged arteries in the heart during angioplasty[20]
Pulse oximeters that measure oxygen in the blood, an indicator of how well the heart and lungs are working[21]
Speculums, an instrument used during women's annual gynecological exams[22]
Surgical gowns and examination gloves[23]
Wheelchairs[24]

The FDA's Dr. Margaret Hamburg told an audience at Peking University that China is the biggest exporter of medical devices to the United States. Four thousand Chinese medical device firms are registered with the FDA, and nearly twenty thousand products are listed for sale.[25]

Medical devices are a lucrative business. The Advisory Board Company™, a healthcare consulting firm, opined about the "rampant proliferation of expensive devices," whose costs are rising faster than hospital employee wages and benefits.[26] China wants a bigger slice of this profitable US market for medical devices and will probably get it.

China's 13th Five-Year Plan, presented by the state council of the People's Republic of China in 2016, targeted medical devices as one of the strategic emerging industries for investment and development. Medical imaging machines and radiation therapy equipment are among the products slated for domestic manufacture for China and the global market.[27]

US companies exported $1.7 billion in cardiac stents (to prop open clogged arteries), ultrasound machines, and MRIs to China from 2008 to 2012, according to the US International Trade Commission.[28] But the Chinese government was already signaling that big changes were coming.

In 2007, the Chinese government ordered new safety inspections for foreign-made devices but not for domestic-made ones.[29] Seven years later, in another salvo in the government's strategy to bolster domestic companies, China sent a clear message to Western firms: build manufacturing and assembly plants in China if you want to sell in China. China's discrimination in favor of domestic companies was evident when the government announced that it would "strongly advocate health ministry organizations to use domestically-made medical devices."[30]

As part of its "Made in China" initiative, government funding is boosting its domestic medical device industry. The American Chamber of Commerce in China (AmCham China) says the government's goal is to increase the use of locally made, high-end medical devices in its county hospitals to 70 percent by 2025.[31] Domestic content in core components is slated to grow to 80 percent by the same year. The headline in AmCham China's analysis is revealing: "Foreign Business' Critical Components, Technologies and Business Models Are Needed to Support the Development of Domestic Firms."[32]

US and European medical device manufacturers are creating their own competitors by establishing joint ventures with Chinese firms, moving manufacturing to China, transferring intellectual property, and opening up their global distribution channels to Chinese companies. From 2008 to 2012, US multinationals invested in at least thirty projects to establish new research and development facilities, manufacturing centers, and education and training programs for Chinese workers, according to the US International Trade Commission.[33]

The General Electric™ (GE) website boasts pride in a China-developed CT scanner, and commitment to developing highly skilled employees and suppliers who can meet international quality standards.[34] A *China Daily* article about the company's investment in research and development is accompanied by a photo of GE's Chinese engineers assembling an MRI in Beijing.[35]

Medical device-maker Medtronic™, which moved its headquarters from Minneapolis to Ireland for tax advantages, bought a Chinese orthopedic implant manufacturer, Kanghui Holdings, in 2012. Kanghui makes products for spine and joint reconstruction.[36] Two years later, Medtronic announced a deal with Lifetech Scientific to coproduce pacemakers in China.[37] At first, the pacemakers will be sold in China, which will benefit many people with heart conditions. But the deal includes Medtronic helping Lifetech commercialize its pacemakers, which means they will be made available for sale around the world. In another deal, Medtronic is helping Lifetech achieve China's ambition to sell its own global brand of sophisticated devices at home, in Europe, and in the United States. Lifetech has been developing a device for people born with atrial septal defect, which is a hole in the wall between the two upper chambers of the heart.[38]

In a press release, the company was candid about the challenge of Westerners trusting a Chinese-made medical device. When employees were studying the use of the device, a Lifetech engineer recalled his experience in an operating room in Germany in 2008:

> At that time, the doctor and patient were ready for the operation and we, as the engineers, were recording the data on product use within the operating theater, but when the patient on the operating table heard me and my colleagues talking in Chinese, he . . . refused to undergo the surgery. It was a heavy blow for us at the time but it also motivated us to work harder and increase confidence in our products.[39]

Six years later, Lifetech announced that Medtronic bought the first batch of the device, the first time a Chinese company's product entered the Western medical device market, a Lifetech press release said.[40] Medtronic will use its sales network in the United Kingdom, Germany, Italy, France, and other Western countries to distribute the product. The company expressed pride, saying,

> Just five years ago or even five months ago, it might have been hard to imagine implanting a medical device made in China into the body of a pediatric patient that would remain with them for the rest of their lives. But in the near future, such an event will become a reality in advanced western countries such as the UK, Germany, Italy, and France.[41]

Before sophisticated products like this can be sold in the United States, the FDA evaluates their safety and effectiveness. When we searched the FDA website, no Lifetech products in this category had been approved by the agency for use in the United States.[42] The FDA has approved other Lifetech devices for sale in the United States that doctors use in surgical procedures, which have a lower threshold for approval.[43]

How long will it take before cardiac stents, hip and knee replacement joints, CT scanners, and other sophisticated medical devices and equipment made in China are loaded off even bigger cargo ships when they dock at US shores, if they aren't already? Is a homegrown industry on track to never come back?

The Chinese government has a plan to grow a core industry, but the United States has no plan to keep an advanced technology sector at home. In testimony to the US-China Economic and Security Review Commission, Robert D. Atkinson, president of the Information Technology and Innovation Foundation, said he met with political appointees during the Obama administration who couldn't obtain documents translated into English about the Chinese government's long-term strategy to target core technology in the medical device industry.[44]

If current trends persist, an increasing share of the more than $3 trillion spent on healthcare in the United States will be spent on Chinese-made products.[45]

FROM TRADE TO OWNERSHIP IN THE UNITED STATES: SOMETHING ELSE IS GOING ON

China has pivoted from trading with the United States to owning in the United States, and the pace is staggering. From 2000 to 2016, cumulative Chinese foreign direct investment totaled more than $100 billion, according to New York–based Rhodium Group, which tracks cross-border investment flows.[46] Recent investment is dramatic. "Chinese companies invested a record $45.6 billion in the US economy in 2016, triple the amount recorded for 2015 and a tenfold increase of annual investment just five years ago," the Rhodium Group wrote.[47]

One of the poorest counties in Alabama is one of the destinations of Chinese investment, a place bereft of meaningful industrial investment for nearly four decades.[48] The Chinese company GD Copper USA that makes copper tubing received about $20 million in incentives from the state to create jobs. Surely the residents of the community are grateful for work and a revitalized local economy. But something else is going on. The manager of the Chinese-owned factory was quoted in *Bloomberg* as saying, "The best way to beat the enemy is probably to go to their homeland. As our former leader Deng Xiaoping put it, we'll cross the river by touching the stones."[49]

DRUG SAFETY AND THE US-CHINA BILATERAL INVESTMENT TREATY

As China goes on a spending spree, the United States and China agreed in 2013 to negotiate a bilateral investment treaty. Lauding the move, the US-China Business Council said, "Investment barriers in China are market access barriers, so a meaningful bilateral investment treaty would expand market access in China for American manufacturers, services providers, and agriculture companies."[50]

Cheering the agreement, the Obama administration's Treasury Department said, "This marks an important step in opening China's economy to US investment by eliminating market barriers, and leveling the playing field for American workers and businesses."[51] As with other investment treaties, the US-China treaty will likely include arbitration provisions to allow US companies with investments in China to bring claims against the Chinese government for violations of protections included in the treaty.

Protections for US investors typically include assurance that they are treated fairly and equitably by the Chinese government, and they can transfer funds related to investments in China freely. Claims are arbitrated in tribunals comprised of lawyers, not courts. The protections afforded US investors in China would also apply to Chinese investors in the United States.

The interests of US investors are not the only considerations when crafting a bilateral investment treaty. It should also serve the public interest. Lori Wallach, director of Global Trade Watch at Public Citizen, a consumer rights advocacy group and think tank, played out various scenarios of what could happen to drug safety under arbitration provisions in a bilateral investment treaty with China.[52]

Let's assume a drug made by a Chinese manufacturer in the United States is found to be harmful and it's taken off the market. The company could use arbitration provisions in a bilateral investment treaty to seek compensation from the US government. It could challenge the alleged adverse events reported to the FDA, saying any alleged harm was not because of the drug but because of the patient's condition or how a doctor prescribed it.

In this scenario, the Chinese company would bring a case before an arbitration tribunal comprised of three corporate attorneys, one appointed by the company, another by the government, and a third by agreement of the parties. It could seek compensation from the US government for lost revenue after the drug was taken off the market. The lawyers could order the US government and taxpayers to pay the Chinese firm for its losses. If the product is a widely used brand-name drug, the bill for taxpayers could be staggering.

"The most pernicious thing about the system is that it allows a foreign company to skirt domestic laws and courts," Wallach says.[53] "And the compensation isn't just actual damages," she adds. "They get compensated for future profits, which is outrageous."

Here's another scenario. If the FDA conducts an inspection in a Chinese-owned drug-manufacturing plant in the United States and finds violations of federal standards that compel the agency to shut it down and stop the sale of its drug, the Chinese owner could bring a case to a tribunal. It could claim the agency was overzealous, or treated the Chinese-owned firm differently than similarly situated domestic manufacturers.

Or if a Chinese drugmaker produced a shoddy drug that harmed patients, and those injured filed a class action lawsuit and collected damages, the Chinese manufacturer could seek compensation from the US government for the damages it had to pay patients, claiming the FDA regulatory approval process for the drug was ineffective.

Or take the case of a Chinese firm in the United States that obtains a patent for a new drug and obtains FDA approval to sell it. After the product is on the market, let's assume the FDA finds out the drug is not what the company claimed it to be. The data used to justify the new drug was fraudulent, and the patent is revoked in this scenario. The Chinese firm could allege unfair treatment with respect to patents and make a claim for compensation.

When it comes to food safety, Public Citizen laid out a scenario in which Shuanghui International, the Chinese company that bought Smithfield Foods™ in Virginia, could use provisions in a bilateral investment treaty to challenge new food safety standards Congress might enact that would increase the company's costs.[54]

The concerns are not theoretical. Consider a high-profile dispute between Germany and the power company Vattenfall™, owned by the Swedish government. After the Fukushima nuclear disaster in Japăn in March 2011, the German parliament voted to phase out nuclear power by 2022.[55] The decision led to the immediate closure of Vattenfall's two power plants in Germany.[56] Vattenfall is seeking compensation under the arbitration provisions in a European energy treaty. The company says the treaty gives "companies the security to make major investments without having to take political risks. . . . Germany can naturally decide to reorient its energy policy, but foreign investors should not have to pay the price for such a decision and lose money."[57]

Compensation to Vattenfall could reach nearly $6 billion for past and future lost profits, according to the International Institute for Sustainable Development, which has been tracking the case.[58] Vattenfall says the amount of compensation it is claiming is confidential under terms of the treaty. The case is pending.

Government policies to protect the public from the harms of smoking were at risk under a bilateral investment treaty between Switzerland and Uruguay. Tobacco company Philip Morris International™, whose operational headquarters are in Lausanne, Switzerland, claimed $22 million in compensation from the government of Uruguay.[59] Its anti-smoking laws caused the company to lose revenues, Philip Morris claimed. Government regulations required graphic warnings covering 80 percent of a cigarette pack.[60] Philip Morris lost the case, and its famed Marlboro Red sub-brands were reportedly slated for withdrawal from stores in Uruguay.[61]

In another case, using provisions of a 1993 Hong Kong–Australia bilateral investment treaty, Philip Morris Asia demanded compensation from the Australian government for its 2011 plain packaging law that prevents tobacco companies from using attractive colors and designs on cigarette packs.[62] The tobacco maker claimed the government expropriated its property by removing the brand name on the packaging. Philip Morris Asia lost the case. The mere threat of a claim at a tribunal had a chilling effect on new public health and safety regulations. New Zealand's government postponed implementing regulations similar to those in Australia until that case was decided.

The staid *Economist* labeled arbitration provisions in treaties "disastrous" for giving multinational companies access to a "secretive tribunal of highly-paid corporate lawyers for compensation whenever a government passes a law to, say, discourage smoking, protect the environment, or prevent a nuclear catastrophe."[63]

The US Office of the Trade Representative under the Obama administration acknowledged the Philip Morris case in Australia and the concern that companies could use arbitration panels to challenge legitimate US regulations.[64] It said it sought to ensure treaties do not impinge on legitimate regulation to protect public health. Nonetheless, companies will go to great lengths to protect their investments, and arbitration provisions in bilateral investment treaties can be a means to try to do so.

Because many Chinese companies are owned or controlled by the Chinese government, arbitration provisions could in effect allow a foreign government to nullify the application of a US law intended to protect the American public. A bilateral investment treaty with China is still on the drawing board. It is not the highest priority in the Trump administration, said Secretary of the Treasury Steven Mnuchin, according to a *Wall Street Journal* report.[65] The administration wants China to open up its market to US beef, biotechnology, and energy exports.

IF YOU THINK IT CAN'T HAPPEN HERE

A Vermont state legislator has an alarming tale to tell about how far the Chinese government will go to undermine US laws to protect the public. About a decade ago, Senator Virginia Lyons introduced a bill in the Vermont legislature to ban the disposal of computers, televisions, and other electronic waste in state landfills and incinerators. The bill mandated recycling of electronic products to prevent environmental contamination from lead, cadmium, and other hazardous materials that leach into the ground.[66]

"I received several emails from the Chinese government," Senator Lyons said.[67] "They were in Chinese. I scrolled down and saw a message in English from the Ministry of Commerce." The government told her to not consider the bill. "They claimed that if the state legislature acted on the bill, we would be violating WTO [World Trade Organization] technical barriers to trade rules."

In a Vermont state senate press release, Senator Lyons explained the Chinese interference:

> I received an email from Beijing. . . . And right on the front of that mailing from China was my home address and telephone. . . . The People's Republic of China questions the authority of the Vermont legislature to enact legislation to protect human life and the environment. This attempted interference by the People's Republic of China in the democratic process in Vermont is alarming and threatens basic principles of our system of government. Common sense solutions to health issues at the state and local level should not be subject to international pressure. . . . It's simply not OK for other governments to feel that they have a right to intervene in our state legislative process.[68]

Senator Lyons was "flabbergasted" to be contacted by the Chinese government as she sought to serve the citizens of her state.[69] She wrote to the US Trade Representative to ask why the Chinese government objected to her bill and was told it would destroy manufacturing in China by eliminating its ability to produce computers and other electronics. The Chinese government was apparently concerned that recycling products, rather than dumping them in the trash, would reduce sales of new products. Of course, that hasn't happened as China has cornered the markets for smartphones, computers, televisions, and so much more.

This was not the first time the Chinese government objected to the democratic process in state legislatures. China tried but failed to kill state legislation introduced in Maryland to protect the public from toys containing toxic levels of lead.[70]

The National Conference of State Legislators (NCSL) unanimously passed a resolution against China's meddling, saying, "NCSL deplores China's interference in the normal exercise of state lawmaking authority by raising the specter of possible trade challenges to state measures that are designed to limit the exposure of children to possible carcinogens and toxic chemicals."[71]

Vermont voted to ban electronic waste from its landfills and incinerators, joining other states with similar laws.

THE AMERICAN PUBLIC VS. THE GLOBALISTS

Globalists are at odds with the majority of the American public. In Gallup^{SM} polls, Americans overwhelmingly say China is a growing economic threat. In 2005, 64 percent considered China an economic threat, while 85 percent did so in 2015.[72] America helped create the middle class in China and at the same time destroy the middle class at home. Chinese workers became richer while American workers became poorer. Every time an American buys medicines, vitamins, clothes, computers, or anything else made in China, that money goes into the wallets of Chinese workers, not American workers.

Cities and towns with abandoned factories struggle under the weight of unemployment and underemployment. Billions of dollars in federal income and payroll tax revenues are foregone that would pay to repair bridges and dams, shore up the finances of Medicare and Social Security, and strengthen defense and cybersecurity against an increasingly aggressive China.

Nobel Prize–winning economist Joseph Stiglitz downplays the US trade deficit with China and advises the United States to look at its total trade balance with all of its trading partners.[73] Stiglitz was chairman of the Council of Economic Advisors during President Bill Clinton's administration. In 2015, he wrote in *Vanity Fair* that if China grows faster, it will buy more US goods and add to American prosperity.[74] With a $3.6 trillion cumulative trade deficit with China since 2000, the prediction that China would buy more from the United States has clearly not come to pass.

Former treasury secretary Henry Paulson is bullish on the belief that the United States will reform China, a theme echoed during the lobbying messages in the run up to the vote in 2000 on granting China permanent normalized trade status. A consummate China insider, Paulson wrote in his book, *Dealing with China*, that if the United States negotiates hard to open up China to competition, it will help reformers in the country succeed.[75] Perpetual wishful thinking ignores China's ascendency as an economic power and the deformation of American industries.

While secretary of the treasury during the George W. Bush administration, Paulson tried to tamp down tension when China irked American businesses, including the medical device industry, for blatantly favoring domestic companies and cutting out foreign ones. As the former chief executive of Goldman Sachs[SM], Paulson sees opportunity for investors looking for financial returns by accessing China's burgeoning market. The outcome is more likely to benefit Wall Street, not Main Street.

Making investment deals is a skill different from strategically guiding the US economy in its long-term best interests. By their very nature, investment deals deploy tactical thinking that benefit individual investors. America needs strategic thinking that looks out for the nation's long-term interests. The stakes are high. A country that loses its economic status surrenders its leverage and respect in the world.

The turning point in this lopsided trade relationship was the US-China Trade Relations Act of 2000. President Clinton's predictions are tragic for how wrong they were. To reject permanent normal trade relations with China would be a mistake of hugely historic proportions, he said.[76]

The truth is that history will judge free trade with China, rather than fair trade, to have been a blunder of truly historic proportions from which America will never recover.

PART III

THE HIDDEN COST OF CHEAP DRUGS

CHAPTER 9

ARE DRUGS FROM CHINA SAFE?

*"I don't think the information is there to say
they're bad, nor is it there to say they're good."*

Atoy train still chugs around the second floor of St. Louis Children's Hospital on an elevated track, a cheerful, momentary distraction for sick children and worried parents. A three-story-high rainbow-colored hot-air balloon still decorates the cafeteria ten years after the heparin contamination was first discovered. Memories linger. Dr. James Duncan, an interventional radiologist at the hospital who was not involved in the heparin incident, describes "the cold chill when you realize something like this happens. We never think about the possibility that how a drug is made is a risk. It used to be that you could judge a book by its cover, but now anyone can print a nice-looking label."[1]

Tragedies can tear apart what was always believed to be true. Trust in medicines was uprooted like the trees felled by the tornados that swept through central Missouri that fateful January in 2008. Never in a million years would doctors, nurses, and pharmacists have thought that every single batch of a drug sold by a company would have to be recalled. They expect a level of scrutiny and reliability. They trust that all the people who touch the making of a drug do everything right, every pill, every vial, every time. That a company obtained the core component from a facility in China that the FDA had never entered, reviewed, or performed product tests in, shattered their faith in the system. It takes years to earn trust and minutes to breach it.

STOCKPILING AND RECYCLING TOXIC HEPARIN

Now, the FDA scrupulously monitors the blood thinner to assure the safety of this vital drug. And it continues to find highly disturbing problems. How could this happen?

FDA officials and industry sources suspected that Chinese authorities were stockpiling and recycling the toxic drug, according to the House Committee on Energy and Commerce in a letter to then FDA commissioner Dr. Robert Califf in 2016.[2] Chinese firms filed patents for a process to remove the contaminant. Not all of it could be removed.[3] Trace amounts were explicitly permitted in the 2010 official Chinese government specifications for the product.[4] By 2015, trace amounts were no longer allowed, and by that time, all of the recycled product had probably been sold.

The change in the Chinese government's specifications "raises the disturbing question of whether any Chinese authorities were complicit" in allowing the stockpiling and recycling even after the contaminant was associated with deaths and injuries, the committee wrote.[5]

FAKE SUPPLIERS STILL IN BUSINESS

In February 2014, FDA officials went to inspect a facility in Beijing that makes the crude ingredient in heparin but were prevented from conducting the inspection. The FDA wrote in a warning letter,

> You barred the investigators access to the production area and other parts of the manufacturing facility. In several instances, the investigators requested to inspect the facility, but were repeatedly denied access to the production area. Your firm also limited FDA access to certain requested records. For example, the FDA investigators requested batch production records for review, but were refused access to these records repeatedly.[6]

What was it hiding? The company was using a supplier with the same address as a firm the FDA had banned from importing to the United States. That supplier apparently used an alias to hide its identity from the FDA. The name of the supplier is redacted (blacked out) in the warning letter.

> Furthermore, during the review of a list of your suppliers, one of the few documents you did provide, we noted that you are supplied by [redacted], which research indicates has the same physical address as, and is thus an alias of, the [redacted], a firm that is currently on FDA Import Alert.[7]

The warning letter raises a more troubling concern that the company may have been using suppliers whose products the FDA had banned because of their complicity in supplying contaminated product a decade ago. These suppliers could be circumventing the FDA ban and doing business under new company names. The warning letter says,

> If your firm is being directly or indirectly supplied by establishments that are associated with historical oversulfated chondroitin sulfate . . . your firm could be manufacturing heparin and heparin-related drugs that could be subject to import alert.[8]

Inspectors tested the raw material used by the company to make the active ingredient in the blood thinner. DNA from animals other than pigs, such as cows or sheep, was found, which can adversely affect the safety of the drug and is prohibited. Five months later, the company's products were barred from the United States.[9]

HIDE-AND-SEEK

Companies that play hide-and-seek will have their products banned. A company that makes active pharmaceutical ingredients in Beijing tried to hide large drums containing unknown products on its premises. An FDA warning letter to the company said,

> On November 16, 2015, our investigators observed through a window of a warehouse containing numerous drums bearing your company's label. When our investigators requested access to this warehouse, you barred them from entering the warehouse to examine the containers or the material in them without giving a reasonable explanation.
>
> The following day, you gave our investigators access to the warehouse. However, upon entry they observed that a significant number of drums had been removed and were not available for inspection. When they asked about the drums they had observed the previous day, you provided no explanation of the whereabouts or contents of the drums. You delayed [the] FDA's access to the warehouse and limited [the] FDA's inspection by removing the drums before our investigators could inspect them.[10]

The drug products the company was sending to the United States are not named in the warning letter. However, they were banned. An online search of publicly available FDA records reveals that the company makes an ingredient for antihistamines that relieve sneezing and coughs from allergies, hay fever, and the common cold, although we can't be certain what products were subject to the ban.[11]

COPY AND PASTE

Shocking findings from FDA inspections continue. In 2017, a Chinese company shipped active ingredients to the United States, claiming it was the manufacturer when the actual manufacturer was another company whose products the FDA had banned.[12] The company that was shipping the products to the United States had no quality unit to test them. Salespeople signed the documents certifying product quality. Companies that buy the active ingredient, and regulators, depend on these documents for truthful information about the quality and source of the products they buy. The FDA warning letter said, in part,

> Your firm has no Quality Unit. During the inspection, you provided no written documents describing the roles and responsibilities of a Quality Unit. You had no written procedures for quality activities. Your salespeople signed your certificate of analysis (COA) under the title "QC Director." Without performing tests, your salespeople also signed under "Tested By."[13]

The inspection was performed in June 2016 when the city where the products are manufactured enters its hot, humid, and heavy rainy season and the average temperature is eighty-one degrees Fahrenheit.[14] The plant didn't have temperature and humidity control systems, so employees opened the window during the inspection. The standards for making the active ingredient require it to be stored at seventy-seven degrees Fahrenheit.[15] Maintaining proper conditions prevents products from losing purity. The failure to spend money on a temperature and humidity control system is another hidden price of cheap drug products sold in America.

The same year, another company was found to be selling active ingredients from an entity whose products the FDA had banned.[16] The company copied and pasted information from the original manufacturer onto its own letterhead. The FDA warning letter named one of the active ingredients, gabapentin, which is used to make drugs that control seizures in people with epilepsy.[17]

An inevitable question is who is buying products from these businesses and using them to make drugs for US hospitals and pharmacies? Do firms that buy active ingredients for medicines inspect their suppliers? If so, how could they be buying from shady companies? Why aren't buyers finding these remarkable breaches of basic standards and terminating their relationship with the supplier? And what about the product? Are consumers and patients at risk when taking medicines made with these ingredients?

By redacting the names of drug products and suppliers in FDA warning letters and import alerts, unlawful acts are being covered up. Kevin McNeil, chairman of the Pharmaceutical Integrity Coalition, says it is "inexplicable and simply wrong" for the names of the products to be removed from warning letters and import alerts.[18]

When a company is placed on import alert, a violation of federal law or regulation has occurred that is serious enough that the FDA doesn't want the product in the country. The number of companies in China whose products were banned has swelled. From January 2014 to January 2016, eleven were put on import alert, nearly one every other month.[19]

CHINA HAMPERS INSPECTIONS: WHY DOESN'T THE UNITED STATES USE ITS BUYING POWER?

The United States buys billions of dollars' worth of drugs, medical devices, and food from China but fails to use its purchasing power to demand high-quality products and cooperation with the FDA.

Only two full-time FDA staff members are assigned to work in the agency's office in China to inspect drug-manufacturing facilities, said Dr. Christopher Hickey, then head of the FDA China office, in testimony to the US-China Economic and Security Review Commission in April 2014.[20] The bipartisan commission monitors and reports to congress on US-China trade and economic affairs. The former chair of the commission, Dennis C. Shea, called the situation "hopeless."[21]

China blocked visas for additional inspectors in the FDA office in China. Although the FDA's budget included money for additional FDA staff there, China refused to give visas to the staff the agency had hired.[22]

As a stopgap measure, US-based FDA employees have had to travel there to conduct inspections.[23]

This arrangement is far from ideal, according to Robert Walsh, founder of Samsara Biopharma Consulting:

> Friends who work for the FDA in the US have been dispatched . . . for short trips to the hinterlands of China. How effective they are expected to be when working against a language barrier, time constraints, and the wiles of companies seeking to hide deficiencies, I don't know.[24]

Then vice president Joe Biden tried to break the visa logjam during a visit to China in December 2013. The White House declared victory prematurely when the Chinese government agreed to allow a substantial increase in the number of FDA food and drug inspectors stationed in China.[25] But by the time Dr. Hickey testified before the commission in 2014, China still hadn't provided the visas.[26] Eager for additional staff, he said, "This will allow more rapid access to Chinese facilities and will help to increase the number of FDA inspectors who have in-depth knowledge and expertise about current challenges that Chinese industry faces."[27]

In another move, China forced the FDA to close its offices in Guangzhou and Shanghai. The government claimed it was a violation of the Vienna Convention for FDA staff posted in American consulates in the two cities to travel outside the geographic jurisdiction of their consulates to conduct inspections.[28] Forced to relocate, the FDA staff moved out of the two consulates and into the American embassy in Beijing in the fall of 2014. The FDA office in Shanghai is closed, and the Guangzhou office has one locally employed staff member.[29]

When then FDA commissioner Dr. Margaret Hamburg visited China in November 2014, she said, "We have every reason to believe that we will be getting the visas very shortly."[30] The agency had identified nine people to work in its offices in China, but the Chinese government continued to delay visas.[31]

"WHAT WOULD DOCTORS, PHARMACISTS, NURSES, AND PATIENTS THINK OF THIS?"

Chinese-owned companies are not the only ones that get into trouble. American-based pharmaceutical giant Pfizer™ owns a plant in Dalian, China, that ran afoul of federal standards. Employees hid documents from inspectors that revealed two sets of manufacturing records, an official set and an unofficial one.[32]

> During our walk-through inspection of your firm's manufacturing unit, we noted the presence of a stack of documentation approximately eight inches high. We entered the room and proceeded with our inspection. Approximately ten minutes later, upon our return to the location where the stack of documentation was identified, we found that it had been removed. We requested its retrieval and were brought approximately one-third of the original stack. We then requested an interview with the individual responsible for the removal of the documents and found that he had removed the remaining two-thirds stack from the manufacturing area and placed them in the upper floor construction/expansion area within a wood crate.[33]

The unofficial set of manufacturing records had a sticky note saying the materials were past their expiration date.[34] Inspectors also found inadequate washing and toilet facilities.

> During our inspection of your unit, we noted the presence of a stand-alone washing and toilet facility approximately fifty yards from the aseptic manufacturing facility that was in significant disrepair. Upon entrance to the facility we found no handwashing facility was provided and an open pit appeared to be used as a urinal.[35]

We spoke to a pharmaceutical industry consultant who worked for many years in the industry and who said this about "outrageous" sanitation issues such as open-pit toilets: "Can you imagine if this was found in the United States or Europe? Can you imagine what pharmacists, doctors, nurses, and patients would think of this if they knew?"[36] *Bloomberg* reported that Pfizer said the agency's findings had no impact on the quality or safety of products on the market.[37]

WORLDWIDE CHALLENGES

Indian manufacturers have come under intense FDA scrutiny and faced a deluge of warning letters and import alerts for compliance problems, quality control issues, and data integrity concerns. Its pharmaceutical industry moved up the value chain to become the largest supplier of generic drugs to the United States.[38] State-of-the-art manufacturing plants in India make high-quality products, but quality concerns continue.

India is different from China because it is not an existential threat to the United States. It does not have a centralized plan, designed and executed at the highest level of government, to drive out global competitors, dominate the world market, instill fear of retribution, or use its leverage to extract economic and political concessions from countries dependent on it.

Manufacturers in the United States run into manufacturing problems as well. Take the example of Johnson & Johnson, which sells Doxil®, a chemotherapy drug to treat ovarian and other cancers. Johnson & Johnson contracted with German drugmaker Boehringer Ingelheim™ to make it at its factory in Bedford, Ohio. The FDA discovered a litany of problems during an inspection in 2011. Metal particles were discovered in products made at the plant.[39] Bacteria were found in manufacturing areas. Rainwater leaked from the roof into a sterile storage area. The plant was the only one that made Doxil, and the quality problems caused a shortage. Doctors had the unenviable task of rationing the drug, causing enormous distress for 2,700 patients on a waiting list. Since then, the FDA approved a new manufacturer.

The shortage of an essential drug reveals the challenges of managing a supplier in the United States a few hundred miles away that has the same language and culture. Imagine the challenge and cost of managing a supplier located thousands of miles away.

We asked a long-time US industry veteran what a level playing field looks like for manufacturers in the United States, and here is what he said:

> We want a level playing field for all active ingredient and drug product manufacturers. And this means a level playing field for enforcement. Read enough warning letters issued to firms on the other side of the globe and you see outrageous sanitation issues such as open pit toilets. . . . My guess is that the FDA and the US Marshals Service would close the doors on this place immediately. Even if there is a warning letter and import alert put in place, those actions don't happen quickly. Warning letters take, on average, twelve months and import alerts appear to take about half that time. Until these actions are taken, the products continue to be sold in the United States. Because their costs are lower, insurers will choose them for formularies. After all, they are made in FDA-inspected facilities. Until we can get past this point, I don't see how we change things. Congress needs to know. Until then, the playing field will remain tilted to those who are problematic.[40]

And as long as the FDA is not permitted to enter a foreign manufacturing plant unannounced whenever it needs to, the playing field will never be fully even.

CHINA IS ON TRACK TO BECOME A PHARMACEUTICAL POWER. . . .

China is rapidly moving ahead to achieve its aim of becoming a global pharmaceutical power. Many state-of-the-art drug-manufacturing facilities produce high-quality drug products for the United States, and the number of firms sanctioned by the FDA is a small fraction of the total.

China acknowledges it is still at a development phase and has a long way to go to assure drug and food safety. Indeed, it takes decades to instill a culture of quality, safety, and integrity, and rigorously maintain it.

Flexing its muscle, the Chinese government is rooting out bad actors and imposing harsh punishment on wrongdoers. "Powerful supervision makes powerful industries," said Director Bi Jingquan, commissioner of China's counterpart to the FDA, at a press conference in Beijing in February 2016.[41]

Shaming scofflaws is a tactic that appears to be paying off. The Chinese government released the names of 1,622 new medicines awaiting approval for sale in China, and said it will publicize companies submitting fake or bad data to prove their products are safe and effective.[42] Companies were given a one-month amnesty period to withdraw their request for product approval. Eighty-three percent of companies withdrew their applications.[43] Conscientious drugmakers are rewarded. The government is publicizing locally made generic drugs that meet high standards and is using its enormous purchasing power to buy them when procuring medicines for the country's public hospitals.[44]

. . . AND AMERICA'S SHOCKING DEPENDENCE ESCALATES

China's ascendancy as a pharmaceutical power increases US dependence. The extent of dependence was revealed in 2015 when the FDA banned twenty-nine products from Zhejiang Hisun Pharmaceutical Company, one of the largest manufacturers in China, operating on a colossal scale, producing active ingredients destined for America and elsewhere.[45]

The FDA had received sixty-one complaints from Zhejiang Hisun customers about products allegedly contaminated with bacteria and lacking the full amount of therapeutic ingredient.[46] Drugs without full potency are especially dangerous for people with cancer, infections, and other life-threatening conditions. They could die, and the disease, not the inadequate drug, will be listed as the cause.

Hisun dismissed customer complaints about bacterial contamination, according to the FDA. After the inspection, the agency lambasted the company in a follow-up letter:

> From 2012 to 2014, several of your customers complained that microbial results were out-of-specification when they tested your active ingredient upon receipt. In your response, you concluded that the percentage of customer complaints reporting out-of-specification microbial test results was insignificant. You attributed the customers' out-of-specification microbial results to test methods that differ from your own.... [Y]ou did not retest the batches that received out-of-specification microbial complaints, even after we pointed out this deficiency. You lack scientific justification to conclude that your customers' out-of-specification findings are inaccurate or insignificant.[47]

FDA inspectors checked to see if employees properly tested products, recorded the results, and maintained good records, all standard practices for manufacturing safe drugs. They found systemic data manipulation:

> During the inspection, we asked to review your lab's raw analytical data of the lots associated with four of the sixty-one complaints. However, you were unable to provide the raw data because it had been deleted. Without raw test data for the lots associated with these complaints, your firm could not adequately investigate the complaints, nor could you expand your investigation to determine whether other lots were affected by the same problems or take corrective actions, such as recalling drugs if appropriate.[48]

The inspectors witnessed an employee removing a USB thumb drive from a computer. When they asked the employee for the thumb drive, the employee walked out of the room with it. Fifteen minutes later, company management gave inspectors what they said was the original thumb drive.[49] Was it the same one? FDA inspectors will never know.

Of the twenty-nine products banned, the FDA exempted fourteen of them because it feared a shortage. The import alert lists the names of the products exempted. When we showed the list of exempted products to a hospital pharmacist, she said six of them are used to make medicines for children with cancer and another is used for an AIDS-related cancer, Kaposi sarcoma. One of them is an active ingredient used to make daunorubicin, a chemotherapy drug for leukemia and other cancers.[50] At the Cleveland Clinic, the drug was rationed because of inadequate supply, according to a *New York Times* article published four months after the import ban.[51] The article did not mention the reason for the shortage.

A 2010 report prepared for the US-China Economic and Security Review Commission estimated that Hisun supplied 60 percent of the active ingredients for generic chemotherapy drugs in the United States, underscoring American dependence on a single company and concern about banning the product.[52]

Not everyone agrees that banned products should be allowed into the country. The FDA is sending a mixed message by allowing exempted products into the country.

Mark Paxton, then chief executive officer of Rx-360, a nonprofit consortium of manufacturers and suppliers from the pharmaceutical industry that wants to ensure the quality of medicines in the global supply chain, said,

> I don't think drug shortages are an adequate reason to allow adulterated products in the United States. Organizations out there making good products for US patients are not real happy, so there could be a bit of a chilling effect on compliance. It makes for an uneven playing field. Companies can skirt the rules and still get their product sold by taking advantage of a shortage situation.[53]

Pfizer formed a joint venture with Hisun in 2012 to make generic drugs.[54] The banned products were not covered by the joint venture, Pfizer told *Bloomberg*.[55]

WHAT HOSPITALS DON'T KNOW ABOUT THE DRUGS THEY BUY

"You put your orders in and get them," said Paul Levy, former chief executive officer of Beth Israel Deaconess Medical Center in Boston, about how hospitals buy prescription drugs.[56] "Hospitals don't do any secondary testing. The presumption is the FDA is managing all this. To have the capability in a hospital to do that kind of testing would be difficult to assemble," he added.

We asked the chief pharmacist at a large healthcare system if she was aware of the import ban and whether the active ingredient in the daunorubicin her organization buys was made by the Chinese company. We watched as she searched the healthcare system's online pharmacy inventory and found that the daunorubicin it purchases came from Teva Pharmaceutical Industries™, the giant Israeli generic company. She called Teva, and a company representative would not tell her if the active ingredient came from Hisun. "It's proprietary," the representative said.[57]

So, a healthcare system customer that spends hundreds of millions of dollars annually on prescription drugs can't find out if a drug it buys is made with a product that would have been banned had it not been for a shortage. Teva was willing to tell a *Bloomberg* reporter that it doesn't use Hisun as a supplier for products it sells in the United States.[58] The information couldn't be proprietary if it told a major news outlet.

The pharmacist asked the Teva representative for a copy of the certificate of analysis for the active ingredient, the document from the manufacturer of the ingredient that lists each test performed, the acceptance limits, and results obtained. Certificates of analysis are issued for each batch of any ingredient and contain the date of release, expiration date, and signatures of the employees in the company quality control unit.

The Teva representative said the pharmacist should get it from McKesson™, the giant distributor that supplies the healthcare system with its generic and brand-name pharmaceuticals. That required more phone calls, and the chief pharmacist had a lot of work to do, so she never received any documentation. Even if the pharmacist could see the certificate of analysis, its trustworthiness could be in question if the product was made with ingredients from Hisun where the FDA had found systemic data manipulation.[59]

The pharmacist wanted to know if banned products are tested by the FDA to ensure that they meet required standards before they are exempted and allowed into the country. We asked industry experts if the FDA tests banned products before exempting them. Without knowing details of the specific situation with Hisun, which are kept under wraps, Paxton said, "I would imagine if [the] FDA has exempted a set of products coming in from a company outside the US, I would expect them to test batch-to-batch samples before allowing them into the country."[60]

Companies that import active ingredients are responsible for monitoring their suppliers and testing active ingredients to ensure that they meet required specifications. But it took about three years for the complaints to the FDA about Hisun to result in products being banned.[61]

INSPECTIONS ARE NO GUARANTEE OF SAFE DRUGS

Inspections don't guarantee safe drugs. That's a lesson from the Zhejiang Hisun case in which multiple countries conducted inspections and allowed the company to operate for years. Hisun had eighteen inspections conducted by China's FDA, ten inspections by the US FDA, one inspection by the European Union's regulatory body (the European Medicines Agency), and inspections by German, Japanese, and Australian regulatory authorities.[62] A report prepared by NSD Bio™, a biotechnology consulting firm, for the US-China Economic and Security Review Commission said the company's quality control system was reported to be "very close to advanced level internationally."[63] How the company received a clean bill of health for so many years is unclear.

FDA inspections in other countries are different from those it conducts in the United States. One of the biggest differences is that inspectors can't walk into a manufacturing plant in China or any other country without giving advance notice to government authorities, although unannounced inspections can occur.[64]

"Foreign inspections are generally announced in advance because the FDA wants to make sure someone is at the facility," says Peter Saxon, who advises companies around the world on meeting good manufacturing standards.[65] "You don't want to fly ten thousand miles and arrive to an empty factory," he adds. "Foreign companies do considerable maintenance just before the FDA arrives. In the United States, companies can't do that because the inspections are unannounced."

Language barriers can be a problem as well. A former federal official told us that a translator did not accurately communicate a critical message this official intended to convey to Chinese counterparts during sensitive negotiations. Another federal employee present during the meeting was fluent in the language and observed the soft-pedaling of the message. The translator was dismissed.[66]

Barbara Unger, a thirty-year industry veteran, says, "It's difficult to audit even with a good translator. You can't read the documentation and cover as much, so you just try to do your best. You can cover less than 50 percent of what could be covered if all documentation was in English."[67]

Another industry veteran says,

I have friends who have worked in China and have gone to audit plants, and the forthrightness of information is so different from what we do here in our plant in the United States. It takes a lot longer to get information from them, sometimes days. When an auditor asks us for something, we have it in ten to fifteen minutes. My colleagues have told me it would take days, and you know they are scrubbing the data. They're showing you what they want to show you, in many cases.[68]

THE WHISTLEBLOWER

A rare inside story made headline news about how inspections can fail to stop bad medicines from reaching patients. The story was revealed only because a courageous pharmaceutical company employee took a career-derailing risk to force change and protect the public.[69] The story began when the FDA inspected a manufacturing facility in 2002 owned by a subsidiary of British drug giant GlaxoSmithKline™ (GSK), located in Puerto Rico. In a warning letter to the company, the agency said that if problems were not corrected, products could be seized. A follow-up inspection later that year found the company made some corrections.

Cheryl Eckard, a global quality assurance manager for Glaxo, was sent to the plant to help fix the problems. It was a big job. The factory churned out a reported $5.5 billion in drug products a year.[70] Eckard said she found drugs made in unsterile conditions. Medicine bottles were packed with different kinds of drugs. Avandamet® diabetes pills were mixed with over-the-counter Tagamet® antacid tablets. Antidepressant Paxil™ and Avandamet pills were found in the same bottle. She informed the company managers and told them the plant should be shut down, the FDA called in, and trucks leaving the factory should be stopped. That didn't happen. Eckard was fired.[71]

Eckard reported the conditions in the factory to the FDA. She became a whistleblower and filed a lawsuit in February 2004. Meanwhile, the FDA conducted additional inspections in 2003 and 2004 that revealed continuing problems, but the plant remained open. In 2005, the FDA and Justice Department sent armed marshals to seize $2 billion worth of products made at the factory that GSK did not recall.[72] The federal government only takes such drastic steps when a manufacturer refuses to fix problems. Paxil tablets were confiscated because they could split apart and consumers could swallow the part without any active ingredient. Avandamet tablets, the diabetes drug with Avandia® as an ingredient, were seized because they didn't have the proper amount of the key ingredient. Some pills contained too much and others too little.

The GSK subsidiary pleaded guilty in 2010 to distributing adulterated drugs. It paid criminal and civil fines totaling $750 million for selling drugs that didn't meet quality standards to Medicare and the Department of Veterans Affairs[73].

GSK responded to a *60 Minutes* report that aired in December 2010 after the settlement that the company had been working with the FDA since 2001 to fix the plant.[74] Those fixes apparently didn't work since federal officials had to raid the factory four years later. Eckard told *60 Minutes* that the company had received a complaint from a pharmacist after a grandmother picked up a prescription for Paxil for her grandson. She opened the bottle in the store in front of the pharmacist and said the pills had always been yellow. But the month before, the pills in the bottle were pink and he became sick. The pink pills were ten milligrams, and the yellow ones were twenty-five milligrams, two and a half times the prescribed amount. During a mix-up on the production line, bottles labeled as ten milligrams were filled with twenty-five-milligram tablets, Eckard said.

In its response to *60 Minutes*, GSK vigorously denied that people were harmed, quoting US Attorney Carmen Ortiz as saying, "We did not uncover any evidence that patients were harmed from these adulterated batches." The truth is authorities don't go looking for the injured. The injured have to come to them.

LOOKING FOR WHISTLEBLOWERS

Pharmaceutical Integrity Coalition's Kevin McNeil spent decades in the pharmaceutical industry and wants consumers to feel confident and trust their prescription drugs.[75] He cofounded the coalition to identify and correct gross deficiencies in drug manufacturing wherever they occur. The coalition's tagline: "We Are Not Pharma—We Are Fighting Bad Pharma."[76]

He is looking for whistleblowers, and here's why he does it:

We don't know what's in the vials on the shelves of our retail pharmacies and our hospitals right now. It deserves to be discovered and revealed for the greater good of America and the rest of the people in the world who depend on this industry. Right now, it's secret. I'm taking generic drugs right now for various ailments and my cholesterol bounces all over the place, and I don't know the quality of the product. I am sure many of the large companies want to pursue ethical manufacturing. I am sure there are plenty of companies that will overlook things because of convenience or because their manufacturing practices are deficient. The problem is finding them out.[77]

As generic drugs came onto the market and drug manufacturing went global, US companies operated on an uneven playing field, making it difficult if not impossible to compete with low-cost competitors offshore. Says McNeil,

They focused on the bottom line and cut the bottom line. The people with tenure tended to be eliminated. The institutional knowledge was leaving. Loyalty to company was gone. Adherence to good manufacturing practices was compromised. Young people came in with no mentors, no legacy. They weren't inculcated with the ethics of manufacturing the way it should be done.[78]

The Pharmaceutical Integrity Coalition provides a safe harbor for insiders anywhere in the world to report unsafe drugs that don't meet US standards, and connects them with experienced attorneys. McNeil says he does this work in the public interest and receives no money. For him, it's about ensuring that doctors, patients, and the public can trust every pill, tablet, and drug vial in corner drugstores, hospitals, and medicine cabinets in the United States and around the world.

Will whistleblowers report quality problems in companies making drugs in China? The risks of retaliation are high for whistleblowers in the United States and elsewhere, and surely the risks are very high in a country with unwavering intent to bolster its image at home and abroad. In the end, government oversight and enforcement can never substitute for corporate integrity. Susan Winckler, former chief of the staff at the FDA, compared the limits of government regulation to child-rearing:

> It's like a parent telling children to clean their room. They will clean it because of an inspection. But the next day? They are unlikely to keep their room clean unless it becomes part of how they live and internalize it. Regulation doesn't create the internalizing; it can't fix an absence of a culture. We can't inspect our way to assurance of good manufacturing. There has to be an ethos.[79]

THE ETHICS OF MAKING MEDICINE

We wanted to know how a high-functioning drug-manufacturing facility operates, so we asked industry veteran Craig Langdale to describe the gold standard for drug manufacturing.

> The company I work for is very ethical. We test absolutely everything that enters our facility, and we have a vigorous audit program where we audit every vendor. I can't say everyone does that. We're inspected by regulatory agencies from countries all over the world, primarily the United States, Europe, and Japan. If you get those three to inspect your facilities and products, most other countries will use their results. So, we get inspected by all these different countries, and it is very subjective and only a week, and there's no way for them to see everything. We are very proud that we've gone ten years with practically zero observations. We spend a lot of money to make sure we get the best of everything.[80]

ARE MEDICINES FROM CHINA SAFE? HERE IS WHAT INDUSTRY INSIDERS SAY

Industry insiders say progress has been made in assuring safe drugs because of the increase in inspections and the large number of import alerts that can motivate companies to improve. Mark Paxton, former CEO of Rx-360, says, "As China FDA levels the hammer, I think we'll see a higher quality of materials coming out."[81]

When we asked industry insiders and observers what they do when they go to the drugstore to pick up a prescription or buy an over-the-counter product, we received a variety of reactions.

A long-time industry employee, Cheryl Neath, admitted,

I have stopped taking vitamins because the components are mostly Chinese-made even if the tablets or capsules are made in the United States, and there's minimal oversight of supplements like vitamins. With antibiotics, that's scary. I will get the antibiotic with the brand name on it. I sent my husband back to the pharmacy saying, "Don't bring me the generic." Rightly or wrongly, I think the people who work for brand name companies have more invested. When my mom was on a blood pressure medicine and it was going off patent, I told her you don't want that since I knew who would be the generic drug maker, so the doctor left her with the branded medicine.[82]

Mark Paxton said,

As a consumer or healthcare provider, I want to know who makes it. I'll look at the label, and it will say either manufactured by, manufactured for, or distributed by. Reputable firms are well known with well-defined compliant post-marketing processes. But then there are those—especially newer companies—that I wouldn't recognize, and this is especially true of generics, believe it or not. The fact that FDA-approved products from them doesn't address a robust compliance profile, so I'd want to research them a bit more. For reputable firms with large portfolios of drugs, 99 percent of the time they will be good. They have too much at risk.[83]

Steve Dickinson, an attorney who advises US companies that conduct business in China, wrote to us and said,

My wife is a Chinese-born engineer. A good friend of mine in China is a US-trained biochemist who works for a drug manufacturer in Shanghai. I mentioned your question to them today. They both said, "I would not take a drug that I knew was manufactured in China." These people are not ignorant peasants. They are both highly-trained scientists/engineers. This shows what this is all like for us folks who live in China. We all think the Americans are a bit naïve. There is a reason for the China price.[84]

Peter Saxon, who helps companies in China and around the world meet good manufacturing standards, said,

In the companies I assist, all of them have reached an acceptable level of compliance with good manufacturing standards. Those that have not, I refuse to represent during an FDA inspection. I measure acceptance by a simple value judgment. If my ninety-year-old mother needed this medicine, would I have any concerns if she used it? If I am confident in the quality using this yardstick, I am confident the pharmaceutical will be safe and effective. This is my definition of what is acceptable.[85]

Former FDA official David Carter summed up the reason for the wide range of views about the safety of China's medicines. "I don't think the information is there to say they're bad, nor is it there to say they're good."[86]

"PEOPLE HAVE NO IDEA . . ."

Although the FDA has new authority to protect the American public, the risks of outsourcing are changing and pose a threat to the safety and reliability of America's medicines. Even with stepped-up inspections, the super-long supply chain increases the risks exponentially.

A company executive with pharmaceutical-maker Amgen™ described to an industry audience the long links in the global supply chain, saying his job is to monitor "our suppliers' suppliers' suppliers."[87] The complexity is driven by procurement departments in pharmaceutical companies looking for the cheapest products to make drugs. The manufacturers of active ingredients are "beaten up by pharma's procurement departments," Louis Garguilo, editor of *Outsourced Pharma*, wrote.[88]

The drive for cheap has breathtaking consequences. At Peking University, then FDA commissioner Dr. Margaret Hamburg told an audience that the global supply chain for America's medicines "spans not simply different factories or farms, but different nations."[89] She added that "the risks are greater at every step in our increasingly complex global supply chain networks today. Sometimes these hazards are the result of a lack of quality control . . . and sometimes, these hazards stem from intentional acts of diversion, counterfeiting, or adulteration."[90] At a Council on Foreign Relations meeting in 2011, Dr. Hamburg said,

> I think people have no idea in this country and around the world about the vulnerability of things that we count on every day, food, drugs, medical devices, and other related products. And that we have a system that has big gaps in our protective mechanisms and that it's a growing problem.[91]

Threats have become more sophisticated. "The reality is that manufacturers and others in the supply chain around the world may place economic gain above safety and public health or have even more malevolent motivations," said Deborah Autor, then deputy commissioner for Global Regulatory Operations and Policy at the FDA, in a speech to American importers and exporters.[92] "Increasingly, the Agency—as well as industry—must contend with ever-more sophisticated threats of fraud, product adulteration, and even terrorism," she said.[93]

The FDA's job is to prevent the proverbial dam from bursting and stop a flood of lethal products from entering the United States. Its dedicated professionals are far better equipped now to detect a disaster sooner and react to it faster than when the heparin incident occurred. By building closer working relationships with its counterparts in other countries, agency officials receive more timely information about troublesome manufacturers and products.

The FDA says drugs are safe. But the outsourcing of America's medicine making is so complex it seems impossible to ensure that they *are* safe.

CHAPTER 10

MADE IN CHINA, SUE IN AMERICA? GOOD LUCK

*"The reason our work is so cheap is that we are not liable
for consumer protection. If we were liable, the product
would be very, very expensive."*

O ver a waffle and bacon breakfast at the Hilton at Phoenix Sky Harbor
Airport, Charlisa Allen opens a manila envelope filled with a trove of
family photos. Summer has not arrived, but the one-hundred-degree heat
is scorching. From the window, palm trees and flowering lantanas can be
seen decorating the patio.

"My husband loved to fly-fish," she says, smiling at a picture of Bob
holding a rainbow trout and squatting by the edge of the Pecos River in
the Sangre de Christo Mountains in New Mexico.[1] The red granite bands
decorating the riverbank are a striking contrast with the azure sky.

Their daughter Jennifer, petite and lithe, has neatly combed blond hair
that rests below her shoulders. "She was really into soccer," Charlisa says.
"My husband drove her to all her games and never missed a single one."

Joshua's college graduation photo shows he's surely his father's son,
tall, with a thick mop of black hair and a widow's peak at the center of
the forehead. "He looks just like his dad," Charlisa marvels. "When I look
at my son, I think of my husband all the time." Beaming with motherly
pride, she adds, "He got a full academic scholarship to Tulane." She shares
his college admission essay in which he wrote, "My dad always told me
that while he was not the best and the brightest, he was still successful
because he gave all of his effort to every endeavor."

Charlisa met Bob in the summer after her first year at the University of Missouri medical school. She was working in Baltimore and living with her brother who was attending Johns Hopkins medical school with his best friend, Bob. On a hot afternoon, Bob came over and met Charlisa for the first time.

"He was really into sports, and I thought we weren't really compatible," she says with a smile. On their first date, the 6'3" sports enthusiast invited Charlisa to go sailing on Chesapeake Bay. It didn't turn out as Bob had hoped. With a bubbly laugh, Charlisa recounts the day as a total disaster. "The mast collapsed, and we were marooned in the bay. The coast guard had to come rescue us."

With so many active ingredients and finished drugs made in China, we wanted to know if Americans have any legal recourse in the unlikely event of a problem with a product. We asked Steven Dickinson, an attorney with the law firm Harris Bricken in Seattle, who lives in China and whose practice is with foreign companies that conduct business there.

Dickinson said when a US company buys a drug product from a Chinese manufacturer and sells it in the United States, Americans who believe they were harmed by the drug can seek a claim against the US company.[2] In the case of the contaminated heparin sold by Baxter™,[3] people who believed they were harmed could file a claim.

In another scenario, if a drug is made in China by a Chinese firm and distributed in the United States by a US sales and marketing firm, the American consumer has recourse against the sales and marketing firm, says Dickinson.[4] He adds that the US-owned firm is taking a high risk if it doesn't buy insurance, which is likely to be expensive.

Another likely scenario is if a Chinese manufacturer has a US-based subsidiary. An American consumer does have a remedy against that subsidiary. "The problem is that the subsidiary probably has little to nothing by way of assets," said Dan Harris, managing partner at Harris Bricken.[5]

Dickinson advises US companies that do business in China to buy product liability insurance, but most don't. This leaves them and their customers exposed to claims against the Chinese manufacturer.

The Chinese companies know this, and he says their explanation for why their products are so cheap goes something like this: "[W]e are not liable for consumer protection. If we were liable, the product would be very, very expensive. If you want a cheap product, the price is that we do not take any liability for consequential damages."[6]

Dickinson explains that this view is well known in China but typically ignored by US and European drug companies:

> Everyone in the West wants the "China price" but they seldom understand what that means. In many or most cases, if the full set of Western standards is loaded onto the product, the "China price" completely disappears.[7]

Back at the Mayo Clinic™, while Bob Allen was in the operating room undergoing a heart and kidney transplant on February 27, 2008, Charlisa waited with his parents, hoping beyond hope.[8] "I knew intellectually it wasn't going to work," she said. "On the other hand, you're still so hopeful you can't focus on it not working." She wrote to family and friends,

> I received the call early this morning (1:30 a.m.) that a donor heart and kidney had been located in San Diego. Bob was taken into surgery around 5:30 a.m. this morning, while the other team retrieved the organs. I will update everyone when I have more news. We are all fine, tired of course, but in good spirits. Thank you everyone.[9]

As the hours dragged on, a nurse, who took care of Bob in the ICU, came out of the operating room with tears streaming down her face. Soon, the surgeon came and talked with Charlisa and Bob's parents. The heart transplant had failed. The plan to transplant a kidney was abandoned because so much irreversible damage had been done to Bob's body and the transplant would have failed. Bob was moved to the ICU where he remained sedated for the coming days.

The following day, despite all odds, Charlisa tried to keep hope alive.

Bob has undergone the transplant surgery yesterday. Due to the severe complications with his lungs, his new heart had difficulty pumping. . . . He is sedated and the situation is critical. The Mayo Clinic has experience with these types of problems and they are not giving up on him. Please send any positive thoughts and prayers his way.[10]

Four days after Bob's transplant, he remained in critical condition and Charlisa, still hoping beyond hope, wrote,

We are still in the hour-by-hour phase, so this can go either way. I think it is a miracle that he has made it this far. I go from planning his memorial service to planning safety bars for him in our bathroom. I know that all your prayers have gotten us this far and I so appreciate this.[11]

The following day she penned,

Bob continues to improve this evening. He is blinking his eyes when we speak to him now! They are continuing to pull off fluid with dialysis in order to get him ready to come off the lung bypass. It is a miracle that we have come this far with him. My son added a family photo of us on vacation in Hawaii that you can see.[12]

On March 4, more news:

I spoke with the surgeon and medical team today and they are encouraged by Bob's progress. . . . He is not in rejection and no signs of infection. The new heart is functioning well. They tried to wean him off the lung bypass, but he is not ready yet, so plan to try again Thursday. We know that Bob will have a slower recovery than we had hoped if he survives, but we are prepared for this. Thank you for all your continued prayers and support.[13]

On March 6, Charlisa wrote,

Today he goes in for surgery to attempt to close his chest and place him on a ventilator. He continues to fight and we thank you for all your prayers.[14]

That night, as was her routine, Charlisa stayed at the hospital until about eleven o'clock and went home to be with Jennifer and Joshua. The next morning when she woke up, she felt as if someone was standing over her bed. The phone rang, and she knew it was the Mayo Clinic. "You need to get here right now," said a voice on the other end of the phone.[15]

When she arrived at the hospital, a priest and social worker were in the family conference room. The surgeon arrived, tears in his eyes. Charlisa knew the doctors and nurses had done everything humanly possible to save her husband. That evening she wrote,

After a courageous fight and long journey, Bob is gone. He put forth a superhuman effort in this struggle, but it was not meant to be. I will always cherish my memories of him and thank everyone for all your prayers and support. A memorial service will be planned for a later date.[16]

"It was a horrific end," Charlisa says of the three tortuous months. "I wouldn't wish it on my worst enemy."[17]

Bob had been in excellent health and healthier than most men his age. With his medical history, the likelihood of him having a heart attack was 1.7 percent, using the American Heart Association risk calculator.[18] He didn't smoke or have diabetes. He had no family history of heart disease. His blood pressure and cholesterol were normal. The abdominal pain that brought him to the Mayo Clinic emergency department was caused by inflammation in his small intestine, just below the stomach, a condition called duodenitis that is not life-threatening.

When doctors examined Bob's heart after it had been removed from his body, it had no telltale signs of heart disease. Heart attacks can occur because globs of fat, or plaque, accumulate on the inner lining of the heart's arteries. If a piece of plaque detaches from an artery wall, it can block the flow of blood. His arteries were free of blockage caused by heart disease.

In the catheterization lab, pictures of his coronary arteries showed extensive clots in his two largest arteries, and doctors removed the clots. He was given two more doses of heparin, larger than before, at 11:52 a.m. and 11:53 a.m.[19]

Eleven minutes later, his heart began to fail, a condition doctors call cardiogenic shock.[20] He developed severe, life-threatening low blood pressure. Doctors did everything they could to raise his pressure, but his heart could not pump enough blood through his body. He suffered a massive heart attack. The blood clots cascaded to his kidneys and other organs, and they, too, became deprived of oxygen.[21] A medical catastrophe was unfolding.[22]

THE CURSE OF MEDICINE

Bob lived with the curse of medicine. As a physician, he understood the horror of knowing too much. He knew there was virtually no hope he would walk out of the hospital alive. "A doctor couldn't come into the room and say everything will be okay," Charlisa says. "My husband knew the probable outcome, but he was brave and stuck with it anyway. He did it for us," she says, her voice breaking.[23]

Charlisa filed a lawsuit in 2010 against Baxter and Scientific Protein Laboratories™ (SPL), whose company in China supplied the contaminated active ingredient in heparin sold by Baxter.[24] The suit alleged that all of the heparin Bob received on December 2 was contaminated Baxter heparin, and it caused the dramatic medical problems that led to his death.[25]

"This was the only way I could get the truth," Charlisa says.[26] She had to file a lawsuit to receive the 2.5 million pages of his medical records and have expert physicians review them and write their independent assessments of why her husband died.

Charlisa's lawsuit and 573 other lawsuits from around the country were consolidated and transferred to a single federal court in Toledo, Ohio, a common practice in product liability cases.[27] The Toledo court coordinated requests for documents and evidence so plaintiffs didn't have to ask for, and defendants didn't have to provide, the same information to 574 plaintiffs and their lawyers.

The judge appointed in the case, the Honorable James G. Carr, established criteria that cases had to meet before they could proceed to a jury trial. An injured person had to suffer a reaction within sixty minutes of receiving heparin, based on evidence from the Centers for Disease Control and Prevention about the usual timing of reactions from contaminated heparin.[28]

Only people who had certain symptoms known to be associated with contaminated heparin could pursue their cases. If a case did not meet the criteria, it was dismissed. Charlisa's case met the criteria for the case to proceed.

About a year after the lawsuit was filed, Baxter and the other defendants requested that the judge dismiss the case. "The patient could not have received contaminated Baxter heparin," the lawyers for the defendants argued.[29] "[P]urchase records produced by Mayo Clinic Hospital show that the first vials of Baxter 5,000 u/ml heparin were not sent to the hospital until December 11, 2007—*9 days after the patient's alleged receipt of contaminated heparin,*" they claimed.[30]

The defense argument was a knockout blow, it seemed, but it had a fatal flaw. The heparin was shipped from pharmaceutical wholesaler Cardinal Health™ to the Mayo Clinic Hospital at 13400 E. Shea Blvd. in Scottsdale, Arizona. This is the address of the Mayo Clinic, an outpatient facility with 240 exam rooms, an imaging center, and pharmacy.[31] Charlisa's lawyers were quick to point out that defense attorneys had the wrong address. Bob received his care fifteen miles away at the Mayo Clinic Hospital located at 5777 E. Mayo Blvd. in Phoenix.[32] At the disclosure of this information, Baxter's lawyers withdrew their motion to dismiss the case.[33]

Charlisa's aim was to have a jury trial at home in Arizona. "I want the public to hear what happened and decide the outcome," she said.[34] But the path to a jury trial is littered with obstacles. A pocket guide for judges overseeing product liability cases consolidated in federal courts advises judges to encourage mediation and settlement out of court.[35] In Charlisa's case, Judge Carr did just that. "The first thing they tell you in mediation is how little your case is worth," she says. "Then they tell you the risk of going to trial and having your case dismissed is great."[36] Charlisa told the mediators she thought mediation should be an opportunity for the guilty party to admit fault, and then both sides come to a resolution. Of course, that did not happen.

"POURING GAS ON A FIRE"

Charlisa's medical background helped her make her case during mediation. "When Baxter came up with objections, I jumped in to explain to the mediator what happened to my husband medically," she said. "I was the only one in the room who had medical training. It also helped that my dad was a prosecutor, so I know a little bit about the law."[37] Charlisa says she kept asking a question the defendants' lawyers could not answer:

> If you think it wasn't contaminated heparin, how do you explain what happened to my husband? Eleven minutes after getting two large doses of heparin, my husband's heart and all his organs failed, and the more heparin he received, the worse he got, like pouring gas on a fire. What is your explanation?[38]

Charlisa says one of Bob's doctors told him he received contaminated heparin, perhaps because he was a fellow physician and a member of the same professional tribe.[39] Armed with this information, she proceeded with confidence that she had a solid case. Charlisa went to mediation three times and refused to settle.

> Other people settled for as little as $10,000 or $50,000 when they lost a limb or a kidney. That won't begin to cover the cost. They'll be on dialysis for the rest of their lives and may not be able to work. They settled because they had little choice. If they didn't take the offer, their cases would be dismissed. They couldn't know what questions to ask because they aren't physicians, and there's no reason they should know.[40]

After unsuccessful mediation, the defendants tried again to have Charlisa's case dismissed in October 2015. They claimed that her lawyers had not established that the heparin Bob received was Baxter's heparin, or that it was contaminated.[41] Charlisa's lawyers filed a statement opposing the companies' motion for dismissal. Because many supporting documents are filed under confidential seal, it is impossible for the public to know the basis for the defendants' request to dismiss the case.

Judge Carr denied the defendants' request. In a May 2016 ruling, the judge said Charlisa's lawsuit could proceed to a jury trial in Arizona where her lawyers could present evidence in support of her case. Delighted with the judge's decision, Charlisa said, "I'll get to talk about it in a trial," which was not possible during the pretrial phase that occurred 1,900 miles away in Toledo, Ohio.[42]

Judge Carr wrote in his decision, "If plaintiff can prove any harm Allen suffered within sixty minutes after the 11:52 a.m. and 11:53 a.m. heparin administration was of a kind that normally occurs from contaminated heparin, and Allen's health problems were, at least, in part due to receiving contaminated heparin, she will prevail."[43] But if the jury finds that the heparin doses at 11:52 a.m. and 11:53 a.m. didn't contribute to Allen's health problems, the defendants would prevail, the judge added.

Charlisa's progress on the journey to justice is a rare bright spot. Of the 574 cases in the Ohio federal court, it appears that hers is the only one that will be heard by a jury.[44] The other cases were settled or dismissed, according to court statistics maintained by the Federal Judicial Center in Washington, DC.[45]

We emailed the Ohio Federal District Court Clerk's Office to find out how many cases were dismissed and how many were settled, and were told the court does not have the information readily available because it requires a painstaking review of court documents for every case.[46]

Charlisa is dismayed the companies have spent millions of dollars defending a case like hers. "What they should do is what any normal person would do and say, 'Oh, gosh, I made a mistake, I feel terrible,' rather than try to hide everything and sweep it under the rug." Charlisa's case progressed because she is a doctor and could explain to her lawyer what happened medically to her husband. "It shouldn't take someone like me, a widow with two children who happens to be a physician, to hold people accountable," she says.[47]

The trial is scheduled to begin in Phoenix, Arizona, in March 2018. "I want people to know how bad this really was," she said. "What they did was wrong. My husband had a horrific death."

Back at Sky Harbor Airport, Charlisa's voice turns wistful, trailing off: "We were together twenty years. We had a great life, we really did. My husband was a wonderful dad. Some people never have that. We swam with dolphins. I tell my kids that I'm lucky to have had the time with him that I did."[48]

Bob was a bird lover, and cardinals, with their brilliant red plumage, were his favorite. "This may seem crazy, but when I flew to New Orleans to celebrate my son's graduation from Tulane, a cardinal suddenly appeared in the backyard where we were gathered," Charlisa says. And it happened again.

A few weeks later when I received the judge's ruling granting a jury trial, I was sitting on my patio thinking about all that's happened. Suddenly, above my head I heard a northern red cardinal's distinctive chirp. I looked up and saw a flash of red in the cluster of ivy that hangs on the wall separating my yard from my neighbor's. I had never seen one at my house before, and they're rare in Phoenix. I feel as if my husband is still here, watching over us.

CHAPTER 11
THE PERFECT CRIME

"In healthcare we usually operate like a mom-and-pop shop and don't aggregate information about bad reactions to medicines, or investigate for shared causes and commonalities."

Apoorly made or deliberately contaminated prescription drug is a perfect crime. It is hard to detect. Manufacturers keep the public in the dark. Regulators are tight-lipped so they don't offend manufacturers. Perpetrators are rarely caught. Most victims are unaware.

Here's a best guess of how many people received contaminated heparin based on publicly available information. We have to guess because no one counts, and no one is accountable for knowing.

In January 2008, Baxter™ recalled more than ten million vials, according to a study published in the *New England Journal of Medicine*.[1] Some could not be recalled, of course, because they had been given to patients. An unknown number of additional vials were recalled by Baxter on February 28, 2008.[2] When the FDA tested samples of the toxic blood thinner, contaminant levels ranged from 2 to 50 percent of the total content of the active ingredient.[3] The higher the level of contaminant in the vial that a patient received, the greater the risk of harm.

Millions of people probably received a dose from the affected vials.[4] If the dose was small, serious ill effects may not have occurred. If the dose was large, and multiple doses were administered, the harm could have been catastrophic.[5]

When we first met Charlisa Allen, one of the first things she said was the number of people harmed would fill a football stadium.[6] Because serious safety concerns with drugs are underreported, she might be right.

SERIOUS DRUG REACTIONS VASTLY UNDERREPORTED

Sheer luck triggered the heparin investigation. At St. Louis Children's Hospital, two children were given the same drug, at the same time, in the same clinic, and had the same bad reactions. If only one child had a bad reaction, doctors would have reasonably thought the child was allergic to something and would have never considered the possibility that a toxic drug was the cause.

Doctors rarely think that a poorly made or contaminated drug might be a cause of a patient's deteriorating condition, especially in the fast-paced, task-oriented healthcare workplace. But the astute and proactive doctors at the hospital pulled the emergency break.

"In healthcare we usually operate like a mom-and-pop shop and don't aggregate information about bad reactions to medicines, or investigate for shared causes and commonalities," said Dr. James Duncan, from the children's hospital.[7] "Other industries use reports of what appear to be flukes to look for patterns and identify the causes. We should do the same thing in healthcare, but all too often we simply go on to the next patient."

Two hundred forty-six reports were made by healthcare professionals to the FDA about deaths associated with heparin from January 1, 2007, to May 31, 2008.[8] As with all reports it receives, the agency makes no claim of certainty that a death was caused by a drug. It doesn't review patient medical records or investigate the cause of death. The person who makes a report doesn't have to prove that a drug was the cause of death.[9]

The FDA briefed the media on conference calls during the height of revelations about the contamination. During a briefing on March 19, 2008, the FDA's Dr. Janet Woodcock told reporters, "On adverse events, fortunately, since Baxter's expanded recall on February 28, we have received no reports of deaths related to allergic reactions to the heparin that occurred after that date."[10] Bob Allen died on March 8, 2008. Apparently, his death was not reported to the FDA by March 19, 2008, the day of the call with the media.

Dr. Woodcock did not discuss the number of people harmed, or the nature of the injuries. "The information is too complicated to present over the phone," she told reporters.[11] "And therefore, we are going to be posting that on our website for people to look at so that they will have the numbers and timing of the reports of deaths and when the deaths occurred and so forth."[12]

According to the FDA website, seven deaths were reported in March 2008, presumably after March 19, the day of the media briefing.[13] Charlisa Allen wants to know if her husband's death on March 8 was eventually counted. She will never know because the FDA does not release the names of hospitals that report serious drug reactions.

Hospitals are expected, but not required, to report to the agency any serious drug reactions that result in death, life-threatening injury, hospitalization, or disability.[14] The agency doesn't have regulatory oversight of hospitals, and there is nothing it can do to require hospitals to report, according to Madris Tomes, who worked at the FDA tracking reports of problems with hip and knee implants and other medical devices.[15] Reporting is voluntary for doctors, nurses, and pharmacists.[16]

Only drug manufacturers, distributors, and packagers are required by federal regulation to report to the FDA, and they have to do so within fifteen days of finding out about a problem.[17] Tomes said, "Manufacturers underreport and misreport. Not all of them. There are some good apples."[18]

MedWatch is the agency's online go-to place to report safety concerns. "It's a nightmare," says industry veteran Barbara Unger, referring to the valuable but voluminous information asked for on the reporting form. "I live and breathe this stuff, and I got two-and-a-half pages into writing a report, and I said to myself I'm not going to finish it. For anyone who is not trained, it's overwhelming. I did end up finishing it, but you have to be really dedicated."[19] This is one of the reasons that only about 10 percent of serious problems are reported.

DEATHS NOT COUNTED

When analyzing reports to the FDA on medical devices, Tomes says, "Even when problems with a device are reported, they might be misreported as injuries when, in fact, the patient died."[20] She adds,

> Some cases where there were deaths, they were reported using words like "the patient passed away" or "autopsy." The FDA doesn't count these as deaths unless the person who makes a report checks the "death" box.[21]

Tomes says that agency employees don't change or correct reports submitted because of concern about liability if a manufacturer's stock price drops after a lot of deaths are associated with a product.[22]

Brian Overstreet is the founder and chief executive officer of Adverse-Events based in Santa Rosa, California. His firm cleaned up more than three million reports to the FDA about drug safety concerns and made them easily searchable on a website.[23] Problems with a drug can be quickly spotted, and prompt regulatory action can be taken to protect the public. Overstreet said, "Such underreporting and delays make it extremely difficult for the FDA or any other interested party to effectively identify and publicize current adverse event risks."[24] Timely action can save lives. Nearly 10 percent of drug adverse events reported to the agency in 2010 resulted in deaths, and 21 percent caused people to be hospitalized.[25]

FDA data is a treasure trove, if it were fully used for the public's benefit. AdverseEvents looked at 150,000 reports of serious muscle and tendon problems associated with cholesterol-lowering statin drugs. Some statins had a much higher rate of reports than others, but the FDA doesn't inform doctors or the public. The pharmaceutical industry exerts substantial control over the agency and prefers to keep problems with their products out of public view.

The AdverseEvents website is available by subscription to pharmaceutical, insurance, and other healthcare firms, and the company plans to start a service for patients. But pharmaceutical firms didn't want to see his data, Overstreet said.[26] He told *Xconomy*, which covers San Francisco-based business and technology news, that pharmaceutical companies ran away from it and didn't want to pay for it.[27]

Madris Tomes says that the FDA reports should be open to the public and easy to search. She left the FDA and founded Device Events, a software application that makes it easier to understand the 5.9 million medical device adverse event reports and recalls in the FDA's data system. She says it takes the FDA two months to two years to act on problem reports it receives.[28] About the FDA reporting system, she says,

> You should be able to search reports to the FDA in a meaningful way, but they're not presented that way. . . . No physician or consumer can possibly understand the risks of a device because the FDA's system is too cumbersome. This is hard for me to say. I worked at the FDA. I know the analysts care. But they don't have the tools to do better.[29]

Kevin McNeil, chairman of the Pharmaceutical Integrity Coalition, says, "All adverse events reported to the FDA should be transparent and searchable. You should be able to search them by product and by deaths."[30]

TRUST BUT VERIFY, BUT WHO'S VERIFYING?

Conscientious manufacturers of drugs, and everything that goes into them, spend a lot of time ensuring product safety. All manufacturers are required by the FDA to test their products. Usually a small sample is tested, so in a batch of two million pills, a hundred might be randomly chosen for testing.[31] Companies that buy an active ingredient or finished drug from a supplier are required to retest it.

McNeil questions the quality of the testing, especially of imported drug products. "I am not confident that all companies test every incoming lot of imported active ingredients or drug products," he said.[32] "I think they use the documentation that comes with the product and don't test it when it comes into the United States."

Joe and Terry Graedon found out that drugs aren't always tested as they should be. They are the founders of the People's Pharmacy®, the consumer-friendly website and radio program. Consumers contacted them about problems when they switched from a brand-name antidepressant to a generic that had just come on the market. It was causing unusual side effects and didn't seem to be effective.[33] The generic was Budeprion XL™ 300 mg, an extended release pill taken once a day, marketed by generic giant Teva Pharmaceutical Industries™. It was supposed to gradually release its active ingredient throughout the day.

The Graedons contacted ConsumerLab.com℠, a privately held company in Westchester County, New York, that conducts independent tests of health and nutrition products.[34] In 2007, ConsumerLab. com tested the product and released its easy-to-understand report to the public.[35] It used samples from pharmacies where consumers buy them, not from the manufacturer who might pretest a sample and send the best.

The generic made by Teva was tested against the brand-name Wellbutrin XL® 300 mg. Within the first two hours of testing, Wellbutrin XL 300 mg released 8 percent of the active ingredient. Teva's generic released 34 percent in the same time period, which might have explained the unusual side effects users reported.[36] The early burst of the generic faded later in the day, putting patients on an "unexpected roller coaster ride," said Todd Cooperman, MD, president of ConsumerLab.com.[37]

The results defied everything the public had been told about generic drugs. The generic was not the same as the original. It took five years for the FDA to announce that Teva's generic was not equivalent to the brand-name product.[38] Teva pulled its drug off the market.[39]

PATIENT NONCOMPLIANCE OR BAD DRUG?

A former FDA official named David Carter told us how patients can be blamed for noncompliance in taking their prescription drug in the manner and dosage indicated by the manufacturer or their physician when it doesn't have the expected result. "The medical community may understandably think if a drug doesn't work, it's a patient compliance problem and not a problem with a drug. It can be very difficult to know what is going on."[40]

Publicly reporting the results of FDA tests can assure doctors and the public of the quality of the medicines. "We're relying on the scruples of the industry," he said. "I tell my wife, if something doesn't work, maybe you need another manufacturer."[41] The problem might be an inactive ingredient, also called an excipient, that can affect the drug.

FDA TESTING OF YOUR DRUGS

The FDA had been dramatically underfunded with respect to testing drugs and their active ingredients, a mere $2 million a year, according to *Bloomberg*.[42] In 2012, the FDA reportedly received a tenfold increase, which is still a miniscule amount.[43]

Most drug products tested by the agency meet federal requirements, according to data on its website. From 2003 to 2013, the FDA tested batches of nearly four thousand drug products. One percent, or forty-four, failed.[44] It is impossible to conclude if a one percent failure rate is good news or bad news. Were millions of people exposed to high risks, or were a small number of people at minor risk?

As the agency increases its testing, it finds substandard products. In 2014, it tested an active ingredient sold by Medisca™, a Plattsburg, New York, company, after FDA inspectors visited the company's facility earlier that year. The inspection was triggered by reports the agency received that people were suffering serious medical problems after receiving a drug made with the active ingredient L-Citrulline, an amino acid. Inspectors collected six samples of the active ingredient. An FDA laboratory analysis found that two of the samples were a different amino acid, N-Acetyl-Leucine. The falsely labeled product could kill someone.[45] The company was not the manufacturer. It repackaged and relabeled the active ingredient before selling it, according to the FDA warning letter to the company.[46]

We wanted to know where the active ingredient L-Citrulline was made. The FDA lists its test results on FDA.gov and says the product was "imported by Ningbo, China."[47] We wondered if this was an error and should have read "imported from Ningbo, China." An online search found multiple suppliers of the active ingredient located in Ningbo, China. The public interest is served when accurate information is available about the country of origin of a toxic ingredient sold in the United States.

SO MUCH TO VERIFY

For decades Americans bought medicines with easily recognized brand names like Eli Lilly™ and Johnson & Johnson™ on the package. Today, consumers, hospitals, and pharmacies have a dizzying array of choices.

In the case of Lipitor®, a statin, and the generic atorvastatin, they are prescribed to lower the level of cholesterol in the blood. The FDA website lists seven generic sellers and one brand-name seller, Pfizer™.[48]

Consumers can choose a generic made in Seymour, Indiana, by Kremers Urban Pharmaceuticals™, according to a company customer service representative who answered the phone at its manufacturing plant.[49] Or they can buy a generic version made in Slovenia by the generic arm of Swiss pharma giant Sandoz™, according to the DailyMed website.[50] The brand-name Lipitor sold under the Pfizer name is made in Ireland.[51]

As the heparin tragedy revealed, medicines are differentiated by more than price. The ethics of a company, the education and training of the people who work in the plant and oversee quality control, and the cultural norms of a company and the country where it is made make a difference. These attributes are invisible to a doctor who prescribes a drug, a pharmacist who fills a prescription for it, a nurse who administers it, and a consumer who consumes it.

INFORMATION INEQUALITY

Nobel Prize–winning economist George Akerlof explained the advantage that sellers have over buyers with the example of the used-car market.[52] Sellers know if a vehicle for sale on a used car lot was flooded in New York City during Hurricane Sandy, or has been in an accident that damaged the frame. The average buyer can't know the quality of a car by looking at it. The seller can take advantage of this information asymmetry, as Akerlof calls it, and sell a low-quality product as a high-quality one.

Fortunately for consumers, the used-car market has morphed considerably since Akerlof wrote his paper in 1970 while at the University of California at Berkeley. The business model for CarMax[SM] and other companies is based on reducing buyer uncertainty. A company guarantees that vehicles have never been flooded or structurally damaged in an accident. Rather than take a risk of buying a used car advertised on Craigslist, many consumers are willing to pay a piece of mind dividend for the added assurance.

As a regulatory agency, the FDA tries to fix Akerlof's conundrum of information inequality between buyers and sellers of medicines. It sets standards of quality for all branded and generic drugs and enforces them with inspections and product testing. But the agency is virtually inaccessible to the public that pays its bills. Many people who work there are dedicated to serving the public interest, but the pharmaceutical industry has positioned itself as the agency's primary client. Industry influence explains why doctors, hospitals, and the public, who spend billions of dollars a year on prescription drugs, don't receive better information about the quality and performance of the medicines they prescribe, purchase, administer, or consume.

Public-spirited ConsumerLab.com tests different brands of vitamin supplements to find out if a brand contains 100 percent of the labeled amount, whether any contaminant is found, and if the supplement dissolves properly. Test results for twenty-nine supplements containing vitamin C are posted online, each with an overall rating of "approved" or "not approved."[53] Price comparisons are available, and a list of all the ingredients in each product is provided.

For a modest subscription fee, the public can see the test results. The information fills a huge gap since no federal or state agency routinely tests the quality of vitamin supplements before they are sold, says Consumer Lab.com.[54]

ENJOY A CHEMICAL COCKTAIL WITH YOUR GOJI BERRIES

Consumers have more luck finding information on the quality of food products from China than their prescription drugs. Greenpeace East Asia had samples of goji berries from China that were sold in the United States, including the Washington, DC, suburbs in Northern Virginia, independently tested. Results revealed they were laced with thirteen pesticides including carbofuran, considered a highly hazardous pesticide by the World Health Organization and banned on food crops in the United States.[55]

Another Greenpeace East Asia investigation found traditional Chinese herbs collected from stores in London, Paris, Amsterdam,

Hamburg, Milan, Toronto, and Vancouver that were spiked with pesticide cocktails.[56] Almost all tested positive for three or more pesticides, many considered highly or extremely hazardous by the World Health Organization, and some contained residues from twenty-six toxic chemicals.

Consumers in China are paying to have drugs independently tested, according to local Chinese media.[57] An investigation into a fake drug racket began when a husband, whose wife had heart disease and diabetes, became concerned when her condition worsened after he had spent nearly $5,000 on medicine.[58] He questioned the authenticity and quality of the drugs and had them tested. All of them were fake. After he notified authorities, they uncovered a $2.2 million scam drug operation. Is it only a matter of time before hospitals, doctors, and consumers in the United States pay for independent testing of drugs and other medical products when their performance is in question?

Dr. Stephen Tower, an orthopedic surgeon in Alaska, had hip replacement surgery, and he later learned that the manufacturer of the hip implant was forced to recall the device from the market. The so-called metal-on-metal hip implant was made with cobalt, which leached toxic material into the bloodstream and wreaked havoc on the health of many people whose doctors had used it. After Dr. Tower had a second surgery to remove the toxic product and replace it, he sent the "explant" (a term for devices that are removed from the body) to the Thayer School of Engineering at Dartmouth for independent testing. He sends implants he removes from his patients there, too. The results are not released to the public.[59]

Design defects and surgeon error, rather than manufacturing quality, have been the usual causes of implant failures.[60] Looking ahead, as China increases the sale of its medical devices in the United States, who is testing them and how will the public know if they meet high standards for design, manufacturing, and performance?

"GOOD ENOUGH FOR AMERICA"

For most of America's history, medicines were downright dangerous. Most drugs were imported, and America was known as a dumping ground for shoddy products. "Good enough for America" is how Jacob Bell, a member of the British Parliament and a pharmacist, characterized the United States in the 1800s because of its willingness to tolerate imported drugs contaminated by ingenious tampering or sheer decay.[61]

A member of Congress and physician, Dr. T. O. Edwards, presented a report in the US House of Representatives on adulterated medicines in 1848.[62] The country had become "the grand mart and receptacle of all the refuse merchandise of that description, not only from the European warehouses, but from the whole Eastern world," he said.[63] Back then, Congress didn't hesitate to criticize American businesses that bought adulterated medicine into the country and sold it to unsuspecting customers. Dr. Edwards said,

> Our country . . . is the market par preference, of these worthless, adulterated and misnamed drugs . . . [of] various quality, from a little below the standard to the most worthless trash [that] finds its way to this country. This traffic once commenced and found to be extremely profitable, has increased to a frightful degree. Nor need we try to throw the blame exclusively on the foreign manufacturer. If the demand for these low-priced and inferior articles did not exist among our own traders, they would not be supplied.[64]

The Drug Importation Act of 1848, the first law to stop adulterated imported drugs, was signed by President James Polk.[65] Government inspectors were posted at New York, Boston, Baltimore, and other major ports to check the quality of drugs coming into the country. After a year, more than ninety thousand pounds of substandard drugs from England, France, Germany, China, and other countries had been denied entry into the Port of New York. Political cronyism soon drove out competent inspectors, and enforcement was watered down.

The first standards for a modern drug regulatory system were written into the 1906 Pure Food and Drug Act that prohibited buying and selling adulterated and misbranded food and medicines. More than thirty years later, after more than one hundred people died from consuming a drug that contained a toxic solvent, President Franklin D. Roosevelt signed the Food, Drug, and Cosmetic Act of 1938 that required inspections of manufacturing facilities and a safety review of all new drugs before they could be sold.[66]

With ingenuity and determination, the United States created the gold standard for protecting the public against unsafe drugs. It was easier back then. The FDA oversaw what became a homegrown industry. American companies operated factories and employed skilled chemists, engineers, and production managers. Manufacturers knew their suppliers, which were located down the street or a short plane ride away. Language barriers didn't exist. The agency's highly trained field staff conducted high-stakes inspections every two years.

Kevin McNeil of the Pharmaceutical Integrity Coalition describes his experience in the industry this way:

> I went into the industry in the early 1980s. At that time, there were not that many companies. Manufacturing was largely contained in the US by companies at home. They put physical plants near where they were doing business. They could see who was making what. I would want to believe from some of my early manufacturing that they were very compliant, highly professional. They would never think twice about cutting a corner. The older folks in manufacturing appeared to be religiously compliant with their discipline and were proud of it. And they would show you. As we would tour their manufacturing facilities, they were proud of what they had established, even with antiquated facilities; they tried to keep them up to date.[67]

WHEN THE AMERICAN PRICE MEETS THE CHINA PRICE

"Too many Americans want their prescription drugs filled just like they want their food at McDonald's[™]—fast and cheap—and the order better be right," says Dr. Lucinda Maine, the chief executive officer of the American Association of Colleges of Pharmacy.[68] As long as America demands the lowest price, China will be more than happy to oblige. And more heparin-like cases will likely occur.

In 2016, medical device-maker Boston Scientific™ was sued under the Racketeering and Corrupt Organizations Act (RICO) for allegedly masterminding a conspiracy to sell a product made with raw material smuggled from China.[69] A lawsuit filed in federal district court in Charleston, West Virginia, claims Boston Scientific bought four thousand pounds of substandard raw material, not approved by the FDA, from a Chinese company. Boston Scientific is alleged to have used it to make a product called surgical mesh that is implanted in women for stress urinary incontinence. Boston Scientific has denied the allegations. As of this writing, a grand jury has been convened.[70]

IS "MADE IN THE USA" REALLY "MADE IN CHINA"?

Soldiers and veterans who had back surgery at a military or Department of Veterans Affairs hospital from 2007 to 2014 may have instruments or devices in their bodies made in China and sold illegally to the US government. Medical device-maker Medtronic™ sold products used in spine surgeries and other items that it certified were made in the United States.[71] Company employees told a different story, however. Workers at a Medtronic distribution facility in Memphis claimed they were instructed to repackage devices and put fake country-of-origin labels on them as if they were made in the United States.[72]

According to whistleblowers who worked at the company and filed a lawsuit in federal court in Minnesota, Medtronic sold and delivered bone screws to the Walter Reed Army Medical Center in Washington, DC, that "had been manufactured in China, stored in inventory as 'finished goods' at the Medtronic-Weigao Joint Venture in China, then shipped from there to the Memphis Distribution Center, where it was repackaged and relabeled as US-made before shipment to the customer."[73] The complaint alleges that this is one of thousands of transactions where Medtronic relabeled products.

According to the complaint, "many products that Medtronic sells under its Government contracts are manufactured by a Chinese company, Weigao Orthopaedic Device Co., located in Weihai City in Shandong Province, China" and other manufacturers in China and other countries not permitted under the federal law. "Medtronic has close ties to Weigao Orthopaedic Device. In 2008, Medtronic and Weigao Orthopaedic Device formed a joint venture [the MedtronicWeigao Joint Venture] in China. Medtronic owns 51% of the joint venture; Weigao Orthopaedic Device owns 49%."[74] In a settlement with the US Department of Justice, Medtronic paid a $4.4 million fine and denied the charges.[75]

FOR THE COST OF TWO LATTES

If Americans like a bargain, they will like the FDA. Its funding from Congress is $2.6 billion a year, and it also receives about $2 billion in fees paid by regulated companies.[76] This is a pittance considering that the FDA is tasked with assuring the safety of more than $1 trillion worth of food, drugs, and other products coming from a vast and complex web of suppliers.

Former FDA commissioner Dr. Margaret Hamburg reminded members of Congress that taxpayers get a "bargain" by paying a mere eight dollars a person for protecting drug and food safety.[77] The FDA is compelled to appear thrifty when it faces the anti-government, pro-industry crowd in Washington that blames the agency for safety failures caused by the negligence of companies and their executives. Bargain-basement prices may appeal to ideologues, but the person sitting in a chair during a chemotherapy treatment for cancer would not be thrilled about getting a bargain when it comes to assuring the safety of life-saving medicines.

IT'S ABOUT TRUST

The federal government acknowledges that America's demand for cheaper Chinese products has caused drug safety problems. The FDA's budget request to Congress in 2014, which asked for more money for inspectors in China, said, "The result will be fewer import safety emergencies . . . and earlier identification of safety problems associated with foods, drugs, and ingredients manufactured in China."[78]

Globalization has turned back the clock on decades of hard-won gains to ensure the quality of America's medicines. Years ago when the United States was a dominant global manufacturer of prescription drugs and active ingredients, it was unthinkable that so many companies would receive warning letters from the federal government because their manufacturing processes didn't meet required safety standards. Now, the FDA has the task of fixing what the free market has created and it's not easy. Industry veterans say the situation is getting better. As quality and safety appear to be improving, another big problem has been created. US dependence on China is increasing, and so is the risk to national security.

CHAPTER 12

WHERE DOES THE SECRETARY OF DEFENSE PROCURE HIS MEDICINE?

*"If . . . the enemy was distributing viruses or bacteria
to society, and it was the source of the drug to fight
those bugs, you could find yourself in deep trouble."*

Aboard the USS *Theodore Roosevelt* on patrol in the South China Sea in the fall of 2015, then US secretary of defense Ashton Carter asserted freedom of navigation in international waters in the western Pacific where China had militarized artificial islands. In the Trump administration, the United States is continuing to patrol the South China Sea security hotspot, Rear Admiral James Kilby told the *Military Times*.[1]

As China's dominance has escalated there, a pharmaceutical industry veteran we spoke to wondered aloud about where the secretary of defense procures his medicine. We tried to find the answer.

After the September 11, 2001, terrorist attacks on the World Trade Center and the Pentagon, and after letters laced with anthrax spores were sent to congressional offices and media companies a week later, the US government needed to buy vast amounts of the anthrax antidote doxycycline to treat anthrax. It turned to the Portuguese company Hovione™,[2] which made the active ingredient for doxycycline at its plant in Macau, a former Portuguese colony that was transferred to China in 1999.[3] The American government bought enough of the antibiotic to treat twenty million people for two months, company chief executive officer Guy Villax told *Bloomberg* at the time. More than ten years earlier, before

Operation Desert Storm, "[i]t was exactly the same situation," Villax added.[4] "Every soldier that went to Desert Storm had their doses of doxycycline in anticipation for bio-warfare."

As a veteran of Operation Desert Storm in 1991, and as a senior army military intelligence officer, Brigadier General John Adams (US Army, ret.) understands the military's dependence on China for components in equipment critical to national defense. Adams served as deputy United States military representative to the North Atlantic Treaty Organization (NATO) military committee in Brussels. He is the author of the report *Remaking American Security: Supply Chain Vulnerabilities and National Security Risks across the US Defense Industrial Base.*[5]

In his book, General Adams identified raw materials and components supplied by China for equipment used in national defense.[6] For example, night vision goggles are made with the rare earth element lanthanum, and 91 percent of it comes from China. Also, the chemical needed to produce the fuel used to propel Hellfire missiles comes from a single Chinese company. As US supplies dwindle, the military is dependent on a Chinese firm to provide butanetriol, the chemical needed to make the fuel.[7]

General Adams described the risks and their impact on military preparedness:

> America's vulnerability today is frightening. This report is a wake-up call for America to pay attention to the growing threat posed by the steady deterioration of our defense industrial base. Excessive and unwise outsourcing of American manufacturing to other nations weakens America's military capability. As a soldier, I've witnessed first-hand the importance of our nation's ability to rapidly produce and field a sophisticated array of capabilities. There is a real risk that supply chain vulnerabilities will hamper our response to future threats.[8]

Product quality could be compromised and endanger the men and women who serve in the military. China could extort a higher price or pressure the United States to resolve disputes in China's favor.

When we contacted General Adams to tell him about US reliance on China for drugs and critical ingredients in them, he immediately grasped the significance.

> I see this as a real vulnerability for our country. . . . We twisted ourselves in twenty-five different directions about Ebola. Imagine a large-scale attack? It would cause complete disruption to American society and to our national security. If an enemy releases anthrax and they control the antidote, the prospect send[s] chills up my spine.[9]

The Pentagon Defense Logistics Agency buys medicines for the military and their dependents stationed all over the world. They must be made in the United States or in an approved country, according to the federal Trade Agreements Act (TAA) of 1979. China is not a designated country. The TAA allows for exceptions when no other source is available.

We contacted the Department of Defense to find out which prescription drugs the Pentagon has purchased that are made in China because no other source is available. A spokesperson replied that the department has had to buy thirty-one prescription drugs from China.[10]

> Prior to October 2012, the Defense Logistics Agency (DLA) met all its customers' requirements for pharmaceuticals without the need to make non-availability determinations for pharmaceuticals produced in China. Due to the increasing commercial trend to rely on China for supply of active pharmaceutical ingredients, the DLA was compelled to make its first non-availability determination for a pharmaceutical of Chinese origin in October 2012. From that date to [the] present, DLA has made determinations of non-availability for thirty-one drugs produced in China.[11]

These drugs include an antibiotic cream, erythromycin, for eye infections such as pink eye (also called conjunctivitis); donepezil for Alzheimer's disease; and gentamicin cream and ointment for eye infections.

Because China makes so many active ingredients and chemical building blocks, it would seem that the military is far more dependent on China than the department's list initially suggests. We went back and asked the department's press office for further clarification but received no reply.

India's military is dependent on China for more than 90 percent of the active ingredients and chemical building blocks needed to make at least fifteen essential drugs, according to a Boston Consulting Group^{SM} and Confederation of Indian Industry report in 2014.[12] The drugs manufactured with China-made therapeutic ingredients include common antibiotics such as amoxicillin, ampicillin, ciprofloxacin, and levofloxacin, which treat a wide range of infections, and the diabetes drug metformin. "Chinese Active Pharmaceutical Ingredients Are Already a Security Threat for India," a headline blared in the India-based PharmaCompass blog.[13]

PHARMACEUTICAL INDUSTRY ADVOCACY FOR CHINESE-MADE DRUGS FOR VETERANS?

The pharmaceutical industry appears to have advocated for the Department of Veterans Affairs (VA) to buy drugs made in China.

The Coalition for Common Sense in Government Procurement is an association of commercial contractors advocating for what it calls "common sense" government procurement.[14] Members include brand-name and generic pharmaceutical companies such as Abbott™, Johnson & Johnson, GlaxoSmithKline™, Genentech™, Pfizer™, Teva™, and others. The law firm Morgan, Lewis & Bockius, which is a member of the coalition, identified changes in policies and procedures to allow the VA to buy drugs made in China and other countries not permitted under the Trade Agreements Act.[15]

It recommended changing US customs law, which requires prescription drugs to be labeled "Made in China" if their active ingredients are made there.[16] This change would obliterate information about the source of active ingredients for all drugs sold in the United States, and to allow imported drug products from China to be given to veterans. Another proposed solution was a statutory waiver of the Trade Agreements Act, which would also allow the VA to buy drugs made in China.[17]

In a sudden policy shift, the VA announced in April 2016 that while it previously required all drugs to be made in the United States or a designated country,

> We are now requiring that all covered drugs, regardless of count[r]y of substantial transformation, be available. . . . In other words, we now accept covered drugs that were formally excluded due to their "TAA non-compliant" nature.[18]

The change signaled that companies can sell drug products made in China to the VA. We contacted the department's public affairs office for comment, and here's what they said:

> [Y]ear after year, more and more pharmaceutical products are being manufactured outside the United States and designated countries, leaving the VA and other government entities struggling to easily obtain pharmaceuticals consistent with commercial practices and at prices set by statute.[19]

The VA had no option, it seems. Is the US military in the same predicament?

GONE IN A GENERATION

In 1988, scientists at Oak Ridge National Laboratory, a preeminent federally funded science and technology laboratory near Knoxville, Tennessee, had an emergency preparedness plan to assure the continuous manufacture of antibiotics in the event of a nuclear attack on the United States.[20]

The names, addresses, and telephone numbers of manufacturing plants owned by seventeen companies making penicillin and other antibiotics were carefully documented, along with a "how-to" guide to quickly build or repair plants if they were damaged or destroyed. The contact information for plants owned by the Upjohn Company in Kalamazoo, Michigan; SmithKline Beckman in Conshohocken, Pennsylvania; F. Hoffmann–La Roche™ in Nutley, New Jersey; Pfizer in Groton, Connecticut; Burroughs Wellcome in Greenville, North Carolina; Eli Lilly™ in Indianapolis, Indiana; and Abbott Laboratories in North Chicago, Illinois, were among those listed. That was 1988. Today, China dominates world production of chemical building blocks to make antibiotics.

The Department of Homeland Security (DHS) commissioned an assessment of US dependence on foreign suppliers of pharmaceuticals, medical devices, and surgical equipment. In a survey conducted for DHS by the Department of Commerce Bureau of Industry and Security that was published in 2011, 73 percent of companies said they relied on non-US based suppliers for at least one component or active ingredient essential for making their products.[21] For most of the imported components or ingredients, there is no US-based supplier and only one global supplier. Cost and product availability were the reasons for foreign sourcing. The top concern among pharmaceutical companies was disruption in the supply of active ingredients.

Nearly one-third of companies surveyed said they had a significant supply disruption or shortage from 2007 to 2010. One company employee wrote, "We do not have redundant sources for the majority of our purchased product, and some supply is provided from non-US sources [so] we are currently vulnerable to such disruptions."[22] China was named as the country where disruptions occurred most often.[23] Some firms say disruptions are just another risk of doing business. One company said it is no more vulnerable than its competitors.[24]

Environmental laws were blamed as the primary reason why most supplies of pharmaceutical active ingredients are obtained from other countries. Strict environmental protections in the United States increase manufacturers' cost of production, making it difficult for them to compete with countries such as China where environmental laws are weak. A company that relies on non-US suppliers for chemicals said that environmental regulatory reform is needed so manufacturing in the United States becomes a viable option.

A company employee summed up the challenges this way:

> We realize today's business world is global, but it is sad to see so much of our manufacturing go off-shore and decisions being made more and more based on purchase price rather than quality. And purchase price isn't including the price of managing the off-shore source, something that is an ever-increasing expectation from the FDA, and it is very, very expensive.[25]

Another company said labor costs and lower corporate tax rates are a reason for offshoring:

> [A]s more firms outsource production to offset high labor costs and tax rates, companies that perform final assembly and test have to source more product overseas, lengthening our supply chain and introducing risk.[26]

A NATIONAL SECURITY VULNERABILITY

We asked two senior industry veterans who have worked in China if they believe a shutdown in exports of Chinese-made drugs and ingredients would cause the collapse of America's healthcare system. Both agreed that such a scenario is possible but unlikely. China wants to become a pharmaceutical partner and must prove it is a reliable business partner, they said. But such a scenario can happen. "We can't be naïve about it," said former federal official Ted Kirk about the centralization of America's drug supply in a single country.[27] Trade sanctions or a trade blockade could stop essential drugs from reaching hospitals and retail pharmacies. A public health crisis could require the US government to buy a large volume of drugs, and it may have to stand in line behind other countries.

Brand-name drugs are not immune to periods of scarcity. "Some of the starting material for them is no longer made in Western countries," said Guy Villax of Hovione.[28] "In terms of security, there is a big issue that nobody is acknowledging."[29]

"WHY ISN'T IT A NATIONAL SECURITY ISSUE?"

At a 2014 meeting of the FDA Science Board, whose members are comprised of outside experts who provide advice to the agency's commissioner on complex scientific and technical issues, FDA official Dr. Janet Woodcock acknowledged a shortage of heparin.[30] Members of the board identified America's dependence on China for heparin as a national security concern that needs to be elevated to the highest levels of government. In a transcript of the meeting, board member Dr. Lynn Goldman, dean of the Milken Institute School of Public Health at George Washington University, commented on the ubiquitous use of heparin in hospitals:

> I'm thinking about the ubiquity of use of heparin and medical care, and for people hospitalized for anything, not just major problems. Almost any surgical procedure . . . you're going to have some heparin. . . . And so, I'm trying to imagine medical care without heparin, and it's hard to.[31]

Dr. Goldman wondered aloud about the national security implications:

> If we have all the heparin virtually coming from a single country . . . there are shortages already, why isn't it a national security issue? . . . I mean, there's no government agency that can order people to put all of their pig guts after slaughter into heparin production.[32]

The Centers for Disease Control and Prevention (CDC) has a stockpile of medicines containing antibiotics, vaccines, chemical antidotes, antitoxins, and other critical medical equipment and supplies. It is used during public health emergencies such as the September 11, 2001, attack on the World Trade Center. "The repository is intended to provide a minimum level of federal coverage as a supplement to state and local resources," says the National Academy of Medicine.[33] It is not intended to respond to widespread drug shortages.

Stepping up its game, the federal government invested in building vaccine manufacturing facilities at home to avert a public health crisis. "Ten years ago, there were only three US-licensed influenza vaccine manufacturers," said Dr. Jesse Goodman, then chief scientist at the FDA, in testimony to congress in 2013.[34] "In 2004, significant manufacturing difficulties with one manufacturer resulted in limited supplies." To avert a shortage, three facilities in Maryland, North Carolina, and Texas were funded by the federal government to increase domestic capacity to make vaccines.

Domestic manufacturing is also needed for essential, everyday drugs used in hospitals and sold in retail drugstores. National security is at stake, said Dr. Goodman in an interview with Diane Rehm on National Public Radio after he left the agency:

> It is a matter of national security that we have the essential drugs we need. Like in defense, we don't say that we can make all our tanks in one place and can't make them in the United States. And I think it is time for an examination, for some of the most critical drugs, and it's not just drugs, medical supplies, masks are all made overseas. Do we need to think about having at least some resilient manufacturing capacity built in this country?[35]

ESSENTIAL MEDICINES AS A STRATEGIC WEAPON

If you drive on Interstate 95 in southeastern Connecticut, you will see a sign that proudly reads, "Groton—Submarine Capital of the World." Electric Boat[SM], a subsidiary of General Dynamics[TM], builds one of the most complicated engineering feats in the world, the nuclear submarine, at the Groton shipyard overlooking the Thames River. Not far from Electric Boat is the Pfizer campus where its penicillin fermentation facility once stood. America's military used to rely on antibiotics made by Pfizer. Now, those who serve on nuclear submarines built in Groton are likely dependent for antibiotics on a geopolitical rival that seeks to dominate the United States economically and militarily.

Making submarines at home is a national security priority. Billions of dollars are invested in assuring domestic production. Essential medicines are a strategic asset, no less than a nuclear submarine.

Paul Levy, former chief executive officer of Beth Israel Deaconess Medical Center in Boston, immediately grasped the strategic vulnerability associated with centralization of the nation's drug supply:

> If we ever did get into an era of biowarfare, and the enemy was distributing viruses or bacteria to society, and it was the source of the drug to fight those bugs, you could find yourself in deep trouble. You can think about it with troops who might be a likely subject of a bio warhead, as well as citizens and the impact on cities.[36]

Assuring the quality of medicines is equally important, Levy says,

> All you have to do is degrade the potency of the drug and no one will notice. Imagine a situation where a country had a surrogate that was doing something bad to our society or other country in the world, and they could be pretending to provide you with the antibiotic, but they could have intentionally degraded the potency so we wouldn't know it is not working. We're taking pills thinking they're curing us and they are not. Or maybe they're intentionally poisoning us.[37]

CONGRESS ACTS TO PROMOTE LESS CONSEQUENTIAL AMERICAN-MADE PRODUCTS

Congress has prodded the US military to buy American-made products with far less strategic consequence. When the Defense Department couldn't find athletic shoes for new recruits made with components from the United States, it had to work around federal law that requires food, clothing, and fabric to be purchased from America when domestic sources exist. Army, navy, and air force recruits were given eighty-dollar vouchers to buy their own shoes for training.[38] Since most shoes are made outside the United States, service members were buying shoes made in China and other countries.

To fix the problem, members of Congress added a provision in the 2017 National Defense Authorization Act to require the Pentagon to buy American-made shoes.[39] New England–based shoe manufacturer New Balance™ stepped in and developed a fully made-in-America athletic shoe.[40]

Much more needs to be done. When Master Sergeant Steve Adachi was deployed to Kabul, Afghanistan, as an advisor to the Afghan air force, he was issued boots made in China and refused to wear them.[41] In a letter to the *Air Force Times*, Adachi wrote, "This is about the countless Americans who are struggling to feed their families, Americans whose livelihoods have been taken away in this so-called global economy. This is about patriotism. . . . This is about American soldiers wearing our country's uniform made by Americans."[42]

After the *Air Force Times* article appeared, Senator Sherrod Brown, Democrat from Ohio, wrote a letter to the undersecretary of the air force and asked that service members be provided uniforms and boots made in America. In a press release, Brown said, "I believe that if we're going to spend taxpayer dollars, we should be doing so in a way that supports American businesses. . . . It just makes plain sense to put US tax dollars back into the US economy, and to have our troops wear the highest-quality boots and uniforms made in America."[43]

SELF-SUFFICIENCY FOR NATIONAL SECURITY

The United States is one of the few countries in the world that can produce enough of its own food.[44] Self-sufficiency helps ensure national security. Starving the enemy into submission by plunder or cutting supply routes is a time-honored military strategy. A Roman military maxim says, "To distress the enemy more by famine than by the sword is the mark of consummate skill."[45]

During World War II, Germany's Atlantic blockade tried to starve food-import-dependent Britain.[46] Germany could hardly forget Britain's Royal Navy blockade of the German coast in World War I to starve its citizens into submission.[47]

When it comes to energy, America is on track to be energy independent and a net exporter.[48] Domestic energy production met 91 percent of domestic consumption in 2015, according to the US Energy Information Administration, which tracks energy production and consumption around the world.[49]

Prescription drugs are a different story, however. The private market has handed control over America's drug supply to China. Economic benefits for American workers have been surrendered. China gains economic leverage and, with it, political power as it charts its path to become the pharmacy to the world.

Congress gave the FDA authority to inspect manufacturing plants in China to help assure the *safety* of Chinese-made drug products. But Congress has been silent on assuring the *security* of an unfettered supply. If the US relationship with China deteriorates, and China blocks exports, severe shortages could cause devastating harm to civilians and military personnel.

"My biggest concern is that we'll do nothing, we'll keep going on, and our options will be constrained and [we'll] soon find ourselves with no option," says General Adams. "We will be coerced in the future, implicitly or explicitly. The same end will be achieved without armed conflict."[50]

China doesn't hesitate to flex its monopoly power in the marketplace to achieve political aims. In 2010, it reportedly restricted exports of rare earth elements, which are ubiquitous in advanced military and civilian technologies such as defense radar systems, satellites, mobile phones, hybrid car engines, and wind turbines.[51] Their name belies their abundance in the earth's crust, but they are costly to mine and process.[52]

From the 1950s until the 1980s, the United States produced most rare earth elements until Chinese companies, with financial support from the Chinese government, sold rare earths on the global market at lower prices.[53] Soon, China was producing 97 percent of the world supply.[54]

The Chinese government reportedly suspended exports of rare earth elements to Japan after that country allegedly detained the captain of a Chinese fishing boat that had collided with two Japanese coast guard vessels in the disputed East China Sea.[55] Japanese auto manufacturers such as Toyota® depend on rare earths from China to make the Prius® hybrid car and other high-tech products. Concerned about the economic impact, Japan released the fishing captain.[56]

A month after the ban on exports to Japan, China blocked exports of rare earth elements to the United States, according to the *New York Times*.[57] It broke the story based on interviews with three rare earth company officials who confirmed the ban. All insisted on anonymity because they were afraid of retaliation by Chinese authorities.

The timing of the ban coincided with an announcement the previous week by the US Trade Representative that it would investigate whether China's reductions in rare earth exports in the prior five years, and high export taxes on them, were illegal actions intended to force companies to make more high-tech products in China.[58]

A LAST-RESORT TREATMENT FOR SUPERBUGS MADE IN CHINA

Superbugs are an international concern and rightly so. They are killers, and as antibiotic resistance increases, the existing arsenal of drugs will eventually cease to work. Only about 10 percent of staph infections, for instance, can be treated successfully with penicillin.[59]

Vancomycin is a treatment of last resort against multi-drug-resistant bacteria. Pfizer-owned Hospira™ sells vancomycin, and it obtains the active ingredient from the Chinese company Zhejiang Medicine, according to the industry newsletter *in-PharmaTechnologist.com*.[60] A Pfizer spokesman confirmed to *in-PharmaTechnologist.com* that Zhejiang Medicine supplies the active ingredient.[61]

The FDA wrote a warning letter to Zhejiang's chief executive officer in August 2016, saying, "Your quality system does not adequately ensure the accuracy and integrity of data to support the safety, effectiveness, and quality of the drugs you manufacture."[62] The company was told to assess the "risks to patients caused by the release of drugs affected by a lapse of data integrity and risks posed by ongoing operations."

The FDA didn't ban the company's products from the United States, which suggests that the agency believed they were safe. A Pfizer spokesperson said it did not find any issues with the ingredient, according to the industry trade letter.[63]

The untold story is that a prominent US-based pharmaceutical company depends on China for a critical component in a drug to treat superbugs.[64] While companies turn to Washington for financial incentives to discover new antibiotics to treat superbugs, no one seems to care about offshoring the manufacture of last-resort generic antibiotics to China.

AMERICAN TAXPAYERS HELP A CHINESE COMPANY MAKE AN IMPORTANT DRUG

Doctors Without Borders, the Nobel Prize–winning humanitarian group, says 80 to 85 percent of the active ingredients to make tuberculosis medicines used worldwide are produced in China.[65] When a shortage of the tuberculosis drug capreomycin occurred in 2011, American taxpayers paid to help a Chinese company make it.

Here's what happened. With money from the US Agency for International Development, a consultant traveled to China to train employees of Zhejiang Hisun Pharmaceutical Company, at no cost to the company, in good manufacturing practices so it could make capreomycin and meet FDA standards.[66] In 2015, when the FDA banned fourteen products from Zhejiang Hisun because it was systematically manipulating quality data, capreomycin was one of them.[67] If this is how the United States deals with a drug shortage, it is not an auspicious sign of how it will handle future shortages.

RELIANCE ON CHINA FOR ANTHRAX ANTIDOTES

A week after the September 11, 2001, terrorist attacks on the World Trade Center and the Pentagon, anonymous anthrax-laced letters were sent to the office of Senate Majority Leader Tom Daschle. Three of the nation's major television networks, CBS, ABC, and NBC, were also targeted. Postal workers and others were not so fortunate. Five people died from inhaling anthrax spores, and seventeen others became infected.[68]

Cipro® became a household name as the anthrax antidote of choice. A generic version of Cipro, called ciprofloxacin, is available now because the patent on the brand-name drug expired. We tried to find out where the chemical building blocks come from to make the active ingredient.

"It's really hard to get a handle on this information," said former federal official Ted Kirk. "It is not tracked very specifically."[69] Then he added, "I bet they get it from China."

A public-spirited pharmaceutical company employee showed us how to search international trade information using the code number for the chemical product needed to make the active ingredient in ciprofloxacin. The trade information revealed that China is the largest global exporter.[70] Another anthrax treatment, doxycycline, also depends on Chinese-made chemical starting materials.[71]

If the supply of essential drugs to treat an anthrax outbreak were to be cut off, the specter of social upheaval is real. Citizens will scramble for a limited supply of life-saving medicines for themselves and their families. Transporting, stocking, and administering essential medicines would require intense security measures.

Sick people have no time to wait for investors to respond to market signals and produce alternative supplies. They need medicines right away. A pharmaceutical company employee told us, "No country can sustain its healthcare system if China shuts down. We are sitting on a problem, and it is just a question of time before the world realizes it."[72]

It will take time to ramp up manufacturing at home. "You don't build manufacturing plants overnight; it requires a great deal of skill," said Bharat Mehta of PharmaCompass.[73] "You need trained people to do it."

If supplies were greatly diminished, the market for counterfeit drugs would skyrocket. As the largest global source of counterfeit drugs, Chinese companies could speed up production of counterfeits and sell them on the internet to a frightened American public. From a geopolitical perspective, a country can use its monopoly production of a medicine to gain power, says General Adams. Wielding that power "can disrupt the entire civil society," he added.[74] An industry veteran, acutely aware of America's vulnerability, added another scenario: "If we have an anthrax attack, what if China was the anthrax attacker?"[75]

CHAPTER 13

CHINA BASHING? TAKE A LOOK AT THIS

"These campaigns consist of state-sponsored and supported criminal cartels ... designed to accelerate China's entry and domination of each key global industry."

On a crisp, sunny January morning, a spellbinding hearing on Capitol Hill in room 419 of the Dirksen Senate Office Building provided the answer we were looking for. We wanted to know how a huge part of a core American industry has been offshored to China. Was there more to it than lower labor costs in China, bad trade deals, cartels, and currency manipulation by the Chinese government?

In testimony before the US-China Economic and Security Review Commission, Jeffrey Johnson, president and chief executive officer of cybersecurity firm SquirrelWerkz, presented an analysis of the breadth and depth of China's systematic cyber-economic campaigns to gain control of strategic global industries and supply chains.[1] Based on his incisive investigations of twenty industries that are among those targeted by China's campaigns, Johnson revealed a common pattern in the Chinese government's strategy:

> These campaigns consist of state-sponsored and supported criminal cartels focused on leveraging cyber-enabled espionage and sabotage to execute industry-wide fraud, market manipulation, and anti-trust schemes designed to accelerate China's entry and domination of each key global industry.[2]

China's aim is to assert monopoly-like control of key industries and the global economy by infiltrating companies, research enterprises, and governments to gain insider access to sensitive intellectual property, Johnson said.

DISNEY™

Johnson cited Disney as an example. It spent $5.5 billion to create its first park resort in mainland China, the Shanghai Disney Resort, which opened in June 2016 after five years of construction.[3] The month before the opening, CNN aired an interview with Wang Jianlin, chairman of Dalian Wanda Group, which has its own theme parks in China. "Billionaire Vows to Crush Disney in China," the story headline said.[4] He told CNN, "We have a strategy. One tiger cannot compete with a pack of wolves."[5]

In another CNN interview two weeks later, Wanda's chairman suggested that Disney was "cloning" its intellectual property.[6] But when Wang's company opened a new entertainment complex located 350 miles southwest of Shanghai, characters looking very much like Snow White and Captain America were seen at the Wanda theme park, CNN reported.[7]

Disney's Chinese competitor appeared destined to make life difficult for the iconic American company. Johnson described the Chinese government's strategy this way:

> You saw they lured them [Disney] in. The enticement stage. They let them go in. Now you have to look at Wanda. Wanda starts using the same intellectual property and now they are starting to put their parks in strategic areas to stop attendees to Disney parks.[8]

In pin-drop silence, Johnson described how the campaigns are carried out:

They are persistent, intense, patiently executed, and include the simultaneous execution of such a large and diverse set of legal and illegal methods, individuals, and organizations, there's little chance the targeted US competitors can effectively defend or compete in the future without significant support of the US government.[9]

Other iconic companies with global brand-name recognition have not had an easy time in China: Google™, Siemens™ (the German engineering company), and Apple®, among many others. Headwinds have forced some to trim their sails, or exit an unfriendly Chinese market, steered by the not-so-invisible hand of the government.

Google

The search engine of internet giant Google in China was short-lived. Google started its China-based Google.cn search engine in January 2006. Four years later, the company's official blog released a bombshell. "[W]e detected a highly sophisticated and targeted attack on our corporate infrastructure originating from China that resulted in the theft of intellectual property from Google."[10]

The hackers stole computer source code by breaking into the personal computers of a small number of Google employees who controlled the source code management systems, Reuters reported.[11] Online technology news source ITWorld described the theft this way: "When you're a search engine, intellectual property is the whole product."[12]

The company had been required by the government to censor content on Google searches in China, acknowledging that "self-censorship is a non-negotiable legal requirement."[13] For example, an internet user in China doing a Google search for "Tiananmen," or "tank man," referring to the 1989 Tiananmen Square protests and a lone man standing in front of a convoy of tanks the morning after the Chinese military had quashed the protests, would obtain censored results.

After the cyberattack, Google said on its official blog it was no longer willing to censor results on Google.cn. "We recognize that this may well mean having to shut down Google.cn, and potentially our offices in China."[14] To work around China's censorship, Google automatically redirected users to servers in Hong Kong so they could continue to receive uncensored information.[15] Less than a week later, Google searches in mainland China were banned.

Google's foray into China lasted four years. Its share of the search engine market peaked at about 35 percent. Filling the vacuum is Baidu, China's own search engine "that kicked Google's butt out of China, with an assist from the Communist Party," *Bloomberg* opined.[16] Baidu now commands 80 percent of the Chinese market.

Siemens

The German engineering company Siemens was awarded a contract to build sixty passenger trains for a railway from Beijing to Tianjin worth $919 million.[17] In a typical requirement set by the Chinese government, it built the passenger trains with a Chinese partner.[18] The first three trains were built in the Siemens plant in Germany, and the remainder were made in China. Siemens brought hundreds of Chinese technicians to Germany for training. Passenger service began in August 2008 in time for the Olympic Games.

A year later, Siemens announced a follow-on project to provide one hundred trains for the Beijing-Shanghai high-speed railway. The Chinese Ministry of Railways denied the existence of the deal, saying the project would use Chinese technology, according to a report by the US Chamber of Commerce.[19] Siemens was granted a token $1 billion contract for components rather than a nearly $6 billion contract to build the trains. The German company created a global competitor for itself and every other train manufacturer in the world. Now, Siemens is competing with China and its lower-cost labor and government subsidies.

Apple

If you own an iPhone®, you've seen the iconic Apple logo on the back and the words, "Designed by Apple in California, Assembled in China." In June 2016, the Beijing Intellectual Property Office ruled that the exterior designs of the iPhone 6 and 6 Plus were a copycat of a domestic company's phone and constituted an infringement of that firm's patent. Patently Apple, a website that "celebrates" Apple's spirit of innovation, showed pictures of the two phones and remarked, "No disrespect to the Chinese court, but Apple's iPhone 6 and 6 Plus have absolutely no resemblance to Baili 100C."[20] Website 9to5Mac observed, "Bizarre intellectual property rulings are not unusual in China . . . but this one does appear to set a new record, as the iPhone 6 looks nothing like the Baili 100C."[21]

Apple was nevertheless ordered to halt the sale of the models in Beijing. The company appealed the decision to the Beijing Intellectual Property Court. The injunction was on hold pending review, and affected iPhones were still for sale in Beijing. Eventually the Beijing Intellectual Property Court ruled that the iPhone 6 and iPhone 6 Plus did not violate patents owned by the local Chinese company.[22]

The injunction came on the heels of another ruling in May 2016 that took another bite out of Apple. If you buy a phone case in China, it might have "IPHONE" embossed on it. But it won't be an Apple product. That's because Apple lost the exclusive use of the "iPhone" trademark in China. A local leather goods producer successfully challenged the Apple trademark, which can now be used on purses, wallets, and other leather goods.[23]

In yet another salvo, in April 2016 Apple's iTunes® movies and iBooks® store went dark, just six months after launch.[24] The company can't sell e-books and movies in China. The move is seen as a government step to censor and control the country's internet.

In 2017, Apple celebrated the tenth anniversary of the iPhone. At the iPhone debut a decade earlier, cofounder, chairman, and CEO Steve Jobs introduced the world to a technology breakthrough, an iPod®, mobile phone, and internet communication device bundled into a consumer-friendly, handheld device. Now, the iPhone has only 10 percent of China's smartphone market.[25] Following China's standard playbook, domestic competitors quickly gained market share, selling comparable products at lower cost.[26] America's most innovative products are not rewarded with substantial market share in China.

Billionaire investor Carl Icahn said in a 2016 interview with CNBC about Apple's prospects in China, "You worry a little bit, and maybe more than a little, about China's attitude," later adding that China's government could "come in and make it very difficult for Apple to sell there."[27]

Johnson & Johnson™ (J&J)

American pharmaceutical companies are hardly immune. Johnson & Johnson (J&J) had been selling OneTouch® blood glucose monitoring products in China for people with diabetes. A domestic company brought a case to the Chinese trademark authority alleging J&J's trademark for its OneTouch products violated Chinese law. In December 2013, the trademark authority ruled that J&J violated the law and revoked the trademark.[28]

The Chinese company that brought the case was allegedly counterfeiting J&J OneTouch products and selling them in the United States and other countries, according to a *Bloomberg* account.[29] A criminal investigation of the company had been ongoing since 2007 for allegedly making fakes, *China Daily* reported.[30] The reportedly fake glucose testing strips were said to cause inaccurate readings that could lead to improper treatment, serious injury, or death.

As China's population adopts a more Western lifestyle and the number of people with diabetes soars, the ruling meant J&J would lose access to the largest market in the world and Chinese companies would fill the void. J&J appealed the decision. We could find no public information about the outcome of the appeal. We contacted J&J in China, and a customer service representative said OneTouch strips are available for sale.[31]

THE ENDGAME

The endgame for American and other Western companies is clear. China aims to destroy their market share in China, the United States, and around the world, and its long-term strategy is to take over vital industries. Robert D. Atkinson, president of the Information Technology and Innovation Foundation, said during testimony at the US-China Economic and Security Review Commission,

> It's become clear that the path we thought China was going on becoming more market-oriented, more rule of law, more respectful of intellectual property—that path hasn't emerged. You could argue there's significant backsliding. Not enough people understand. The old strategy was about gaining commodity production, largely in manufacturing, largely through low cost, largely through inducing US firms and others to go there. That was very successful. . . . The new strategy is to go after our core competencies and technology. That's a very different strategy. We could have a trade balance with China tomorrow and it wouldn't address that problem, which is going after the kinds of advanced industries in which the United States is still competitive in. That's the new war.[32]

LAWFARE: DECIMATING AMERICAN BUSINESS

Patrick Jenevein is the chief executive officer of Dallas-based Tang Energy Group™, which invests in, and develops, clean-energy projects around the world. In January 2017, Jenevein gave riveting testimony to the US-China Economic and Security Commission about his experience in a joint venture with a Chinese state-owned company.[33]

In 2008, after years of success working together, Jenevein's Tang Energy and the Chinese state-owned enterprise AVIC established a venture called Soaring Wind to bring wind energy projects to market worldwide. AVIC reportedly committed $600 million to the venture. Jenevein testified that his company soon discovered that AVIC was setting up separate companies to develop wind energy projects around the world, contrary to provisions in their joint venture.[34] Tang Energy brought a case to the American Arbitration Association's International Centre for Dispute Resolution. A nine-member panel ruled in its favor and awarded the company $70 million. It is the only US company to win a significant arbitration award against a Chinese state-owned enterprise, he told the commission.

But the nightmare was just beginning. Jenevein called it "lawfare." He described how AVIC sought to undermine the arbitration proceedings by alleging the panel engaged in misconduct and was "stacked" against AVIC.[35] AVIC subsidiaries in China ignored orders from the panel to produce evidence.[36] Jenevein is being sued personally. "Already AVIC has sued me personally for invasion of privacy, and in Delaware for breaching my fiduciary capacity here in the United States. And in China, they are withholding dividends payable, and liquidating the joint venture company's assets.... Central control is fairly absolute, isn't it?" he asked rhetorically in an understated remark.[37] AVIC's campaign erased the value of Tang's investment holdings in China.[38]

A fundamental difference exists in the American and Chinese understanding of the purpose of law, Jenevein said. "We as Americans look at law...to protect individuals, but the Peoples' Republic of China...look[s] at laws as a way to protect the Communist Party," he explained.[39]

Jenevein's experience is a lesson for US companies that expect positive outcomes from the US-China Bilateral Investment Treaty and its arbitration provisions. When taking a case to arbitration, American companies must navigate China's opaque multinational corporate structures that limit liability for bad behavior. American businesses go up against the full faith and credit of the Chinese government. "With access to China's treasury...Chinese firms command significant financial and political resources that produce material imbalances favoring them against US companies during legal proceedings in America," he said.[40]

"HOW COME I DON'T KNOW THIS?"

When we talk with friends and colleagues about this book and how so many medicines are made with Chinese-produced ingredients, a common retort has been, "How come I don't know this?"

In his tell-all book, *Bad News*, Tom Fenton, veteran foreign correspondent and former London bureau chief for CBS News, said that in the first ten months of 2004, the year when the US trade deficit with China jumped, *CBS Evening News* ran four stories from China, two of them about pandas.[41] Fenton wrote that the failure of network news to cover important stories in the rest of the world adds to America's isolation and false sense of security. "Foreign correspondents like myself came to be regarded as alarmists . . . trying in vain to attract attention."[42] US media conglomerates have financial interests in China that trigger self-censorship and the cover-up of important events in China.

Bloomberg held back publishing a blockbuster investigative report that documented an intricately woven web of corruption between China's politicians and its wealthiest businessmen. In an account published in the *Columbia Journalism Review* (*CJR*), *Bloomberg*'s editor in chief and cofounder, Matthew Winkler, said the spiking was no different than foreign reporters in Nazi Germany who censored their reports so they could remain in the country and continue reporting.[43]

The truth was revealed when *Bloomberg* chairman Peter T. Grauer said in a speech in Hong Kong that it had strayed too far with its reporting in China, and its business of selling computerized terminals in China that provide financial information was at risk, *CJR* reported. Grauer "warned the *Bloomberg* staff that the company would 'be straight back in the shitbox' in China if 'we were to do anything like that again.'"[44]

The owners of the three major television networks in the United States have financial interests in China. The Walt Disney Company, which built the Shanghai theme park, owns the ABC television network.[45] The CBS television network is part of the CBS Corporation, which has an international division, CBS Interactive^{SM}.[46] It provides online entertainment and information content in China and other countries.[47] And NBC is owned by NBCUniversal™, which is building a theme park in China scheduled to open in 2020.[48]

CENSORING CYANIDE CONTAMINATION OF MEDICINE DESTINED FOR THE UNITED STATES

Censorship in China is nothing new. When its censorship extends to unfavorable news about its medicines exported to the United States, concerns for the health and safety of Americans cannot be effectively addressed.

Three days before Christmas in 2015, the FDA issued an alarming alert to US-based companies importing drug products from China.[49] Unspecified levels of hydrogen cyanide contamination were found in two shipments of drugs from a company located near the port city of Tianjin. Hydrogen cyanide is the toxic chemical used in the Nazi gas chambers. The contaminated shipments were stopped and barred from entry into the United States.

Four months earlier, massive explosions at a Tianjin chemical warehouse created fireballs so huge that they were detected by satellites in outer space. More than one hundred people were reportedly killed. A noxious chemical brew rained down upon the region, contaminating everything and everyone in its wake. More than forty different types of chemicals were discovered at the site. Companies that purchased drug products from the area were urged by the FDA to ensure all shipments "are free from contamination associated with the explosion and not contaminated in any way."[50] The task was impossible without knowing what to test for. Companies were advised to contact their supplier for information.

The contaminated drug shipments came from Tianjin Tianyao Pharmaceuticals. The FDA didn't reveal the names of the drugs that were contaminated. An online search found that the company makes prednisone and other anti-inflammatory products for a range of ailments including severe allergies, arthritis, asthma, and flare-ups from multiple sclerosis.[51]

China Digital Times (*CDT*) reported on its website that the Chinese government authorities issued "censorship instructions" that were leaked and distributed online.[52] *CDT*, based in Berkeley, California, says it translates and makes available for English readers content that has been censored or blocked in Chinese cyberspace.[53] According to *CDT*, the instructions to journalists stated, "All websites [should] strictly adhere to information from the Chinese Food and Drug Administration and the Tianjin municipal government. Do not hype, do not exaggerate. In addition, media from other regions are not to go to Tianjin to cover the story."[54]

In January 2016 we filed a Freedom of Information Act (FOIA) request with the FDA for the names of the forty contaminants. FOIA requests often take months or even years to wend their way through the federal bureaucracy, so we asked for expedited processing because to us the situation appeared urgent. A month later, the FDA denied our request for expedited processing. The letter, signed by Sarah Kotler, director of the Freedom of Information Division, said we had not demonstrated "a compelling need that involves an imminent threat to the life or physical safety of an individual . . . [nor] any urgency to inform the public."[55]

CENSORING JOURNALISTS WORKING IN CHINA

China's long arm of authoritarianism stretches deep into corporate boardrooms and major media outlets in the United States and other countries.

The Foreign Correspondents' Club of China, the professional association of journalists from foreign countries reporting from China, conducts an annual survey of its members. Nearly all who responded to its 2014 survey said China does not meet international journalism standards.[56] One of four said Chinese authorities exerted pressure on their editors in their home country over news coverage. A Japanese reporter explained the pressure this way:

> On quite a few occasions, officials from the Chinese embassy in Tokyo have told our editors that they were not pleased with some reports by our reporters in China. Their complaints cover a wide variety of topics, from domestic incidents such as suicide attacks in Xinjiang to international affairs including China's recent confrontations in the South China Sea with Vietnam and the Philippines. . . . The Tokyo headquarters of other Japanese media have received similar visits.[57]

A reporter for a European newspaper wrote, "Diplomats contacted my editor several times. They also had a meeting where the Chinese embassy sent three people including a lawyer."[58]

About two-thirds of respondents said they experienced interference, harassment, or violence while trying to cover stories in China. A *USA Today* reporter said, "I and several other journalists were manhandled away from the Malaysian Embassy in Beijing by plainclothes and uniformed police when reporting on the MH370 relatives' protest in April 2014," referring to the mysterious disappearance of the ill-fated Malaysia Airlines flight that literally fell off the radar.[59]

In a compelling article about Chinese government censorship outside China, the *Economist* wrote, "Watch What You Say, Even at Home." It opined, "Today the Communist Party wields its now formidable leverage in all manner of ways, successfully muting or softening criticism from CEOs and world leaders."[60]

During China's stock market crash in July 2015, Britain's *Daily Telegraph* reported, "Western banks say they are coming under heavy pressure from Chinese officials to refrain from negative comments. They are effectively gagged if they wish to do business in China."[61]

A CNN presenter in Hong Kong, Kristie Lu Stout, tweeted about what happened when she asked a group of MBA students if they would "spike" a story critical of China to secure market access. The students responded with a "resounding yes."[62]

But censorship does not make facts disappear. As President John Adams quipped long ago, "Facts are stubborn things, and whatever may be our wishes, our inclinations, or the dictates of our passion, they cannot alter the state of facts and evidence."[63]

We asked journalists in the United States if their colleagues working for US-based media companies are surveyed to find out if they have spiked news reported in the United States because of pressure from the Chinese government. No survey exists, we were told, but there should be. Then again, its findings might be censored, too.

WHAT'S AT STAKE

On a chilly November day, a month before Christmas, members of the Washington elite gathered outside the Smithsonian on the National Mall to admire the work of Chinese artist Cai Guo-Qiang.[64] His exhibition consisted of a four-story-high pine tree covered with two thousand fireworks that exploded in a series of three loud, smoky bursts. The flashes from the fireworks looked like lights on a Christmas tree. Soon, black smoke billowed and covered the tree. The artist said through a translator, "Now it looks like a Chinese ink painting."[65] The *Washington Post* described the event as the "Christmas tree explosion." *Smithsonian* magazine memorialized the event as "What a Blast!"[66] Then secretary of state Hillary Clinton awarded the artist with the State Department Medal of Arts for contributions to the advancement of understanding and diplomacy.

The symbolism is profound, but the Washington establishment, caught up in itself, missed it. Everyone applauded as a symbol of American prosperity and happiness was blown into blackness, forming a Chinese image.[67]

As we have documented, another symbol of American prosperity is at risk, ingenious industries that make products to help people live longer, healthier, happier lives.

PART IV

BRING IT HOME

CHAPTER 14

A TEN-STEP PLAN TO BRING IT HOME

Without firing a missile or hacking the
electric grid, China can take America down
by disrupting access to essential drugs.

China has been one of America's bankers, buying US Treasury bonds, and is now America's drugmaker. The centralization of the global supply of key ingredients for America's medicines in a single country poses enormous risks that must be mitigated.

Free market advocates may contend that the United States is better off outsourcing medicine making to China and allowing Americans to keep more of their money to spend on other goods. But medicines are essential for life. A country needs them to function. Prescription drugs are made by private corporations, but many serve a public purpose. Everyone expects that medicine given to restart the beating of a heart is always available in hospital emergency rooms. Antibiotics prevent the spread of deadly infectious diseases. Both the government and industry considered penicillin a public good during World War II when they worked together to ensure a sufficient supply before D-day.

Not unlike the manufacture of other consumer products, business decisions about manufacturing essential drugs and their therapeutic ingredients have been left to the invisible hand of the market. Financial and human capital have migrated to countries with the lowest cost of doing business. Corporate executives and their boards have determined that for them, the benefits of dependence on China outweigh the risks.

These decisions are too important to leave to the invisible hand. As

China rapidly pursues a determined strategy to become a pharmaceutical power, US dependence on a single country will rise dramatically. China could become a fierce rival to India and eventually overtake it in the global market for generic drugs.

What could be on the horizon? Chinese investors are buying US hospitals, which are among the largest purchasers of prescription drugs. A Chinese billionaire is the largest shareholder of Tennessee-based Community Health Systems (CHS), which owns 158 hospitals in twenty-two states, mostly in rural America.[1] A Securities and Exchange Commission filing revealed an intent to possibly "request board seats or otherwise get involved in CHS operations," the industry trade journal *Modern Healthcare* reported.[2] The move could signal a positioning to influence the country of origin of the prescription drugs that hospitals purchase.

Looking ahead, Congress and the White House have given the FDA more authority to help assure the *safety* of Chinese-made drug products. While progress has been made, much work remains to be done. Action is needed now to assure the *security* of an uninterrupted supply of essential medicines. Without firing a missile or hacking the electric grid, China can take America down by disrupting access to essential drugs.

Here are ten steps to advance America's health security, economic vitality, and national security.

1. CONSIDER MEDICINES A STRATEGIC ASSET, NOT A COMMODITY TO BE BOUGHT AT THE LOWEST PRICE

Medicines and their key ingredients should be considered a strategic asset, not a cheap commodity purchased by drug companies and middlemen from the lowest bidder. A strategic asset for a country is one that enables people to enjoy a high quality of life, and its absence places a country in jeopardy.

2. TRACK AND FORECAST VULNERABILITIES IN THE SUPPLY OF AMERICA'S MEDICINES

Food and energy are treated as strategic assets in the United States because the country would cease to function without them. The government and industry use sophisticated methods to track and forecast their availability.

To ensure enough food is available to fill grocery store shelves, the US Department of Agriculture and industry track and forecast the supply of wheat, corn, meat, and many other commodities. Similarly, the government and industry track and forecast the supply and demand of oil to ensure gas stations have enough fuel so Americans can go to work and businesses can transport goods.

When it comes to medicines, "[n]obody owns the idea of understanding who has control of our drug supply, and it won't be resolved until it hits a crisis point," former federal official Ted Kirk said.[3] Information exists about the drug supply, but it isn't used to strategically map vulnerabilities. In the private sector, business intelligence firm Thomson Reuters™ has proprietary manufacturing intelligence for sixty thousand generic drug products containing more than ten thousand active ingredients and the companies that make them.[4]

The FDA has information on the countries and companies that supply medicines and their key ingredients. "To my knowledge, I don't think FDA sits back and looks at tetracycline or vancomycin and figures out where all our ingredient suppliers are," said Kirk, referring to widely used antibiotics.[5] "The agency doesn't see this as within its mandate."

A tracking and forecasting system to serve the nation's interest is needed to identify the companies and the countries that supply America's essential medicines and their ingredients. Risk assessments can and should be made about their reliability as suppliers of quality products. The political risks of foreign government-sponsored cartels and censorship about the causes of supply interruptions can and should be evaluated.

Drug products that are at persistent risk of shortages should be identified in advance. Hospitals and other large purchasers of drug products, which are not usually informed by drug manufacturers of pending drug shortages, should be informed of possible disruptions so they can plan for shortages and not be caught off guard.

Long-term forecasting will identify vulnerabilities on the horizon and generate long-term solutions. Take heparin as an example. It is derived from natural sources rather than produced synthetically. Population growth and global demand are on track to outstrip the availability of animal sources to make heparin in the future. US researchers have developed a synthetic alternative that doesn't rely on pig intestines harvested on the other side of the globe and that isn't fraught with suppliers operating fake factories.[6] A synthetic version could be made in the controlled environment of a manufacturing facility. The investment required to bring a synthetic alternative to market is lagging because the price of naturally derived heparin remains relatively cheap, at least for now. To compensate for the market's failure to maintain the supply of heparin or any other critical medicine, strategic public investment in alternative sources warrants consideration.

3. PRIORITIZE A LIST OF MEDICINES FOR WHICH A SUPPLY INTERRUPTION POSES AN IMMEDIATE DANGER TO PUBLIC HEALTH

A private, nongovernmental organization, perhaps the National Academy of Medicine, an arm of the National Academy of Sciences that advises the nation on issues related to science and technology, can be urged to convene expert physicians and public health leaders to quickly prioritize medicines for which an interruption in supply poses an immediate danger to the health of the public.

This process will create needed awareness among the physician and public health communities about the underlying causes of many current and future drug shortages, and the national security risks of America's dependence on China for essential drugs, active ingredients, and chemical building blocks. It will stimulate a call to action to ensure that these drugs are available when needed.

4. INVESTIGATE CHINESE DRUG CARTELS TO FIND OUT IF THEY CAUSE DRUG SHORTAGES IN THE UNITED STATES

The US federal appeals court ruling in September 2016, which absolved Chinese companies of undisputed antitrust actions to control exports and the price of vitamin C in the United States, opens the door to unfettered cartel behavior affecting the supply of America's medicines. Prudence warrants an investigation conducted in the public interest to determine if Chinese companies that sell prescription drugs, active ingredients, and chemical building blocks operate cartels that contribute to drug shortages in the United States. Drug shortages can kill. It is imperative to understand the impact of the concentration of the global supply chain in a single country.

5. PROVIDE INCENTIVES TO BRING DRUG MANUFACTURING HOME

Pharmaceutical-manufacturing plants are among the thousands of US plants that have shut their doors since China joined the World Trade Organization in 2001. The United States is rapidly losing its manufacturing capacity for generic drugs and the active ingredients that provide the therapeutic value for them and some brand-name drugs.

"Nothing is being built here," says Craig Langdale, a pharmaceutical company executive.[7] "I talk with absolutely everyone we hire, and they've been downsized because the facility where they were working was moving overseas. I hear over and over again, 'We just built a brand-new multimillion-dollar facility, and we never got it up and running.'"

The future of drug manufacturing in the United States may be limited to new brand-name drugs. "There is virtually no generic active ingredient synthesis currently performed in the United States," says industry manufacturing consultant Peter Saxon. "In ten years, only new drugs from research-based companies will be made here; nothing else will be synthesized in the US."[8]

Most prescriptions today are filled using generics—89 percent. As China gains market share in generics, it will garner a larger cut of the money Medicare spends on generic drugs for people covered by the program.[9] Public policies should reward domestic manufacturing. Lower corporate taxes, regulatory reform, and trade deals that level the playing field for domestic companies can bring jobs back home.

In 2016, Congress passed the 21st Century Cures Act to accelerate new drug discovery, development, and delivery of innovative treatments and cures.[10] But we must not forget about the vast majority of prescriptions that are filled with generics. There are no television commercials and multibillion-dollar advertising campaigns for these drugs because they have become commodities. Yet they can save our lives.

Generic drugs have saved consumers and taxpayers $1.46 trillion in the decade from 2006 to 2015, according to the Association for Accessible Medicines, formerly the Generic Pharmaceutical Association.[11] A small fraction of the savings to Medicare could be allocated to provide incentives for domestic manufacturing of high priority generic drugs and their active ingredients. By bringing manufacturing home, the United States can reclaim a minimum capacity to make essential medicines that millions of Americans need every day.

6. ENSURE THE US MILITARY DOES NOT DEPEND ON CHINA FOR ESSENTIAL MEDICINES

The US military should not depend on China for its medicine. The United States spends billions on nuclear submarines and fighter jets but depends on a country that is an adversary to make medicines for the men and women who operate them. While it is difficult to completely turn the clock back on globalization, it is not too late to identify the most critical vulnerabilities and remove them.

Federal government procurement requirements should be changed to encourage American manufacturing, not to rubber-stamp offshoring to a country that seeks to dominate the United States economically and militarily. Decisions must be made now to assure domestic supply in the future. Otherwise, in the hands of an adversary, essential drugs can be used as a strategic weapon.

7. STRENGTHEN, DON'T WEAKEN GOVERNMENT OVERSIGHT OF DRUG MANUFACTURERS

Some manufacturers are not as diligent as they should be in making safe and effective medicines. FDA oversight should be strengthened, not weakened. A repeat of a heparin-like disaster is unacceptable, where a vital but underfunded government agency had to clean up, at public expense, the consequences of people taking calculated risks that resulted in calamity.

8. DON'T CEDE US REGULATORY OVERSIGHT OF DRUG MANUFACTURING TO CHINA

The Chinese government bristles at FDA inspections. During the height of the tensions surrounding the heparin tragedy, an official at the Chinese embassy in Washington said inspection agreements should be reciprocal, the *New York Times* reported.[12] "Will the US government accept the Chinese FDA to set up in the United States?" the official was quoted as saying. China was hardly prepared to do so. In the prior year, as we learned in a previous chapter, the first head of the Chinese FDA was executed by his own government for taking bribes in return for approving new drugs. Chinese officials admitted that their regulatory system was at a very early stage.

China is moving quickly to improve regulatory oversight of its domestic manufacturing. If past intentions are indicative of future action, the Chinese government will eventually pressure the US government to recognize inspections of manufacturing facilities in China conducted by China's counterpart to the FDA, similar to how the FDA recently recognized European regulatory authorities' inspections.[13] The United States should not cede its regulatory oversight of drug making in China to the Chinese government.

9. INCREASE FDA TESTING OF MEDICINES

The FDA tests only a small fraction of prescription drugs, over-the-counter products, and active ingredients. Its test results are hard to find and interpret. The agency should be given the resources to expand independent testing and be more transparent about its findings to doctors, hospitals, pharmacists, and the public. Here's why.

When the FDA banned twenty-nine drug products made at the Zhejiang Hisun manufacturing plant because of numerous complaints from American healthcare professionals about the lack of full potency and suspicious particles, the agency was compelled to exempt fourteen products from the ban because of concern about a shortage. Some of the exempted products are used to make medicines to fight cancer. Hospitals that buy these products, and patients who receive them, were unaware of this predicament. Manufacturers who sell finished drugs using banned but exempted products don't tell their hospital customers. That needs to change. "Trust us" doesn't work.

10. LUCK IS NOT A STRATEGY: IDENTIFY PROBLEM PRODUCTS RAPIDLY

The global alert and investigation into the toxic blood thinner heparin was triggered by doctors and nurses at St. Louis Children's Hospital who were concerned about their patients' serious reactions. They contacted federal authorities who began the investigation that identified China as the source of contamination. The year before, the FDA had received reports showing a spike in heparin-related events, but outsiders had to prompt the FDA to protect the public from a bad drug. The FDA has a treasure trove of information about problem drugs, but it is not easily searchable.

Millions of reports from doctors, nurses, pharmacists, manufacturers, and the public can be turned into usable information to rapidly identify patterns showing a potentially lethal product. The FDA requires financial and human resources to create and sustain this kind of analytical capability. More than that, it needs freedom from pharmaceutical industry influence to do what is right for patients and their doctors. We may not be so lucky next time if a toxic drug is undetected for months or even years.

American medicine making is a vital part of the country's health security, economic prosperity, and national security. As manufacturing goes, so goes the workforce and the skills to innovate, build, and operate manufacturing plants. Reshoring can bolster employment and maintain a workforce with the skills necessary for a rapid buildup in production in anticipation of a public health emergency or national security event.

A long-time industry leader in pharmaceutical manufacturing who has witnessed the closure of many manufacturing plants asks, "Who's going to do this after my generation retires? We have to turn it around."[14] He is right, and he will have the last word. "We have to get back to making things here."

HOW TO FIND OUT WHERE YOUR MEDICINES ARE MADE

Here are tips to find out where your medicines are made. Some companies consider the information proprietary while others will gladly tell you.

Companies build trust with their customers when they openly state where their products come from. It shows that the drug companies have confidence in where they are made. When companies don't tell, customers will naturally wonder why.

Here's what you can do to find out where your medicines are made. You may not always be successful, but it's worth a try.

CALL THE COMPANY LISTED ON THE DRUG PACKAGE

Look on the label of your medicine for the name of the manufacturer, distributor, or packager. The FDA requires companies to disclose this information. Some labels may tell you the country where the product is made. If the label on your product doesn't say, go online and find the company's customer service phone number and speak to a representative. Ask for the country of origin of the pills and the active ingredients because they are often different. Some pharmaceutical companies have nurses and pharmacists who answer questions, and if so, you might get more information by speaking to one of them.

If your prescription drug comes in an amber-colored bottle or another type of container without a company name on the label, ask your pharmacist for the name of the manufacturer, distributor, or packager, which is found on the drug package. If you go to a pharmacy to pick up a prescription, ask the pharmacist to show you the package and snap a picture with your smartphone or ask the pharmacist to photocopy the package for you.

GO TO DAILYMED

Go to the website DailyMed, which is an authoritative website maintained by the National Library of Medicine at the National Institutes of Health in Bethesda, Maryland. It is the official source of information printed on the labels of drug packaging. The FDA obtains the information from manufacturers and provides it to DailyMed.[1]

In the search box on DailyMed, type the name of your prescription drug. A list of the companies that make it will appear. You can click on each product, and many products will have pictures of the drug package with the name of the manufacturer, distributor, or packager. Call the company and ask where the finished drug and the active ingredient are made.

ONLINE WEBSITES

When we searched Drugs.com™ for a generic of the brand-name antidepressant Wellbutrin XL®, the brand-name product and the names of about a dozen generic companies that sell it appeared.[2] You can look up each company to find out where its generic is made.

Be aware that online information isn't always accurate. The generic blood pressure medicine losartan potassium is listed for sale on Good Rx. The website says the generic is made by a US company, Pack Pharmaceuticals.[3] In fact, a search on DailyMed for the label revealed that Zhejiang Huahai makes the drug and Pack distributes it.[4]

When we searched for an over-the-counter pain reliever, WellPatch® capsaicin patches, Amazon™ sells it, but the image of the package on the Amazon website doesn't say where it is made.[5] A legal disclaimer on Amazon's web page says, "Actual product packaging and materials may contain more and different information than what is shown on our website."[6] We called Mentholatum™, in Orchard Park, New York, the company that sells the pain patch. A customer service representative told us the product is made in China because the ingredients are not available in the United States.[7] DailyMed shows an image of the product with "Made in China" on the package.[8]

HOW TO REPORT SAFETY CONCERNS TO THE FDA

If you have a problem with a medicine, talk with your doctor. You can also tell the FDA. Report serious side effects such as new or worsening symptoms. If you notice a problem after switching to a drug made by a different company, or have problems with the quality of a drug, report it. Call the FDA toll-free line 1-800-332-1088 to find out how you can report, or go online at www.fda.gov/medwatch.

WHEN CO-PAYS AND DEDUCTIBLES DETERMINE THE MEDICINE YOU TAKE

You may not have a realistic choice when deciding whether to take a brand-name or generic drug because out-of-pocket costs can be very expensive, depending on your insurance plan. A woman we know who worked in the pharmaceutical industry told us she had been paying a forty-dollar co-pay for a brand-name drug, a price she could afford. When she became eligible for Medicare, the out-of-pocket cost for the brand-name drug jumped to $300, while the generic drug cost a couple of dollars. She switched to the generic because it was more affordable.

Whatever medicine you take, be assured that the US drug supply is among the safest in the world. Hundreds of thousands of people go to work every day to make medicines as high quality and safe as they can be. One of those dedicated people said that many in the industry remind each other that the products they make might be for their children, parents, or themselves. If you have questions or concerns, always talk to your healthcare provider before stopping or switching your medicines.

NOTES

PREFACE

1. Guy Villax, in discussion with author, April 5, 2016.
2. Gardiner Harris, "Drug Making's Move Abroad Stirs Concerns," *New York Times*, January 19, 2009, http://www.nytimes.com/2009/01/20/health/policy/20drug.html (accessed March 2, 2017).
3. Department of Pharmaceuticals, *Recommendations of the Task Force on Development of Manufacturing Capabilities in Each Medical Vertical in Pharmaceutical Production* (New Delhi: Government of India, Ministry of Chemicals and Fertilizers, 2015), p. 38, http://pharmaceuticals.gov.in/sites/default/files/3rd%20TF%20Inside%20pages1.pdf (accessed March 2, 2017); Tony Scott and Chris Oldenhof, *A 25-Year Landslide in the Manufacture and Business of Active Pharmaceutical Ingredients (API) in Europe between 1983 to 2008* (Brussels: European Fine Chemicals Group, 2009), http://ec.europa.eu/DocsRoom/documents/12086/attachments/1/translations/en/renditions/native (accessed March 5, 2017).
4. Bharat Mehta, in discussion with author, February 2016.
5. *Hearing, Before Subcommittee on Oversight and Investigations Committee on Energy and Commerce*, 110th Cong. (2008) (statement of Marcia G. Crosse, director of public health and military health issues, US Government Accountability Office), https://www.gpo.gov/fdsys/pkg/CHRG-110hhrg52415/html/CHRG-110hhrg52415.htm (accessed March 23, 2017).
6. Keith Bradsher, "Amid Tension, China Blocks Vital Exports to Japan," *New York Times*, September 22, 2010, http://www.nytimes.com/2010/09/23/business/global/23rare.html (accessed December 8, 2017).
7. Christopher Nelson, Anna Bruse, et al., *Reliance on Foreign Sourcing in the Healthcare and Public Health Sector* (Washington, DC: US Department of Commerce, December 2011), p. 30, https://www.bis.doc.gov/index.php/forms-documents/doc_view/642-department-of-homeland-security-dhs-assessment-impact-of-foreign-sourcing-on-health-related-infra (accessed January 15, 2017).

NOTES

CHAPTER 1: "THEY TOOK MY HEART AWAY"

1. Charlisa Allen, etc. v. American Capital Ltd., et al., No. 1:10HC60098 (N.D. Ohio 2016), http://www.leagle.com/decision/In%20FDCO%2020160518E03/IN%20RE%20 HEPARIN%20PRODUCTS%20LIABILITY%20LITIGATION (accessed March 30, 2017).
2. Charlisa Allen, in discussion with author, April 2016.
3. *Charlisa Allen*, p. 2.
4. Ibid., p. 6.
5. Ibid., p. 3.
6. Ibid., p. 3.
7. Ibid.
8. Allen, in discussion with author.
9. *Charlisa Allen*, p. 3.
10. Ibid., p. 6.
11. Allen, in discussion with author.
12. Allen, in discussion with author.
13. *Charlisa Allen*, p. 4.
14. Allen, in discussion with author.
15. Charlisa Allen, CaringBridge, December 8, 2007.
16. Allen, in discussion with author.
17. Charlisa Allen, CaringBridge, December 18, 2007.
18. Charlisa Allen, CaringBridge, December 27, 2007.
19. Allen, in discussion with author.
20. Charlisa Allen, CaringBridge, January 1, 2008.
21. Charlisa Allen, CaringBridge February 1, 2008.
22. Dr. Alexis Elward, in discussion with author, February 2016.
23. Beth Miller, "Drama in the Dialysis Unit," *Outlook*, Washington University, St. Louis School of Medicine, January 14, 2008, https://outlook.wustl.edu/2009/spring/dialysis.htm (accessed March 2, 2017).
24. Ibid.
25. Elward, in discussion with author.
26. Ibid.
27. Ibid.
28. Ibid.
29. US Food and Drug Administration, "Updated Questions and Answers on Heparin Sodium Injection (Baxter)," June 18, 2008, https://www.fda.gov/Drugs/DrugSafety/Postmarket DrugSafetyInformationforPatientsandProviders/ucm112606.htm (accessed December 8, 2017).
30. Lisa Richwine and Susan Heavey, "Families tell US Lawmakers about Heparin Deaths," April 29, 2008, https://www.reuters.com/article/idUSN29333077 (accessed December 9, 2017).

31. Elward, in discussion with author.

32. Ibid.

33. US Food and Drug Administration, "Updated Questions and Answers."

34. Ibid.

35. US Food and Drug Administration, FDA press conference, transcript, February 11, 2008, https://wayback.archive-it.org/7993/20170112230037/http://www.fda.gov/downloads/NewsEvents/Newsroom/MediaTranscripts/ucm122115.pdf (accessed December 8, 2017).

36. Ibid.

37. *Hearing, Before Subcommittee on Oversight and Investigations Committee on Energy and Commerce,* 110th Cong. (April 29, 2008) (testimony of Robert L. Parkinson, chief executive officer of Baxter International), http://www.baxter.com/assets/downloads/RLP_testimony.pdf (accessed March 2, 2017).

38. Allen, in discussion with author.

39. *Hearing, Before Subcommittee on Oversight and Investigations Committee on Energy and Commerce* (Parkinson).

40. Ibid.

41. Ibid.

42. US Food and Drug Administration, Changzhou SPL, Form 483 Inspectional Observations, February 26, 2008, https://www.fda.gov/ucm/groups/fdagov-public/@fdagov-afda-orgs/documents/document/ucm056155.pdf (accessed March 2, 2017); Walt Bogdanich, "Blood Thinner Might Be Tied to More Deaths," *New York Times*, February 29, 2008, http://www.nytimes.com/2008/02/29/us/29heparin.html?_r=0 (accessed March 2, 2017).

43. US Food and Drug Administration, Changzhou SPL, Form 483.

44. Ibid.

45. *Hearing, Before Subcommittee on Oversight and Investigations Committee on Energy and Commerce*, 110th Cong. (2008) (statement of Janet Woodcock, MD, director of the Center for Drug Evaluation and Research, Food and Drug Administration), https://www.gpo.gov/fdsys/pkg/CHRG-110hhrg53183/pdf/CHRG-110hhrg53183.pdf (accessed December 23, 2017).

46. Takashi Kei Kishimoto et al., "Contaminated Heparin Associated with Adverse Clinical Events and Activation of the Contact System," *New England Journal of Medicine* 358, no. 23 (April 23, 2008): 2457, http://www.nejm.org/doi/pdf/10.1056/NEJMoa0803200 (accessed March 2, 2017).

47. Jacob Goldstein, "Making Heparin Is a Dirty Job," *Wall Street Journal*, February 21, 2008, http://blogs.wsj.com/health/2008/02/21/making-heparin-is-a-dirty-job/ (accessed March 3, 2017).

48. Walt Bogdanich, "Tainted Blood Drug to Face Import Tests," *New York Times*, March 15, 2008, http://www.nytimes.com/2008/03/15/health/policy/15fda.html (accessed December 8, 2017).

49. *Hearing, Before Subcommittee on Oversight and Investigations Committee on Energy*

and Commerce, 110th Cong. (2008) (testimony of David Nelson, senior investigator of the Committee on Energy and Commerce), https://www.gpo.gov/fdsys/pkg/CHRG -110hhrg53183/html/CHRG-110hhrg53183.htm (accessed March 2, 2017).

50. *Hearing on Examining the US Food and Drug Administration, Focusing on Its Ability to Ensure the Safety of Food and the Drug Supply in the United States, Before the Committee on Health, Education, Labor, and Pensions,* 110th Cong. (2008) (testimony of Janet Woodcock, MD, director of the Center for Drug Evaluation and Research, Food and Drug Administration), https://www.gpo.gov/fdsys/pkg/CHRG-110shrg42153/html/CHRG-110shrg42153.htm (accessed March 2, 2017).

51. Gardiner Harris, "US Identifies Tainted Heparin in 11 Countries," *New York Times,* April 22, 2008, http://www.nytimes.com/2008/04/22/health/policy/22fda.html (accessed March 2, 2017).

52. *Hearing, Before Subcommittee on Oversight and Investigations Committee on Energy and Commerce,* 110th Cong. (2008) (testimony of William Hubbard, associate commissioner of the Food and Drug Administration), https://www.gpo.gov/fdsys/pkg/CHRG-110hhrg52415/html/CHRG-110hhrg52415.htm (accessed March 23, 2017).

53. Associated Press, "China and US Disagree over Tainted Heparin," *New York Times,* April 22, 2008, https://mobile.nytimes.com/2008/04/21/business/apee-heparin.html (accessed December 8, 2017).

54. US Food and Drug Administration, Changzhou SPL, Form 483.

55. Allen, in discussion with author.

CHAPTER 2: WHAT'S IN YOUR MEDICINE CABINET?

1. Barbara Morris, in discussion with author.
2. Pfizer customer service representative, in discussion with author.
3. Bob Kennedy, "China Increases Activity in Regulated Markets," Thomson Reuters, 2012, http://thomsonreuters.com/content/dam/openweb/documents/pdf/pharma-life -sciences/misc/china_increases_activity_regulated_markets.pdf (accessed March 2, 2017).
4. Ibid.
5. "Levonest," DailyMed, last updated September 5, 2017, https://dailymed.nlm. nih.gov/dailymed/drugInfo.cfm?setid=be7000f1-5bf1-4de5-a256-e4436c37f0a1 (accessed November 29, 2017).
6. "Levonest," GoodRx, https://www.goodrx.com/levonest/ images?quantity=1&dosage=28-tablets&form=package&label_override=levonest and https://www.goodrx.com/levonest?quantity=1&dosage=28-tablets&form=package&label_override =levonest (accessed March 2, 2017).
7. "About DailyMed," National Institutes of Health, National Library of Medicine, https://dailymed.nlm.nih.gov/dailymed/about-dailymed.cfm (accessed March 2, 2017).

8. "Levonest," DailyMed.

9. Breckenridge Pharmaceutical, "Breckenridge Signs Generic Agreement with Zhejiang Huahai Pharmaceuticals Co., Ltd.," PR Newswire, May 4, 2012, http://www.prnewswire.com/news-releases/breckenridge-signs-generic-agreement-with-zhejiang-huahai-pharmaceuticals-co-ltd-150203195.html (accessed March 2, 2017).

10. Ibid.

11. Nicholas Zamiska, "US Opens the Door to Chinese Pills," *Wall Street Journal*, October 9, 2007, http://www.wsj.com/articles/SB119187230072652477 (accessed March 2, 2017).

12. Ibid.

13. "Donepezil Hydrochloride," DailyMed, last updated October 20, 2015, https://dailymed.nlm.nih.gov/dailymed/drugInfo.cfm?setid=042a59ea-131a-4806-b0f4-2f791d4414e2 (accessed March 2, 2017).

14. Kennedy, "China Increases Its Activity," p. 4.

15. Prinston Pharmaceuticals, http://www.prinstonpharm.com/ (accessed March 2, 2017); Huahai US, Inc., http://www.huahaius.com/history.html (accessed March 2, 2017); Solco Healthcare, http://www.solcohealthcare.com/ (accessed March 2, 2017).

16. "Risperidone," DailyMed, https://dailymed.nlm.nih.gov/dailymed/search.cfm?labeltype=all&query=risperidone&pagesize=20&page=2&vfile= (accessed March 2, 2017).

17. "Amlodipine Besylate," DailyMed, last updated July 27, 2017, https://dailymed.nlm.nih.gov/dailymed/drugInfo.cfm?setid=3518853a-4c5b-4161-a178-8da7f656f009 (accessed November 22, 2017).

18. Beijing Second Pharmaceutical Company, 2009, http://english.saike.com.cn/English/AboutUs.aspx?cid=3 (accessed March 2, 2017).

19. Kennedy, "China Increases Its Activity," p. 5.

20. "Losartan Potassium," DailyMed, last updated October 1, 2015, https://dailymed.nlm.nih.gov/dailymed/drugInfo.cfm?setid=3D6A61CD-77C4-4F52-B826-C030DF979270 (accessed March 2, 2017); Pack Pharmaceuticals was purchased by Rising Pharmaceuticals: "Rising Pharmaceuticals to Acquire PACK Pharmaceuticals for $100 Million," PharmaBiz, March 29, 2014, http://www.pharmabiz.com/NewsDetails.aspx?aid=81120&sid=2 (accessed March 2, 2017).

21. Globe Newswire, "Sagent Pharmaceuticals Announces Reintroduction of Irinotecan Hydrochloride Injection," press release, August 5, 2014, https://globenewswire.com/news-release/2014/08/05/656057/10092909/en/Sagent-Pharmaceuticals-Announces-the-Reintroduction-of-Irinotecan-Hydrochloride-Injection-USP.html (accessed March 2, 2017).

22. Sandoz Global Communications, "Sandoz Launches First Generic Version of Cyclophosphamide Injection," press release, November 10, 2014, https://www.sandoz.com/news/media-releases/sandoz-launches-first-generic-version-cyclophosphamide-injection-usp (accessed March 2, 2017); "Cyclophosphamide Injection," DailyMed, https://dailymed.nlm.nih.gov/dailymed/drugInfo.cfm?setid=369e6911-66bd-4544-9901-cf887fdf1dc2 (accessed March 2, 2017).

23. Prinston Pharmaceutical, "Prinston Pharmaceutical Announces the Approval of Generic Wellbutrin SR® Extended Release Tablets in the United States," press release, May 26, 2015, http://www.prinstonpharm.com/Bupropion%20SR%20Tabs%20Press%20Release.html (accessed March 2, 2017).

24. "Levetiracetam," DailyMed, last updated February 24, 2015, https://dailymed.nlm .nih.gov/dailymed/drugInfo.cfm?setid=d818ef84-9b3e-434b-92d9-910cfa8af7da (accessed March 2, 2017).

25. Prinston Pharmaceutical, "Prinston Pharmaceutical Introduces Doxycycline Hyclate Delayed-Release Tablets 150mg and 200mg," press release, November 15, 2016, http://www .prinstonpharm.com/Doxycycline%20Hyclate%20DR.html (accessed March 2, 2017).

26. "Clindamycin Phosphate Topical Solution," DailyMed, last updated October 30, 2017, https://dailymed.nlm.nih.gov/dailymed/drugInfo.cfm?setid=f7480256-8b32-419a-8983 -e2c413040dba (accessed November 22, 2017).

27. Prinston Pharmaceutical, "Prinston Announces Approval of Generic Diovan-HCT® Tablets from the US Food and Drug Administration," press release, February 15, 2016, http:// www.prinstonpharm.com/Valsartan%20and%20hydrochlorothiazide.html (accessed March 2, 2017).

28. *Generic Drug Savings in the United States*, 7th annual ed. (Washington, DC: Generic Pharmaceutical Association, 2015), http://www.gphaonline.org/media/wysiwyg/PDF/GPhA _Savings_Report_2015.pdf (accessed March 2, 2017).

29. "Lisinopril," DailyMed, https://dailymed.nlm.nih.gov/dailymed/search.cfm?label type=all&query=LISINOPRIL&pagesize=50&page=1 (accessed January 14, 2018).

30. "Regular Strength Tylenol," Tylenol.com, https://www.tylenol.com/products/tylenol -regular-strength-tablets#other-information (accessed March 2, 2017)

31. NSD Bio, "Potential Health and Safety Impacts from Pharmaceuticals and Supplements Containing China-Sourced Raw Ingredients," prepared for the US-China Economic and Security Review Commission, April 2010, p. 2, http://www.uscc.gov/sites/default/files/ Research/NSD_BIO_Pharma_Report-Revised_FINAL_for_PDF-14_%20April_2010.pdf (accessed March 29, 2017).

32. "Imbruvica," DailyMed, last updated August 7, 2017, http://dailymed.nlm.nih.gov/ dailymed/drugInfo.cfm?setid=0dfd0279-ff17-4ea9-89be-9803c71bab44 (accessed November 22, 2017)

33. Kennedy, "China Increases Activity," p. 3. Victoria Slind-Flor, "Lilly, Apple, Deckers, Pella: Intellectual Property," *Bloomberg*, January 24, 2011, https://www.bloomberg.com/ news/articles/2011-01-24/lilly-apple-deckers-pella-intellectual-property-update1- (accessed December 30, 2017).

34. Gareth McDonald, "Pfizer Vancomycin Supplier Zhejiang Medicine Warned By US FDA," *in-PharmaTechnologist.com*, August 17, 2016, https://www.in-pharmatechnologist.com/ Article/2016/08/17/Pfizer-vancomycin-supplier-Zhejiang-Medicine-warned-by-US-FDA (accessed December 30, 2017).

35. *Reference for Business, Encyclopedia for Business*, 2nd ed., s.v. "Medicinal and Botanical Manufacturing, Industry Snapshot," 2017, http://www.referenceforbusiness.com/industries/ Chemicals-Allied/Medicinal-Chemicals-Botanical-Products.html (accessed March 30, 2017).

36. Eric Palmer, "Dangers Aside, Drugmakers Can't Live Without Chinese APIs," *FiercePharma*, September 3, 2012, https://www.fiercepharma.com/regulatory/dangers-aside -drugmakers-can-t-live-without-chinese-apis (accessed March 2, 2017).

37. Ibid.

38. Ted Kirk, in discussion with author, March 2016.

39. Associated Chambers of Commerce and Industry of India, *Pharmaceuticals Sector in India: Challenges Faced and Suggested Way Forward* (New Delhi: Associated Chambers of Commerce and Industry of India, 2014).

40. B. V. Mahalakshmi, "Indian Bulk Drug Industry Faces Chinese Threat," *Financial Express*, July 28, 2015, http://www.financialexpress.com/industry/indian-bulk-drug-industry -faces-chinese-threat/109041/ (accessed March 2, 2017).

41. Soma Das, "India Relies on China for 90 Percent of Drug Raw Materials," *Economic Times*, October 29, 2014, http://articles.economictimes.indiatimes.com/2014-10-29/ news/55559092_1_essential-drugs-bulk-drugs-apis (accessed March 2, 2017).

42. Mustaqim Adamrah, "Drug Prices Soar on Raw Material," *Jakarta Post*, August 24, 2008, http://www.thejakartapost.com/news/2008/08/24/drug-prices-soar-raw-material.html (accessed March 2, 2017).

43. Elly Burhaini Faizal, "Raw Material Shortage Jacks Up Drug Prices," *Jakarta Post*, March 13, 2012, http://www.thejakartapost.com/news/2012/03/13/raw-material-shortage -jacks-up-drug-prices.html (accessed March 2, 2017).

44. "Local Firms Turn to Government to Cut Imports," *Jakarta Post*, May 21, 2014, http://www.thejakartapost.com/news/2014/05/21/local-firms-turn-govt-cut-imports.html (accessed March 2, 2017).

45. Customer service representative at St. Joseph, in discussion with author, March 2, 2015.

46. Susan Liebeler et al., *Certain Acetylsalicylic Acid (Aspirin) from Turkey* (Washington, DC: US International Trade Commission, 1987), pp. A-4–A-5, http://books.google.com/ books/about/Certain_acetylsalicylic_acid_aspirin_fro.html?id=Q6uKjlIHwrQC (accessed March 3, 2017).

47. International Trade Commission, "Notice of Final Results of Changed Circumstances: Review and Revocation of the Antidumping Duty Order: Bulk Aspirin from the People's Republic of China," *Federal Register* 69 (December 28, 2004): 77726, http://enforcement. trade.gov/frn/summary/prc/E4-3829.txt (accessed March 3, 2017).

48. Ibid.

49. International Trade Administration, "Notice of Antidumping Duty Order: Bulk Aspirin from the People's Republic of China," *Federal Register* 65, no. 133 (July 11, 2000): 42673–42674, http://www.gpo.gov/fdsys/pkg/FR-2000-07-11/html/00-17515.htm (accessed March 3, 2017).

50. Dr. Margaret Hamburg, "Meeting the Challenges of Globalization and Strengthening International Collaboration for Improved Health and Safety" (speech at Peking University, Beijing China, November 17, 2014), https://wayback.archive-it.org/7993/20170111003408/http://www.fda.gov/NewsEvents/Speeches/ucm423280.htm (accessed December 2016).

51. "Common Medicines: Acetaminophen," Acetaminophen Awareness Coalition, http://www.knowyourdose.org/common-medicines/ (accessed March 3, 2017).

52. Anne-Sylvaine Chassany, "Rhodia Shuts Europe's Last Paracetamol Plant as China Prevails," *Bloomberg*, December 29, 2008.

53. Ibid.

54. "India Slaps $787 per Ton Anti-Dumping Duty on Chinese Paracetamol," *Economic Times*, October 30, 2013, http://articles.economictimes.indiatimes.com/2013-10-30/news/43528865_1_anti-dumping-duty-sunset-review-domestic-industry (accessed March 2, 2017).

55. Jeffrey Orenstein, "Country of Origin Compliance: The Top Ten Things Pharmaceutical Companies Need to Know," Reed Smith, February 6, 2014, http://www.reedsmith.com/Country-of-Origin-Compliance-The-Top-10-Things-Pharmaceutical-Companies-Need-to-Know-02-06-2014/ (accessed March 2, 2017).

56. Ibid.

57. Food and Drug Administration, *Title 21: Food and Drugs* (Washington, DC: Department of Health and Human Services, April 1, 2015), subchapter C: Drugs: General, part 201, section g, http://www.accessdata.fda.gov/scripts/cdrh/cfdocs/cfcfr/CFRSearch.cfm?CFRPart=201&showFR=1&subpartNode=21:4.0.1.1.2.1 (accessed March 3, 2017).

58. Ibid.

59. Craig Langdale, in discussion with author, March 2016.

60. Senator Sherrod Brown, "In Wake of New Report Showing Dangerous Gap in Drug Safety Efforts, Brown Calls on FDA to Tighten Oversight of Pharmaceutical Company Outsourcing," press release, June 7, 2011, https://www.brown.senate.gov/newsroom/press/release/in-wake-of-new-report-showing-dangerous-gap-in-drug-safety-efforts-brown-calls-on-fda-to-tighten-oversight-of-pharmaceutical-company-outsourcing (accessed March 2, 2017).

61. Transparency in Drug Labeling Act of 2008, S. 3633, 110th Cong. (September 26, 2008), https://www.congress.gov/bill/110th-congress/senate-bill/3633/titles (accessed March 2, 2017).

62. Cheryl Neath, in discussion with author, March 2016.

63. "As China Pumps Up Drug Exports, FDA Worries About Inspections," *FiercePharma*, October 1, 2015, https://www.fiercepharma.com/manufacturing/as-china-pumps-up-drug-exports-fda-worries-about-inspections (accessed December 8, 2017).

64. Guy Villax, in discussion with author, April 5, 2016.

65. Ibid.

66. Ibid.

67. Ibid.

68. "Novartis Plant Shut Down Creates Urgency to Find Alternatives to Chinese APIs," PharmaCompass, July 30, 2015, http://www.pharmacompass.com/radio-compass-blog/novartis -plant-shut-down-creates-urgency-to-find-alternatives-to-chinese-apis (accessed February 20, 2017).

69. Ibid.

70. Mimi Lau, "Supplies of Chemical Agent 7-ACA Affected by Use of 'Gutter Oil' in China," *South China Morning Post*, September 6, 2012, http://www.scmp.com/news/china/ article/1030395/supplies-chemical-agent-7-aca-affected-use-gutter-oil-china (accessed March 29, 2017).

71. Ibid.

72. Ibid.

73. International Chemical Investors, "International Chemical Investors Group Acquires Sandoz Site in Frankfurt-Hochst," press release, February 24, 2016, http://www.ic-investors .com/news/details/article/international-chemical-investors-group-acquires-sandoz-site-in -frankfurt-hoechst.html (accessed February 20, 2017).

74. Hart Research and Pew Prescription Project, *Americans' Attitudes on Prescription Drug Safety* (Washington, DC: Hart Research/POS for Pew Prescription Project, 2010), http://www.pewtrusts.org/~/media/legacy/uploadedfiles/phg/collection_and_hub_pages/ IBDSPPPAmericanAttiduesonPrescriptionDrugSafetypdf.pdf (accessed March 3, 2017).

75. US Food and Drug Administration, "Melamine Pet Food Recall of 2007," https:// www.fda.gov/AnimalVeterinary/SafetyHealth/RecallsWithdrawals/ucm129575.htm (accessed December 8, 2017).

76. Louis Garguilo, "Biopharma Outsourcing Shall Be Revealed," *Outsource Pharma*, December 16, 2014, http://www.outsourcedpharma.com/doc/biopharma-outsourcing-shall-be -revealed-0001?sectionCode=ffocus&templateCode=Departments&user=3093092&source =nl:42065&utm_source=et_6214173&utm_medium=email&utm_campaign=OUTPH _2015-01-07&utm_term=455fed7d-13a1-4421-9a40-5c93fa6460db&utm_content =Biopharma%2bOutsourcing%2bShall%2bBe%2bRevealed (accessed March 2, 2017).

77. Ibid.

78. Ibid.

79. Customer service representative, in discussion with author, April 24, 2015.

CHAPTER 3: WASHINGTON WAKES UP

1. John Taylor, in discussion with author, March 2016.

2. *Hearing, Before Subcommittee on Oversight and Investigations Committee on Energy and Commerce*, 110th Cong. (2008) (statement of Janet Woodcock, MD, director of the Center for Drug Evaluation and Research, Food and Drug Administration), https://www.gpo.gov/ fdsys/pkg/CHRG-110hhrg53183/html/CHRG-110hhrg53183.htm (accessed March 3, 2017).

3. *Hearing, Before Subcommittee on Oversight and Investigations Committee on Commerce*, 106th Cong. (June 8 and October 3, 2000) (statement of John D. Dingell, representative, D-MI), https://www.gpo.gov/fdsys/pkg/CHRG-106hhrg65846/html/CHRG-106hhrg65846 .htm (accessed December 15, 2017).

4. *Hearing, Before Subcommittee on Oversight and Investigations Committee on Energy and Commerce* (Woodcock).

5. Chemjobber, in discussion with author, September 11, 2015.

6. James Campbell, in discussion with author, November 2017.

7. *Hearing, Before Subcommittee on Oversight and Investigations Committee on Energy and Commerce*, 110th Cong. (2008) (statement of David Nelson, senior investigator of the Committee on Energy and Commerce), https://www.gpo.gov/fdsys/pkg/CHRG-110 hhrg53183/pdf/CHRG-110hhrg53183.pdf (accessed December 14, 2017).

8. *Hearing, Before Subcommittee on Oversight and Investigations Committee on Energy and Commerce*, 110th Cong. (2008) (statement of Bart Stupak, chairman of Subcommittee on Oversight and Investigations), https://www.gpo.gov/fdsys/pkg/CHRG-110hhrg53183/pdf/ CHRG-110hhrg53183.pdf (accessed December 14, 2017).

9. *Hearing, Before Subcommittee on Oversight and Investigations Committee on Energy and Commerce*, 110th Cong. (2008) (testimony of Robert L. Parkinson, chief executive officer of Baxter International), http://www.baxter.com/assets/downloads/RLP_testimony.pdf (accessed March 3, 2017).

10. *Hearing, Before Subcommittee on Oversight and Investigations Committee on Energy and Commerce* (Nelson).

11. Ibid.

12. *Hearing, Before Subcommittee on Oversight and Investigations Committee on Energy and Commerce* (Parkinson).

13. Associated Press, "Baxter Healthcare to Acquire Wyeth Subsidiary," June 11, 2002, http://www.nytimes.com/2002/06/11/business/company-news-baxter-healthcare-to-acquire -wyeth-subsidiary.html (accessed December 14, 2017).

14. *Hearing, Before Subcommittee on Oversight and Investigations Committee on Energy and Commerce* (Nelson).

15. Philippe Andre, "API Manufacturing Situation in China: An Auditor's Experiences and Views," May 13, 2009, http://webcache.googleusercontent.com/search?q=cache:2PF6NL 8rX_UJ:www.efcg.cefic.org/fdx3d385a03aa.iKc4fa64b36e42f39a/publication_file/api -manufacturing-situation-in-china.pdf+&cd=5&hl=en&ct=clnk&gl=us (accessed March 3, 2017).

16. Philippe Andre, "Supervision of Chinese-Made Drug Substances," March 14, 2011, p. 30, http://magazine.pewtrusts.org/~/media/assets/2012/12/pew_heparin_final_hr.pdf?la=en (accessed December 14, 2017).

17. Andre, "API Manufacturing Situation in China."

18. Ibid.

19. Ibid.

20. Chris Oldenhof, "Falsified Active Pharmaceutical Ingredients," *Chemistry Today*, September–October 2010, https://www.researchgate.net/publication/288410917_Falsified _APIs_Are_we_solving_the_problems (accessed December 14, 2017); Chris Oldenhof, email correspondence with author, March 8, 2017.

21. Oldenhof, email correspondence with author.

22. Nick Taylor, "Falsified Active Pharmaceutical Ingredients and Gangsters in the Pharma Industry," *in-PharmaTechnologist.com*, October 12, 2010, http://mobile.in-pharmatechnologist .com/Processing/Falsified-APIs-and-gangsters-in-the-pharma-industry (accessed March 6, 2017).

23. Oldenhof, "Falsified Active Pharmaceutical Ingredients."

24. *Hearing, Before Subcommittee on Oversight and Investigations Committee on Energy and Commerce* (Parkinson).

25. Ibid.

26. *Hearing, Before Subcommittee on Oversight and Investigations Committee on Energy and Commerce* (Nelson).

27. *Hearing, Before Subcommittee on Oversight and Investigations Committee on Energy and Commerce*, 110th Cong. (2008) (statement of Charlie Melancon, representative, D-LA), https://www.gpo.gov/fdsys/pkg/CHRG-110hhrg53183/pdf/CHRG-110hhrg53183.pdf (accessed December 14, 2017).

28. *Hearing, Before Subcommittee on Oversight and Investigations Committee on Energy and Commerce* (Nelson).

29. *Hearing, Before Subcommittee on Oversight and Investigations Committee on Energy and Commerce* (Parkinson).

30. *Hearing, Before Subcommittee on Oversight and Investigations Committee on Energy and Commerce*, 110th Cong. (2008) (testimony of David G. Strunce, chief executive officer of Scientific Protein Laboratories), https://www.gpo.gov/fdsys/pkg/CHRG-110hhrg53183/ html/CHRG-110hhrg53183.htm (accessed March 3, 2017).

31. Ibid.

32. *Hearing, Before Subcommittee on Oversight and Investigations Committee on Energy and Commerce* (Stupak).

33. *Hearing, Before Subcommittee on Oversight and Investigations Committee on Energy and Commerce* (Woodcock).

34. *Hearing, Before Subcommittee on Oversight and Investigations Committee on Energy and Commerce* (Stupak).

35. *Hearing, Before Subcommittee on Oversight and Investigations Committee on Energy and Commerce* (Woodcock).

36. Virginia Herold, presentation at the meeting of the California State Board of Pharmacy, Department of Consumer Affairs, Enforcement Committee, Sacramento, CA, October 6, 2008, http://www.pharmacy.ca.gov/meetings/minutes/2008/08_oct_enf.pdf (accessed December 14, 2017).

37. *Hearing on Examining the US Food and Drug Administration, Focusing on Its Ability to Ensure the Safety of Food and the Drug Supply in the United States, Before the Committee on Health, Education, Labor, and Pensions*, 110th Cong. (2008) (testimony of Janet Woodcock, MD, director of the Center for Drug Evaluation and Research, Food and Drug Administration), https://www.gpo.gov/fdsys/pkg/CHRG-110shrg42153/html/CHRG-110shrg42153.htm (accessed March 2, 2017).

38. *Hearing, Before Subcommittee on Oversight and Investigations Committee on Energy and Commerce* (Stupak).

39. *Hearing, Before Subcommittee on Oversight and Investigations Committee on Energy and Commerce,* 110th Cong. (2008) (testimony of William Hubbard, associate commissioner of the Food and Drug Administration), https://www.gpo.gov/fdsys/pkg/CHRG-110hhrg52415/html/CHRG-110hhrg52415.htm (accessed March 23, 2017).

40. *Hearing, Before Subcommittee on Oversight and Investigations Committee on Energy and Commerce*, 110th Cong. (2008) (testimony of Deborah Autor, director of the Office of Compliance, Center for Drug Evaluation and Research, Food and Drug Administration), https://www.gpo.gov/fdsys/pkg/CHRG-110hhrg53183/pdf/CHRG-110hhrg53183.pdf (accessed December 14, 2017).

41. *Hearing, Before Subcommittee on Oversight and Investigations Committee on Energy and Commerce* (Woodcock).

CHAPTER 4: "THESE DRUGS CAN REACH ANYONE INCLUDING THE PRESIDENT"

1. Fred Fricke, memo from the FDA Forensic Chemistry Center, July 29, 1996, US House of Representatives, Committee on Commerce, Subcommittee on Oversight and Investigations, June 8 and October 3, 2000, serial no. 106-164, p. 162.

2. Ibid.

3. *Hearing, Before Subcommittee on Oversight and Investigations Committee on Energy and Commerce*, 110th Cong. (2008) (testimony of Carl Nielsen, former director of the Division of Import Operations, Office of Regulatory Affairs, Food and Drug Administration, US Department of Health and Human Services), https://www.gpo.gov/fdsys/pkg/CHRG-110hhrg52415/html/CHRG-110hhrg52415.htm (accessed March 23, 2017).

4. Ibid.

5. Craig Langdale, in conversation with author, April 2016.

6. Ibid.

7. Ibid.

8. Ibid.

9. *Hearing, Before Subcommittee on Oversight and Investigations Committee on Energy and Commerce*, 110th Cong. (2008) (statement of David Nelson, senior investigator of the

Committee on Energy and Commerce), https://www.gpo.gov/fdsys/pkg/CHRG-110hhrg 53183/pdf/CHRG-110hhrg53183.pdf (accessed December 14, 2017).

10. Chris Oldenhof, "API Audits and Inspections: APIC Point of View," (presentation; Paris: 11th APIC/CEFIC European Conference on APIs, October 22–24, 2008), slide 14, http://www.slideserve.com/Patman/api-audits-inspections-an-apic-point-of-view (accessed March 6, 2017).

11. Ibid., slide 17.

12. Nick Taylor, "EMEA Ideas for Preventing Heparin-Like Contaminations," *in-Pharma Technologist.com*, June 9, 2008, https://www.in-pharmatechnologist.com/Article/2008/06/ 09/EMEA-ideas-for-preventing-heparin-like-contaminations (accessed March 5, 2017).

13. US Food and Drug Administration, "Patents and Exclusivity," *FDA/CDER SBIA Chronicles* (May 19, 2015), http://www.fda.gov/downloads/drugs/development approvalprocess/smallbusinessassistance/ucm447307.pdf (accessed March 3, 2017).

14. "Ampicillin," Drugs.com, https://www.drugs.com/ampicillin-images.html (accessed December 14, 2017).

15. Ibid.

16. Jack Mitchell, in discussion with author, March 1, 2016.

17. Joe Graedon, email correspondence with author, April 17, 2017.

18. Dan Stanton, "China-Based Paracetamol Maker Hit with US FDA Warning Letter," *in-Pharma Technologist.com*, January 6, 2015, http://www.in-pharmatechnologist.com/ Ingredients/China-based-paracetamol-maker-hit-with-US-FDA-warning-letter (accessed March 3, 2017); US Food and Drug Administration, warning letter to Novacyl Wuxi Pharmaceutical, December 19, 2014, https://www.fda.gov/ICECI/EnforcementActions/WarningLetters/ ucm427976.htm (accessed March 3, 2017).

19. Senator Sherrod Brown, "In Wake of New Report Showing Dangerous Gap in Drug Safety Efforts, Brown Calls on FDA to Tighten Oversight of Pharmaceutical Company Outsourcing," press release, June 27, 2011, https://www.brown.senate.gov/newsroom/press/ release/in-wake-of-new-report-showing-dangerous-gap-in-drug-safety-efforts-brown-calls-on -fda-to-tighten-oversight-of-pharmaceutical-company-outsourcing (accessed March 3, 2017).

20. Gene B. Sperling, "Permanent Normal Trade Relations and the Potential for a More Open China" (remarks, Dallas Ambassadors Forum, Dallas, Texas, May 12, 2000), https:// clintonwhitehouse4.archives.gov/WH/EOP/nec/html/PunkeChinaSpeech1.html (accessed December 14, 2017).

21. "Full Text of Clinton's Speech on China Trade Bill," *New York Times*, March 9, 2000, http://partners.nytimes.com/library/world/asia/030900clinton-china-text.html (accessed March 4, 2017).

22. Public Citizen, *Purchasing Power: The Corporate-White House Alliance to Pass the China Trade Bill over the Will of the American People* (Washington, DC: Public Citizen's Global Trade Watch, October 2000), p. ii, https://www.citizen.org/documents/purchasingpower.PDF (accessed March 3, 2017).

NOTES

23. Bernie Sanders, "Senate Speech by Sen. Bernie Sanders on Unfettered Free Trade" (speech, Washington, DC, October 12, 2011), https://www.sanders.senate.gov/newsroom/press-releases/senate-speech-by-sen-bernie-sanders-on-unfettered-free-trade (accessed December 14, 2017).

24. Samuel Wagreich, "Lobbying by Proxy: A Study of China's Lobbying Practices in the United States 1979–2010 and the Implications for FARA," *Journal of Politics and Society* 24 (2013): 143, http://dx.doi.org/10.7916/D8S75D9G (accessed March 3, 2017).

25. Ibid.

26. Ibid.

27. "US Shatters Annual Record Trade Deficit," ABC News, January 14, 2004, http://www.abc.net.au/news/2004-01-15/us-shatters-record-annual-trade-deficit/120008 (accessed March 4, 2017).

28. *Wikipedia*, s.v. "US Census Bureau, Foreign Trade Division, US Trade Balance (1980 to 2014)," January 24, 2016, https://en.wikipedia.org/wiki/File:US_Trade_Balance_1980_2014.svg (accessed March 4, 2017).

29. Ronald Hrebenar and Clive S. Thomas, "The Rise of the New Asian Lobbies in Washington, DC: China, India and South Korea," (paper; Seattle: American Political Science Association Annual Meeting, 2011), http://papers.ssrn.com/sol3/papers.cfm?abstract_id=1901573 (accessed March 6, 2017).

30. Jack Mitchell, email correspondence with author, March 25, 2017.

31. *Testimony: Agriculture, Rural Development, and Related Agencies Before Senate Appropriations Comm.*, 107th Cong. (testimony of Bernard Schwetz, acting principal deputy commissioner, Food and Drug Administration, May 10, 2001).

32. US Food and Drug Administration, "FDA Ensures Equivalence of Generic Drugs," August 2002, http://www.fda.gov/Drugs/EmergencyPreparedness/BioterrorismandDrugPreparedness/ucm134444.htm (accessed March 4, 2017).

33. John Taylor, in conversation with author, March 2016.

34. Former FDA official, in conversation with author, July 2017.

35. William Hubbard, "Wrongly Blaming the FDA," *Washington Post*, May 8, 2006, http://www.washingtonpost.com/wp-dyn/content/article/2006/05/07/AR2006050700907_pf.html (accessed March 5, 2017).

36. US Governmental Accountability Office, *Better Data Management and More Inspections Are Needed to Strengthen FDA's Foreign Inspection Program* (Washington, DC: Governmental Accountability Office, September 2008), p. 24, http://www.gao.gov/new.items/d08970.pdf (accessed March 4, 2017).

37. Ibid., p. 32.

38. Joseph Kahn, "China Quick to Execute Drug Official," *New York Times*, July 11, 2007, http://www.nytimes.com/2007/07/11/business/worldbusiness/11execute.html?n=Top%2FNews%2FWorld%2FCountries%20and%20Territories%2FChina&_r=0 (accessed March 5, 2017).

39. "Former SFDA Chief Executed for Corruption," *China Daily*, July 10, 2007, http://www.chinadaily.com.cn/china/2007-07/10/content_5424937.htm (accessed March 5, 2017).

40. John Taylor, in conversation with author, March 2016.

41. Julie Appleby, "Budget Cuts FDA Safety Checks," *USA Today*, February 14, 2005, http://usatoday30.usatoday.com/money/industries/health/2005-02-14-fda-safety-usat_x.htm (accessed March 3, 2017).

42. Food and Drug Administration, *Justification of Estimates for Appropriations Committees* (Washington, DC: US Department of Health and Human Services, 2014), p. 4, http://www.fda.gov/downloads/AboutFDA/ReportsManualsForms/Reports/BudgetReports/UCM347422.pdf (accessed March 5, 2017); Montgomery County, Maryland School District, "Fiscal Year 2019 Operating Budget," http://www.montgomeryschoolsmd.org/departments/budget/ (accessed March 5, 2017).

43. Alastair Wood, "Playing 'Kick the FDA': Risk-Free to Players but Hazardous to Public Health," *New England Journal of Medicine* 358 (April 24, 2008), http://www.nejm.org/doi/full/10.1056/NEJMp0802227 (accessed March 4, 2017).

44. Ibid.

45. Christine Dellert, "Tainted-Toothpaste Alarm Becoming Teeth-Chattering," *Orlando Sentinel*, July 6, 2007, http://articles.orlandosentinel.com/2007-07-06/news/TOOTHPASTE 06_1_florida-hospital-waterman-toothpaste-diethylene (accessed March 4, 2017).

46. Ibid.

47. *Hearing, Before Subcommittee on Oversight and Investigations Committee on Energy and Commerce,* 110th Cong. (2008) (testimony of William Hubbard, associate commissioner of the Food and Drug Administration), https://www.gpo.gov/fdsys/pkg/CHRG-110hhrg52415/html/CHRG-110hhrg52415.htm (accessed March 23, 2017).

48. Walt Bogdanich, "Toxic Toothpaste Made in China Is Found in US," *New York Times*, June 2, 2007, http://www.nytimes.com/2007/06/02/us/02toothpaste.html (accessed March 4, 2017).

49. Ibid.

50. US Food and Drug Administration, "Toothpaste Imported from China May Contain Diethylene Glycol," August 13, 2007, https://wayback.archive-it.org/7993/20170112170 452/http://www.fda.gov/Safety/MedWatch/SafetyInformation/SafetyAlertsforHuman MedicalProducts/ucm153155.htm (accessed January 14, 2018).

51. Ibid.

52. Walt Bogdanich and Jake Hooker, "From China to Panama, a Trail of Poisoned Medicine," *New York Times,* May 6, 2007, http://www.nytimes.com/2007/05/06/world/americas/06poison.html (accessed December 15, 2017).

53. Edie Lau, "US Attorney Recommends $35,000 in Fines, No Prison Time for ChemNutra Owners," *Veterinary Information Network*, June 19, 2009, http://news.vin.com/VINNews.aspx?articleId=13187 (accessed March 4, 2017).

54. Ibid.

55. Senator Richard Durbin and Representative Rosa DeLauro, letter to Ambassador Zhou Wenzhong, April 18, 2007, http://www.humanesociety.org/assets/pdfs/Pet-Food-Recall -Letter-to-China.pdf (accessed March 6, 2017).

56. Former FDA official, in discussion with author, 2015.

57. US Food and Drug Administration, "Melamine Pet Food Recall—Frequently Asked Questions," October 7, 2009, https://www.fda.gov/AnimalVeterinary/SafetyHealth/ RecallsWithdrawals/ucm129932.htm (accessed December 15, 2017).

58. Ibid.

59. US Department of Justice, United States of America vs. Sally Miller et al., Indictment, February 6, 2008, http://online.wsj.com/public/resources/documents/WSJ080206_miller _indictment.pdf (accessed November 22, 2017). See also https://www.fda.gov/Animal Veterinary/SafetyHealth/RecallsWithdrawals/ucm129932.htm.

60. Edie Lau, "Sentences Handed Down in Pet-Food Poisoning Criminal Case," *Veterinary Information Network*, February 9, 2010, http://news.vin.com/VINNews.aspx?articleId=14984 (accessed March 5, 2017).

61. David Barboza, "Death Sentences in Chinese Milk Case," *New York Times,* January 22, 2009, http://www.nytimes.com/2009/01/23/world/asia/23milk.html (accessed December 15, 2017).

62. US Food and Drug Administration, *Guidance for Industry Pharmaceutical Components at Risk for Melamine Contamination* (Washington, DC: US Department of Health and Human Services, August 2009), http://www.fda.gov/downloads/Drugs/GuidanceCompliance RegulatoryInformation/Guidances/UCM175984.pdf (accessed March 4, 2017).

63. *Hearing, Before Subcommittee on Oversight and Investigations Committee on Energy and Commerce* (Hubbard).

64. Andrew Jacobs and Mark McDonald, "FDA Opens New Office in Beijing to Screen Food and Drug Exports," *New York Times*, November 20, 2008, http://www.nytimes.com/ 2008/11/20/world/asia/20beijing.html?_r=0 (accessed March 2, 2017).

65. US Food and Drug Administration, warning letter to Shanghai No. 1 Biochemical & Pharmaceutical Co. Ltd., April 14, 2009, http://wayback.archive-it.org/7993/2016 1023103200/http://www.fda.gov/ICECI/EnforcementActions/WarningLetters/2009/ ucm136668.htm (accessed December 15, 2017).

66. Ibid.

67. US Food and Drug Administration, Import Alerts, https://www.accessdata.fda.gov/ cms_ia/importalert_189.html (accessed March 3, 2017).

68. *Testimony: US Food and Drug Administration, US Department of Health and Human Services, Before US-China Economic and Security Review Commission* (statement of Christopher Hickey, country director of the People's Republic of China, April 3, 2014), https://www.uscc .gov/sites/default/files/Hickey_testimony.pdf (accessed December 15, 2017).

69. "SOCMA's BPTF and CEFIC's EFCG Work with FDA to Protect Public Safety," Society of Chemical Manufacturers, March 8, 2011, http://www.powderbulksolids.com/news/ socmas-bptf-and-cefics-efcg-work-fda-protect-public-safety (accessed December 15, 2017).

70. Howard Sklamberg, "Protecting the Global Drug Supply: FDASIA Title VII," US Food and Drug Administration, FDA Voice (blog), July 10, 2014, https://blogs.fda.gov/fdavoice/index.php/2014/07/protecting-the-global-drug-supply-fdasia-title-vii/ (accessed March 3, 2017).

71. US Food and Drug Administration, *Guidance for Industry Circumstances That Constitute Delaying, Denying, Limiting, or Refusing a Drug Inspection* (Washington, DC: Department of Health and Human Services, 2014), http://www.fda.gov/downloads/regulatoryinformation/guidances/ucm360484.pdf (accessed March 3, 2017).

72. John DiLoreto, in discussion with author, April 2017.

73. *Testimony: US Food and Drug Administration, US Department of Health and Human Services, Before US-China Economic and Security Review Commission* (Hickey).

CHAPTER 5: THE VITAMIN C AND PENICILLIN CARTELS

1. Animal Science Products, Inc. et al. v. Hebei Welcome Pharmaceutical Co. Ltd. et al., No. 1:05-cv-00453 l (E.D.N.Y. 2005), p. 8, https://www.unitedstatescourts.org/federal/nyed/240061/1-0.html (accessed December 15, 2017).

2. DSM customer service representative, in discussion with author, January 7, 2016.

3. Royal DSM, http://www.dsm.com/products/quali-c/en_US/about-quali-c.html (accessed March 5, 2017).

4. Trader Joe's, email correspondence with author, July 1, 2015.

5. Whole Foods customer service representative, in discussion with author.

6. Nature Made customer service representative, in discussion with author, December 22, 2014.

7. *Animal Science Products*.

8. Ibid., p. 10.

9. Ibid., pp 11, 13.

10. Ibid.

11. Ibid.

12. Ibid., p. 11.

13. Ibid., pp. 11–12.

14. Animal Science Products, Inc., Ranis Company, v. Hebei Welcome Pharmaceutical Co. Ltd., North China Pharmaceutical Group Corporation, No. 13-4791-cv (2d Cir. 2014), Amicus brief, http://www.appliedantitrust.com/26_extraterritoriality/cases/animal_science/2cir/animal_sci_2cir_open_amicus_china4_14_2014.pdf (accessed December 15, 2017).

15. Christie Smythe, "Chinese Vitamin C Makers Fixed Prices, US Jury Says," *Bloomberg*, March 15, 2013, https://www.bloomberg.com/news/articles/2013-03-14/chinese-vitamin-c-makers-illegally-fixed-prices-u-s-jury-says (accessed December 15, 2017).

16. US Department of Justice, "F. Hoffman–La Roche and BASF Agree to Pay

Record Criminal Fines for Participating in International Vitamin Cartel," press release, May 20, 1999, https://www.justice.gov/archive/opa/pr/1999/May/196at.htm (accessed March 5, 2017).

17.   United States v. Dr. Kuno Sommer (plea agreement, May 20, 1999), https://www.justice.gov/atr/case/us-v-dr-kuno-sommer (accessed December 15, 2017).

18.   Andrew Longstreth, "US Courts Confront China's Involvement in Price-Fixing," Reuters, March 11, 2011, http://www.reuters.com/article/2011/03/11/us-china-vitaminc-idUSTRE72A4XH20110311 (accessed March 5, 2017).

19.   Ibid.

20.   North China Pharmaceutical Group Company, http://ncpc.globalchemmade.com/ (accessed March 5, 2017).

Animal Science Products, Inc., Ranis Company, v. Hebei Welcome Pharmaceutical Co. Ltd., North China Pharmaceutical Group Corporation, No. 13-4791-cv (2d Cir. 2014), p. 2, http://www.appliedantitrust.com/26_extraterritoriality/cases/animal_science/2cir/animal_sci_2cir_open4_7_2014.pdf (accessed November 22, 2017).

21.   Animal Science Products, Inc., Ranis Company, v. Hebei Welcome Pharmaceutical Co. Ltd., North China Pharmaceutical Group Corporation, No. 13-4791-cv (2d Cir. 2014), plaintiffs brief, p. 18, http://uschinatradewar.com/files/2014/07/VITAMIN-C-PLAINTIFFS-BRIEF-2ND-CIRCUIT.pdf (accessed November 22, 2017).

22.   Animal Science Products, Inc., Ranis Company, v. Hebei Welcome Pharmaceutical Co. Ltd., North China Pharmaceutical Group Corporation, No. 13-4791-cv (2d Cir. 2014), p. 13, http://www.appliedantitrust.com/26_extraterritoriality/cases/animal_science/2cir/animal_sci_2cir_open4_7_2014.pdf (accessed November 22, 2017).

23.   Ibid.

24.   Animal Science Products, Inc., Ranis Company, v. Hebei Welcome Pharmaceutical Co. Ltd., North China Pharmaceutical Group Corporation, No. 13-4791-cv (2d Cir. 2014), Amicus brief, p. 8, http://uschinatradewar.com/files/2014/04/MOFCOM-VITAMIN-C-APPEAL-BRIEF.pdf (accessed March 25, 2017).

25.   Debra S. Dunne, Laurie A. Henry, Madeleine M. McDonough, "China Asks US State Department for Support in Vitamin C Price-Fixing Appeal," Lexology, June 6, 2014, http://www.lexology.com/library/detail.aspx?g=e3b25cfc-1cbd-4849-90eb-7e6e0e1181cb (accessed March 25, 20107); see also Embassy of the People's Republic of China, letter to the US Department of State, April 9, 2014.

26.   Animal Science Products, Inc., Ranis Company, v. Hebei Welcome Pharmaceutical Co. Ltd., North China Pharmaceutical Group Corporation, No. 13-4791-cv (2d Cir. 2016), decided: September 20, 2016, http://caselaw.findlaw.com/us-2nd-circuit/1745603.html (accessed March 5, 2017).

27.   Ibid., pp. 44–45.

28.   Ibid., pp. 43–44.

29.   Wang Yanfei, "Drug Firms Face Industrywide Probe by Price Regulator," *China Daily*,

May 7, 2016, http://europe.chinadaily.com.cn/business/2016-05/07/content_25120304.htm (accessed March 4, 2017).

30. Charles M. Grossman, "The First Use of Penicillin in the United States," *Annals of Internal Medicine* 149, no. 2 (July 15, 2008): 135–36, http://annals.org/aim/article/741794/first-use-penicillin-united-states (accessed March 3, 2017).

31. Ibid.

32. Ibid.

33. Joseph G. Lombardino, "A Brief History of Pfizer Central Research," *Bulletin of the History of Chemistry* 25, no. 1 (2000), http://www.scs.illinois.edu/~mainzv/HIST/bulletin _open_access/v25-1/v25-1%20p10-15.pdf (accessed March 5, 2017).

34. Dr. Lucinda Maine, in discussion with author, May 7, 2016.

35. John Scott, in discussion with author.

36. Kenneth Gosslein, "Pfizer Plans Job Cuts," *Hartford Courant,* June 21, 2006, http://articles.courant.com/2006-06-21/business/0606210435_1_pharmaceutical-giant-pfizer-pfizer -plans-job-cuts-pfizer-s-research-and-development (accessed March 5, 2017).

37. Ibid.

38. Ted Kirk, in discussion with author.

39. Tony Scott and Chris Oldenhof, "A Twenty-Five Year Landslide in the Manufacture and Business of Active Pharmaceutical Ingredients (API) in Europe Between 1983 to 2008," European Fine Chemicals Group, http://ec.europa.eu/DocsRoom/documents/12086/attachments/1/translations/en/renditions/native (accessed December 15, 2017).

40. Ibid.

41. Ibid.

42. Ibid.

43. Chris Oldenhof, "Export Pricing of Strategically Important Chemical Products Made in China: How It Works," 2010, slide 10.

44. Gardiner Harris, "Drug Making's Move Abroad Stirs Concern," *New York Times,* January 19, 2009, http://www.nytimes.com/2009/01/20/health/policy/20drug.html?_r=0 (accessed March 5, 2017).

45. Department of Pharmaceuticals, *Recommendations of the Task Force on Development of Manufacturing Capabilities in Each Medical Vertical in Pharmaceutical Production* (New Delhi: Government of India, Ministry of Chemicals and Fertilizers, 2015), http://www .pharmaceuticals.gov.in/sites/default/files/3rd%20TF%20Inside%20pages1.pdf (accessed March 5, 20107)

46. Shine Jacob, "Chinese Scare Looms over India's Bulk Drug Industry," *LiveMint,* November 3, 2015, http://www.livemint.com/Industry/L8C3Zb8G80FsCxu97IVj1K/Chinese-scare-looms-over-Indias-bulk-drug-industry.html (accessed March 5, 2017).

47. Toni Clarke, "Smithfield's China Deal Spurs Heparin Heart Drug Safety Concerns," Reuters, July 25, 2013, http://www.reuters.com/article/2013/07/26/usa-smithfield-heparin -idUSL1N0FW00P20130726 (accessed March 27, 2017).

48.   Phil Walzer, "Q&A with Larry Pope, President, and CEO of Smithfield Foods," *Virginian-Pilot*, October 19, 2010, http://pilotonline.com/business/q-a-with-larry-pope -president-and-ceo-of-smithfield/article_007186df-3da5-5561-b158-ed90e76c1f82.html (accessed January 15, 2017).

49.   Ibid.

50.   David Barboza, "Chinese Bid for US Pork Had Links to Wall Street," June 2, 2013, *New York Times*, http://www.nytimes.com/2013/06/03/business/global/behind-the-chinese -bid-for-smithfield-foods.html (accessed January 15, 2017).

51.   Daniel Slane, "Chinese Investment in the US, Part I," video, C-SPAN, US-China Economic and Security Review Commission, January 26, 2017, https://www.c-span.org/video/ ?422783-1/forum-focuses-chinese-investment-us (accessed March 6, 2017).

52.   Government official, in discussion with author.

53.   Clarke, "Smithfield's China Deal."

54.   US House of Representatives, Committee on Energy and Commerce, letter to C. Larry Pope, July 24, 2013, https://energycommerce.house.gov/news-center/letters/letter -smithfield-foods-regarding-heparin-safety (accessed March 25, 2017).

55.   Dr. Janet Woodcock, "Introduction of Proposal for Reintroduction of Bovine Heparin in the US Market," June 4, 2014, slides 2, 4.

56.   *China Heparin Industry Report*, ReportLinker, December 2015, http://www.report linker.com/p0354148/China-Heparin-Industry-Report-2012-2014.html#utm_source=pr newswire&utm_medium=pr&utm_campaign=Pharmaceuticalhttp://www.prnewswire.com/ news-releases/china-heparin-industry-report-2012-2014-185273002.html (accessed January 15, 2017).

57.   Woodcock, "Introduction of Proposal," slide 9.

58.   Ibid., slide 5.

59.   Courtney Comstock, "How Goldman Sachs Made $1 Billion on Pig Innards Yesterday," *Business Insider*, May 6, 2010, http://www.businessinsider.com/how-goldman-sachs -made-1-billion-on-pig-innards-yesterday-2010-5 (accessed March 29, 2017).

60.   Seth Horwitz, "Hepalink Signs Agreement to Acquire Scientific Protein Laboratories," Businesswire, December 26, 2013, http://www.businesswire.com/news/home/2013122600 5071/en/Hepalink-Signs-Agreement-Acquire-Scientific-Protein-Laboratories#.VUfYscN0y00 (accessed January 15, 2017).

61.   C. Lee Ventola, "The Drug Shortage Crisis in the United States," *Pharmacy and Therapeutics* 36, no. 11 (2011): 740–42, 749–57, https://www.ncbi.nlm.nih.gov/pmc/articles/ PMC3278171/ (accessed December 15, 2017).

62.   Bharat Mehta, in discussion with author, February 2016.

63.   Emily Kimball, "Antibiotics: Will Changes to Eastern Regulations Impact the West?" CHEManager Europe, June 2012, http://www.chemanager-online.com/en/topics/pharma -biotech-processing/impact-new-regulations-global-antibiotics-production (accessed December 15, 2017).

64. Tan Zongyang, "Pollution Apology Fails to Calm Public Anger," *China Daily*, June 13, 2011, http://www.chinadaily.com.cn/china/2011-06/13/content_12681687.htm (accessed March 5, 2017).

65. Harbin Pharmaceuticals, http://en.hayao.com/product/product.html (accessed January 13, 2017).

66. Emily Bourke, "Penicillin Rationed in Global Shortage," Australian Broadcasting Company, September 26, 2011, http://www.abc.net.au/news/2011-09-27/global-shortage-of -penicillin/2946130 (accessed March 5, 2017).

67. Helen Hollingsworth, email correspondence with author, April 2015.

68. "Nationwide Shortage of Doxycycline Resources for Providers and Recommendations for Patient Care," Centers for Disease Control and Prevention, June 12, 2013, https:// emergency.cdc.gov/han/han00349.asp (accessed March 5, 2017).

69. US Department of Justice, "Former Top Generic Pharmaceutical Executives Charged with Price-Fixing, Bid-Rigging, and Customer Allocation Conspiracies," press release, December 14, 2016, https://www.justice.gov/opa/pr/former-top-generic-pharmaceutical-executives -charged-price-fixing-bid-rigging-and-customer (accessed March 5, 2017).

70. Ibid.

CHAPTER 6: THE CHINA TRAP

1. Rich Kramss, in discussion with author, April 13, 2016.

2. Mark Peters and Eric Gershon, "Bayer Closing Research Facility," *Hartford Courant*, November 10, 2006, http://articles.courant.com/2006-11-10/news/0611100121_1_bayer-ag -bayer-closing-research-facility-bayer-healthcare (accessed March 5, 2017).

3. Kramss, in discussion with author.

4. Sophie L. Rovner, "Still Waiting for Good Times," *Chemical & Engineering News* 91, no. 44 (November 4, 2013), http://cen.acs.org/articles/91/i44/Still-Waiting-Times.html (accessed March 5, 2017).

5. Linda Wang, "Barely Hanging On," *Chemical and Engineering News* 90, no. 45 (November 5, 2012), http://cen.acs.org/articles/90/i45/Barely-Hanging.html (accessed March 5, 2017).

6. Ellen Clark, "The Shift to CROs Continues," *Clark Executive Search Pharma Outsourcing and Movement to China* (blog), July 23, 2012, http://www.clarksearch.com/the -shift-to-cros-continues/ (accessed January 8, 2017).

7. Ibid.; Ellen Clark, "Big Pharma Outsourcing to CROs and Setting up R&D in China," *Clark Executive Search Pharma Outsourcing and Movement to China* (blog), April 17, 2011, http://www.clarksearch.com/big-pharma-outsourcing-to-cros-and-setting-up-rd-in-china/ (accessed March 6, 2017).

8. "Merry Christmas Your Fired!" CafePharma (message boards), December 23, 2014, http://cafepharma.com/boards/threads/merry-Christmas-your-fired.572343 (accessed March 5, 2017).

9. Ibid.

10. *Chemjobber* (blog), http://chemjobber.blogspot.com/ (accessed April 10, 2017).

11. Chemjobber, "The Layoff Project: 'I Seem to Have Lost Purpose,'" *Chemjobber* (blog), October 31, 2011, http://chemjobber.blogspot.com/2011/10/layoff-project-i-seem-to-have -lost.html (accessed March 5, 2017).

12. Tracy Staton, "AstraZeneca Cuts 1,150 US Jobs, Adds on in China," *FiercePharma*, December 8, 2011, http://www.fiercepharma.com/story/astrazeneca-cuts-1150-us-jobs-adds -china/2011-12-08 (accessed March 5, 2017).

13. Stephanie Saul, "Johnson & Johnson Plans to Cut 4,800 Jobs," *New York Times*, August 1, 2007, http://www.nytimes.com/2007/08/01/business/01drug.html?_r=0 (accessed March 5, 2017); Natasha Singer, "Johnson & Johnson Plans Cuts," *New York Times*, November 3, 2009, http://www.nytimes.com/2009/11/04/business/04drug.html (accessed March 5, 2017).

14. Peter Landers, "Johnson & Johnson Looks to Expand in Asia," *Wall Street Journal*, April 3, 2015, http://www.wsj.com/articles/johnson-johnson-looks-to-expand-in-asia-1428 096781 (accessed March 5, 2017)

15. "US Workforce Focus of Merck Cuts," *in-PharmaTechnologist.com*, July 31, 2011, http://www.in-pharmatechnologist.com/Regulatory-Safety/US-workforce-focus-of-Merck-Co -cuts (accessed March 5, 2017).

16. Gareth Macdonald, "Merck & Co. to Set up Asian R&D Hub in China," *in-Pharma Technologist.com*, December 7, 2011, http://www.in-pharmatechnologist.com/Regulatory -Safety/Merck-Co-to-set-up-Asian-R-D-hub-in-China (accessed March 5, 2017).

17. Kate Nagangast, "Pfizer's State Sites Slowly Shut Down," MLive.com, January 21, 2008, http://blog.mlive.com/grpress/2008/01/pfizers_state_sites_slowly_shu.html (accessed December 15, 2017).

18. Jonathan Rockoff, "Pfizer Shuts Six R&D Sites after Takeover," *Wall Street Journal*, November 10, 2009, http://www.wsj.com/articles/SB10001424052748703808904574525644 154101608 (accessed March 5, 2017).

19. Ransdell Pierson, "New Pfizer CEO Slashes R&D to Save 2012 Forecast," Reuters, February 1, 2011, http://www.reuters.com/article/pfizer-idUKN0112596620110201 (accessed March 5, 2017).

20. "New London, Groton Salute Pfizer for Community Role; Plaque Given at Breakfast, *The Day*, November 12, 1954, https://news.google.com/newspapers?id=qqItAAAAIBAJ &sjid=9nEFAAAAIBAJ&pg=6161,2259308&hl=en (accessed March 5, 2017); *Wikipedia*, s.v. "Victory Yard," last edited February 20, 2017, https://en.wikipedia.org/wiki/Victory_Yard (accessed March 5, 2017); "Pfizer Buys War Plant: Chemical Concern Gets WAA Shipyard at Groton for $911,999," *New York Times*, December 19, 1946, http://query.nytimes.com/

gst/abstract.html?res=9904E7D61F3AEE3BBC4152DFB467838D659EDE&legacy=true (accessed March 5, 2017).

21. "New London, Groton Salute Pfizer."

22. Lee Howard, "Pfizer Stuns Officials, Will Demolish Building 118," *The Day*, March 27, 2013, http://www.theday.com/article/20130327/BIZ02/130329658 (accessed March 5, 2017).

23. Lee Howard, "Research Unit Going to China, Pfizer Says," *The Day*, March 16, 2011, http://www.theday.com/article/20110316/BIZ02/303169949 (accessed March 5, 2017).

24. David Shlaes, in discussion with author, May 12, 2016.

25. Lee Howard, "Pfizer Delays Plan for Unit in China to Do Antibacterial Research," *The Day*, November 15, 2011, http://www.theday.com/article/20111115/BIZ02/311159974 (accessed March 5, 2017.

26. Pfizer, "Pfizer Announces Partnership with Shanghai Institutes for Biological Sciences for Drug Discovery Activities," press release, July 29, 2009, http://www.pfizer.com/news/press -release/press-release-detail/pfizer_announces_partnership_with_shanghai_institutes_for _biological_sciences_for_drug_discovery_activities (accessed March 5, 2017).

27. Ibid.

28. Zhou Yan, "Pfizer Grows R&D Work in China," *China Daily*, August 10, 2008, http://www.chinadaily.com.cn/bizchina/2009-08/10/content_8548101.htm (accessed March 5, 2017).

29. Ibid.

30. Lingshi Tan and Cory Williams, "Inside View: Pfizer," *Nature*, October 22, 2014, http://www.nature.com/naturejobs/science/articles/10.1038/nj0437 (accessed March 6, 2017).

31. Steve Krieger, in discussion with author, June 1, 2016.

32. Cynthia A. Jackevicius et al., "Generic Atorvastatin and Health Care Costs," *New England Journal of Medicine* 366, no. 3 (January 19, 2012): 201, http://www.nejm.org/doi/ pdf/10.1056/NEJMp1113112 (accessed March 6, 2017).

33. "Pfizer's CEO Discusses Q3 2012 Results," Earnings Call Transcripts, SeekingAlpha .com, November 1, 2012, http://seekingalpha.com/article/968651-pfizers-ceo-discusses-q3 -2012-results-earnings-call-transcript (accessed March 5, 2017).

34. Herman Saftlas, *Standard & Poor's Industry Surveys Healthcare: Pharmaceuticals* (New York: S&P Capital IQ, December 2012), p. 12, https://securingalpha.files.wordpress.com/ 2014/01/healthcare-pharmaceuticals.pdf (accessed March 6, 2017).

35. "Beatrijs Van Liedekerke, *The Changing Dynamics of Pharma Outsourcing in Asia* (London: PricewaterhouseCoopers, 2008), p. 7, https://www.pwc.com/gx/en/pharma-life -sciences/pdf/change_asia_10_08_08.pdf (accessed March 6, 2017).

36. Deborah Straszheim, "Demolition of Building 118 by Pfizer Begins in Groton," *Day*, July 31, 2013, Reader Comments, http://www.theday.com/article/20130731/NWS01/ 307319936 (accessed March 5, 2017).

37. Ibid.

38. John Scott, in discussion with author, May 11, 2016.

39. Lian Obrey, in discussion with author, March 31, 2017.

40. Tony Simpson, in discussion with author, May 22, 2016.

41. Ibid.; Katie Carolan and Katie Corrado, "Groton Police: Car Dealership Was a Front for Heroin Ring, Owner Arrested," Fox61, May 23, 2016, http://fox61.com/2016/05/23/groton -police-car-dealership-was-a-front-for-heroin-ring-owner-arrested/ (accessed March 5, 20107).

42. Diane Smith, in discussion with author, May 30, 2016.

43. Krieger, in discussion with author.

44. Peter Saxon, in discussion with author, August 6, 2016.

45. Vincent Lui et al., "The Age of the Affluent: The Dynamics of China's Next Consumption Engine," Boston Consulting Group, November 2012, http://www.bcg.com.cn/ export/sites/default/en/files/publications/reports_pdf/BCG_The_Age_of_the_Affluent _Nov_2012_ENG.pdf (accessed March 5, 2017).

46. *China's 12th Five-Year Plan* (Washington, DC: APCO Worldwide, December 10, 2010), p. 7, https://wikileaks.org/gifiles/attach/12/12143_12%20five%20year%20plan%20 -%20apco.PDF (accessed March 5, 2017).

47. "Unpacking Made in China 2025 for US Healthcare Cos," AmCham China, January 15, 2016, http://www.amchamchina.org/news/made-in-china-2025-can-help-us-healthcare -companies (accessed March 30, 2017).

48. Natasha Khan, "GE Ships Ready-Made Drug Factories from Berlin to Beijing," *Bloomberg*, November 1, 2015, http://www.bloomberg.com/news/articles/2015-11-01/ge -ships-ready-made-drug-factories-from-berlin-to-beijing (accessed March 15, 2017).

49. Ibid.

50. Kenneth Jarrett and Carly Ramsey, "China's 12th Five-Year Plan," AmCham China, April 2011, http://www.amcham-shanghai.org/amchamportal/infovault_library/2011/ China's_12th_Five-Year_Plan.pdf (accessed March 28, 2017).

51. "China's Pharmaceutical Industry: Poised for the Giant Leap," KPMG, 2011, p. 36, http://www.elsi-project.eu/fileadmin/user_upload/elsi/brosch%C3%BCren/DD/Chinas _Pharma_Industry_-_KPMG_2011__REPORT_.pdf (accessed January 18, 2018).

52. Scott Cendrowski, "Novartis CEO on Why the Firm Just Opened a Major R&D Facility in China," *Fortune*, June 2, 2016, http://fortune.com/2016/06/02/novartis-ceo-china -facility/ (accessed December 14, 2017).

53. "China's Pharmaceutical Industry," p. 15.

54. Ibid.

55. Pfizer Corporation, "Pfizer and Hisun Announce Launch of Hisun-Pfizer Pharmaceuticals Co., Ltd.," press release, September 12, 2012, http://press.pfizer.com/press-release/ pfizer-and-hisun-announce-launch-hisun-pfizer-pharmaceuticals-co-ltd (accessed March 28, 2017).

56. "Merck and Simcere Sign Agreement to Establish Pioneering China Joint Venture," Merck, July 21, 2011, http://www.merck.com/licensing/our-partnership/Simcere-agree-china

-joint-venture-partnership.html (accessed March 28, 2017); "Merck Hands over China Joint Venture to Partner Simcere Pharma," Pharmaceuticaltech.com, February 10, 2015, https://www .pharmaceutical-tech.com/news/merck-hands-over-china-joint-venture-to-partner-simcere -pharma (accessed March 28, 2017).

57. Jared S. Hopkins, "Pfizer Sells Stake in China's Hisun, Ending Drugs Joint Venture," *Bloomberg,* November 10, 2107, https://www.bloomberg.com/news/articles/2017-11-10/ pfizer-sells-stake-in-china-s-hisun-ending-drugs-joint-venture (accessed December 16, 2017).

58. Bob Kennedy, "China Increases Its Activity in Regulated Markets," Thomson Reuters, 2012, p. 4, http://thomsonreuters.com/content/dam/openweb/documents/pdf/pharma-life -sciences/misc/china_increases_activity_regulated_markets.pdf (accessed March 2, 2017).

59. Beatrijs Van Liedekerke, *The Changing Dynamics of Pharma Outsourcing in Asia* (London: PricewaterhouseCoopers, 2008), p. 13, https://www.pwc.com/gx/en/pharma-life -sciences/pdf/change_asia_10_08_08.pdf (accessed January 5, 2018).

60. "China's Pharmaceutical Industry," p. 27

61. James McGregor, "*China's Drive for Indigenous Innovation: A Web of Industrial Policies*" (Washington, DC: US Chamber of Commerce, July 20, 2010), https://www.uschamber .com/sites/default/files/legacy/reports/100728chinareport_0.pdf (accessed March 28, 2017).

62. Ibid., p. 7.

63. Aaron Kruse, Beata Cichocka, and Joe Mazur, "A Prescription for Growth," AmCham China, February 23, 2017, http://www.amchamchina.org/news/a-prescription-for-growth (accessed March 6, 2017).

64. Kalyeena Makortoff, "We Want to Be Seen as Chinese Novo Nordisk," CNBC, August 6, 2015, http://www.cnbc.com/2015/08/06/novo-nordisk-upbeat-on-china-insulin -market.html (accessed March 5, 2017).

65. Philip Leung, Grace Shieh, and Ellon Xu, *Embracing China's Brave New Pharmaceutical World* (Boston, MA: Bain & Company, 2014), http://www.bain.com/Images/BAIN _BRIEF_Embracing_Chinas_brave_new_pharmaceutical_world.pdf (accessed March 5, 2017).

66. "China's Drug-Price Cuts Are Hitting Big Pharma Where It Hurts," *Bloomberg*, March 8, 2016, https://www.bloomberg.com/news/articles/2016-03-08/big-pharma-s-china-dream -meets-reality-of-price-cutting-campaign (accessed March 5, 2017).

67. Ibid.

68. Laurie Burkitt, "Drug Companies Face Pressure Despite China Price Pledge," *Wall Street Journal*, March 5, 2015, http://www.wsj.com/articles/china-plans-to-lift-price-controls -on-drugs-1425520528?mg=id-wsj (accessed March 5, 20107).

69. Kruse, Cichocka, and Mazur "Prescription for Growth."

70. McGregor, "China's Drive for 'Indigenous Innovation,'" p. 6.

71. *2016 Top Markets Report Pharmaceuticals: Country Case Study: China* (Washington, DC: International Trade Commission, 2016), http://www.trade.gov/topmarkets/pdf/ Pharmaceuticals_China.pdf (accessed March 28, 2017).

72. McGregor, China's Drive for 'Indigenous Innovation, p. 4.

73. "US Companies in China Say Labor Costs Pose Top Business Risk," *Bloomberg*, March 29, 2013, https://www.bloomberg.com/news/articles/2013-03-29/u-s-companies-in-china-say -labor-costs-pose-top-business-risk (accessed March 30, 2017).

74. United States v. Yuan Li, No. 12-cr-34 (D.N.J), http://www.justice.gov/usao/nj/ Press/files/pdffiles/2012/Li,%20Yuan%20Information.pdf (accessed January 1, 2017).

"Yuan Li, Former Sanofi-Aventis Research Chemist Sentenced to Prison for Theft of Trade Secrets," Outlook Series, May 7, 2012, http://www.outlookseries.com/A0993/Security/3557 _Yuan_Li_Sanofi-Aventis_Research_Chemist_Sentenced_Prison_Theft_Trade_Secrets_Yuan _Li_Sanofi-Aventis.htm (accessed March 30, 2017).

75. James T. Areddy, "Scientist Convicted of Stealing Merck Drugs," *Wall Street Journal*, June 5, 2012, http://www.wsj.com/articles/SB100014240527023039182045774482 21514110882?mg=id-wsj (accessed March 5, 2017).

76. Christine Yiu, "Eli Lilly v. Huang: Shanghai Court Issues Interlocutory Injunction against Breach of Trade Secret," Lexology, August 21, 2013, http://www.lexology.com/library/ detail.aspx?g=acd9b712-126e-4081-aecb-f8fcaa1bfa16 (accessed March 28, 2017).

77. Ibid.

78. Jeff Swiatek, "2 Former Eli Lilly Scientists Indicted on Charges of Stealing Trade Secrets," *IndyStar*, October 8, 2013, http://www.indystar.com/story/money/2013/10/08/ 2-former-eli-lilly-scientists-indicted-on-charges-of-stealing-trade-secrets/2948225/ (accessed March 5, 2017).

79. Troy Kehoe, "Charges Dropped against Eli Lilly Scientists Accused of Selling Trade Secrets," WISHTV.com, December 5, 2014, http://wishtv.com/2014/12/05/charges-dropped -against-eli-lilly-scientists-accused-of-selling-trade-secrets/ (accessed March 5, 2017).

80. Jen Weedon, "Searching for the Cure: Targeted Threat Actors Pursuing the Pharmaceutical Industry," FireEye, August 21, 2014, https://webcache.googleusercontent.com/search ?q=cache:RORWNmyyWQgJ:https://www.fireeye.com/blog/threat-research/2014/08/ searching-for-the-cure-targeted-threat-actors-pursuing-the-pharmaceutical-industry.html +&cd=1&hl=en&ct=clnk&gl=us (accessed January 18, 2018).

81. Christina Larson, "China Releases Grim Cancer Statistics," *Bloomberg*, April 9, 2013, http://www.bloomberg.com/bw/articles/2013-04-09/grim-cancer-statistics-from-china (accessed March 1, 2017).

82. Weedon, "Searching for the Cure."

83. Ibid.

84. "Advance Persistent Threat Groups: A Field Guide to State-Sponsored Cyber Attackers, Who They Target and How They Operate," FireEye, https://www.fireeye.com/ current-threats/apt-groups.html (accessed December 16, 2017).

85. Hospital chief executive, in discussion with author.

86. *2016 China Business Climate Survey Report* (Beijing; Boston: Am Cham China, Bain and Company, 2016), p. 6, http://www.bain.com/publications/articles/china-business-climate -survey-report-2016.aspx (accessed January 5, 2018).

87. Robert Atkinson, "Chinese Investment in the U.S., Part 2," video, C-SPAN, January 26, 2017, https://www.c-span.org/video/?422783-2/chinese-investment-us-part-2 (accessed February 26, 2017).

88. Dr. Margaret Hamburg, "Meeting the Challenges of Globalization and Strengthening International Collaboration for Improved Health and Safety" (speech at Peking University, Beijing China, November 17, 2014), https://wayback.archive-it.org/7993/20170111003408/http://www.fda.gov/NewsEvents/Speeches/ucm423280.htm (accessed December 2016).

CHAPTER 7: THE GREAT AMERICAN SELLOUT

1. US Department of Agriculture, "Frequently Asked Questions—Equivalence of China's Poultry Processing System," https://www.fsis.usda.gov/wps/portal/fsis/newsroom/news-releases-statements-transcripts/news-release-archives-by-year/archive/2013/faq-china-08302013 (accessed December 19, 2017).

2. "H5N1 Avian Influenza: Timeline of Major Events," World Health Organization, December 17, 2012, http://www.who.int/influenza/H5N1_avian_influenza_update_20121217b.pdf (accessed February 26, 2017).

3. US Department of Agriculture, "Frequently Asked Questions."

4. Alabama Contract Poultry Growers Association et al., letter to President Barack Obama, May 15, 2009.

5. *Hearing on Food and Drug Safety, Public Health, and the Environment in China, Before Congressional-Executive Commission on China*, 113th Cong. (2013) (statement of Tony Corbo, senior lobbyist for the Food Program at Food & Water Watch), p. 43, https://www.gpo.gov/fdsys/pkg/CHRG-113hhrg81854/pdf/CHRG-113hhrg81854.pdf (accessed March 30, 2017).

6. Renee Johnson and Geoffrey S. Becker, *China-US Poultry Dispute* (Washington, DC: Congressional Research Service, report no. 7-5700 R40706, April 5, 2010), p. 3, http://nationalaglawcenter.org/wp-content/uploads/assets/crs/R40706.pdf (accessed February 27, 2017).

7. "FSIS Announces Final Rule to Permit Export of Poultry Processed in China," *Food Chemical News*, April 24, 2006, https://www.agra-net.com/agra/food-chemical-news/fsis-announces-final-rule-to-permit-export-of-poultry-processed-in-china-1.htm (accessed February 27, 2017).

8. US Department of Agriculture, "Frequently Asked Questions."

9. Alabama Contract Poultry Growers, et al., letter to Obama.

10. Ibid.

11. Ibid., pp. 2–3.

12. Johnson and Becker, *China-US Poultry Dispute*, p. 6.

13. Ibid., p. 7.

14. Ibid., p. 3.

15. Ibid., p. 5.

16. Ibid., p. 8.

17. Jonathan Lynn, "UPDATE 2—WTO Raps US Ban on Chinese Chicken Imports," Reuters, September 29, 2010, https://www.reuters.com/article/trade-chicken/update-2-wto -raps-u-s-ban-on-chinese-chicken-imports-idUSLDE68S1PZ20100929 (accessed December 19, 2017).

18. Office of the US Trade Representative, "United States Wins Trade Enforcement Case for American Farmers, Proves Export-Blocking Chinese Duties Unjustified under WTO," press release, August 2013, http://www.ustr.gov/US-Wins-Trade-Enforcement-Case -AmericanFarmers-Proves-Export-Blocking-Chinese-Duties-Unjustified-Under-WTO-Rule (accessed February 27, 2017).

19. "China: Anti-Dumping and Countervailing Duty Measures on Broiler Products from the United States," World Trade Organization, August 2, 2013, http://www.wto.org/english/ tratop_e/dispu_e/cases_e/ds427_e.htm#bkmk427r (accessed February 27, 2017).

20. *Testimony: National Chicken Council Before US Senate Finance Comm.*, 113th Cong. (2014) (statement of Kevin J. Brosch, international trade lawyer and consultant), https://www .finance.senate.gov/imo/media/doc/NCC%20Senate%20Finance%20Testimony%20062514 .pdf (accessed December 19, 2017).

21. Ron Kirk, "Remarks by United States Trade Representative Ron Kirk Announcing Action against China with Regard to Poultry," transcript, Office of the United States Trade Representative, September 20, 2011, https://ustr.gov/about-us/policy-offices/press-office/ speeches/transcripts/2011/september/remarks-united-states-trade-representative (accessed March 25, 2017).

22. National Chicken Council, "US to Challenge China at WTO over Chicken Duties," press release, May 10, 2016, http://www.nationalchickencouncil.org/us-challenge-china-wto -chicken-duties/ (accessed August 5, 2017).

23. *Food Safety and Inspection System: Final Report of an Audit Conducted in the People's Republic of China* (Washington, DC: US Department of Agriculture, March 4–13, 2013), http://www.fsis.usda.gov/wps/wcm/connect/c3dab827-151d-4373-917f-139db6a2466d/ China_2013_Poultry_Processing.pdf?MOD=AJPERES (accessed March 25, 2017).

24. Andreas Keller, US Department of Agriculture, letter to Li Chunfeng, August 30, 2013, https://www.fsis.usda.gov/wps/wcm/connect/c3dab827-151d-4373-917f-139 db6a2466d/China_2013_Poultry_Processing.pdf?MOD=AJPERES (accessed February 27, 2017).

25. "Constituent Update: Special Alert, Names of Establishments in China Eligible to Export Processed (Cooked) Poultry Products to the United States Posted," US Department of Agriculture, November 5, 2014, https://www.fsis.usda.gov/wps/portal/fsis/newsroom/ meetings/newsletters/constituent-updates/archive/2014/ConstUpdate110514/!ut/p/a1/ jZFRb4IwFIV_DY-1t-IM7o2QOKcTZxa18rJUKNAMWlKKJPv1u7gnt5nZJk3u6bk5

_W5pQjlNtDirQjhltKiGOpm-wxambBbBcjMP5_Ac-_N9ED8x2PloOF4ZZmww7Leb
VRRBEPt39t9YIfzXv7wjYGzX0bqgSSNcSZTODeVa9m0lnZO2pTw1unXKdVI70jWZ
cBJFYdNSnSXlY2ATyqPBs7tcMgYPKB1ocp0NDDdmv00Wy9iH1fSn4Y_hfBtu0yNeUZ
nT5SeOoT75AXJYmUsr7aizKJfONY8eeND3_Sg3JhM66_GVFo-0HBlbeDDQeoA86Yf
URNWNsa4lWGtBrOhJJkVFOlQQsqsvM_mdVprWUX4zhTb1jn-hAtQr_UhaMMvLq
Hb-w!!/?PrinterFriendly=true (accessed February 27, 2017).

26. *Testimony, Before Congressional-Executive Committee on China* (2014) (statement of
Dan Engeljohn, assistant administrator of the USDA's Food Safety and Inspection Service's
Office of Field Operations), https://www.usda.gov/sites/default/files/documents/OCR
-061714-Engeljohn.pdf (accessed December 19, 2017).

27. Tony Corbo, in discussion with author, March 21, 2017.

28. Jonathan Buttram, in discussion with author, August 2015.

29. Bettina Siegel and Nancy Huehnergarth, "Keep Chinese Chicken out of Our Schools
and Supermarkets" (petition) Change.org, https://www.change.org/p/congress-keep-chinese
-chicken-out-of-our-schools-and-supermarkets (accessed February 27, 2017).

30. US Representative Rosa DeLauro, https://delauro.house.gov/media-center/press
-releases/delauro-introduces-bill-protect-our-children-unsafe-food-china (accessed December
19, 2017).

31. US Representative Rosa DeLauro, "DeLauro Introduces Bill to Protect Our Children
from Unsafe Food from China," press release, July 21, 2017, https://delauro.house.gov/media
-center/press-releases/delauro-introduces-bill-protect-our-children-unsafe-food-china (accessed
December 19, 2017).

32. Corbo, in discussion with author, August 7, 2015.

33. US Department of Agriculture, "China Suspends Imports of US Poultry and
Products," Global Agriculture Information Network (GAIN) report no. CH 4006, February
13, 2004, https://apps.fas.usda.gov/gainfiles/200402/146105547.pdf (accessed December 19,
2017).

34. "Va. Officials Hope Visitors from China 'Clear' Poultry," Shenandoah Valley
Partnership, March 16, 2013. Copy in author's possession.

35. Ibid.

36. John Reid Blackwell, "First Poultry Shipments Going to China after Ban Lifted,"
Richmond Times-Dispatch, June 17, 2014, http://www.timesdispatch.com/business/economy/
first-poultry-shipments-going-to-china-after-ban-lifted/article_65f73bd3-d8f9-5edc-ad34
-8bbfbba95fa3.html (accessed February 27, 2017).

37. Bryan Salvage, "China Bans US Poultry and Eggs over HPAI," *Meat + Poultry*, http://
www.meatpoultry.com/articles/news_home/Global/2015/01/China_bans_US_poultry_and
_eggs.aspx?ID=%7BFD6FC543-81B6-42FE-A544-57D9D4BDF601%7D (accessed August 5,
2017).

38. Li Wang and Tylor Babcock, *China: Poultry and Products Annual 2016* (Washington,
DC: US Department of Agriculture GAIN Report, August 1, 2016), https://gain.fas.usda

.gov/Recent%20GAIN%20Publications/Poultry%20and%20Products%20Annual_Beijing
_China%20-%20Peoples%20Republic%20of_8-2-2016.pdf (accessed August 5, 2017).

39. *2013 Annual Report to Congress* (Washington, DC: US-China Economic and Security Review Commission, November 20, 2013), p. 169, https://www.uscc.gov/Annual_Reports/2013-annual-report-congress (accessed February 27, 2017).

40. Ibid., p. 173.

41. Ibid., p. 178.

42. Ibid.

43. Keller, letter to Chunfeng.

44. Corbo, in discussion with author, August 7, 2015.

45. American Meat Institute et al., letter to President Barack Obama, April 30, 2009.

46. Associated Press, "China Promises to Promote US Beef Imports," CBS News, December 20, 2013, http://www.cbsnews.com/news/china-promises-to-promote-us-beef-imports/ (accessed February 27, 2017).

47. Corbo, in discussion with author, August 7, 2015.

48. American Meat Institute, letter to Obama.

49. Joe Roybal, "Chinese Beef Market Surging: US Locked Out," *Beef Magazine*, October 1, 2013, http://beefmagazine.com/blog/chinese-beef-market-surging-us-locked-out-0 (accessed February 26, 2017).

50. Fanny Fung and Alice Woodhouse, "Huge Amounts of Banned US Beef Smuggled through Hong Kong to Mainland China," *South China Morning Post*, March 20, 2015, http://www.scmp.com/news/hong-kong/article/1742727/banned-us-beef-smuggled-through-hong-kong-mainland-china-huge-amounts (accessed February 26, 2017).

51. *2013 Annual Report to Congress*, p. 178.

52. Zoe Li, "China Tainted Meat Scandal Explained," CNN, July 30, 2014, http://www.cnn.com/2014/07/29/world/asia/explainer-china-meat-scandal/ (accessed February 27, 2017).

53. Reuters, "Cost of China Scandal for OSI Nearing $1 Bln—Xinhua," July 1, 2015, https://www.reuters.com/article/osi-china-damages/cost-of-china-scandal-for-osi-nearing-1-bln-xinhua-idUSL3N0ZH2JN20150701 (accessed December 26, 2017).

54. Alice Yan, "CCTV Report Says KFC Chickens Are Being Fattened with Illegal Drugs," *South China Morning Post*, December 19, 2012, http://www.scmp.com/news/china/article/1107804/cctv-report-says-kfc-chickens-are-being-fattened-illegal-drugs (accessed February 17, 2017).

55. Joe McDonald, "KFC Sues over Rumors Company Uses Eight-Legged Chickens with Six Wings," CBS Local, San Francisco, June 1, 2015, http://sanfrancisco.cbslocal.com/2015/06/01/kfc-sues-over-rumors-company-uses-eight-legged-chickens-with-six-wings/ (accessed February 28, 2017).

56. "38 Arrested for Selling Contaminated Chicken Feet," CCTV, August 26, 2014, http://www.cctv-america.com/2014/08/26/38-arrested-for-selling-contaminated-chicken-feet (accessed February 27, 2017).

57. Zhang Yan, "Gangs Smuggle in 40-Year Old '"Zombie"' Meat," *China Daily*, July 2, 2015, http://usa.chinadaily.com.cn/epaper/2015-07/02/content_21163820.htm (accessed February 26, 2017).

58. Author conversation with US Department of Agriculture, Meat and Poultry Hotline, February 27, 2017.

59. Corbo, in discussion with author, February 28, 2017.

60. *Final Report of an Audit Conducted in the People's Republic of China* (Washington, DC: US Department of Agriculture, May 8 to May 28, 2015), https://www.fsis.usda.gov/wps/wcm/connect/bd2f2159-63b2-4846-a738-7983f38f297f/2015-China-Slaughtered-Poultry-FAR.pdf?MOD=AJPERES (accessed February 28, 2017).

61. Corbo, in discussion with author, February 28, 2017.

62. *Final Report of an Audit Conducted*, p. 23.

63. Corbo, in discussion with author, February 28, 2017.

64. *Final Report of an Audit Conducted*, p. 24.

65. Ibid.

66. Yang Wang, et al., "Comprehensive Resistome Analysis Reveals the Prevalence of NDM and MCR-1 in Chinese Poultry Production," *Nature Microbiology* 2, no. 16260 (February 6, 2017), http://www.nature.com/articles/nmicrobiol2016260 (accessed March 22, 2017).

67. Stephen Chen, "Drug Resistant Bacteria Are Rampant in China's Poultry Products, Study Shows," *South China Morning Post*, February 15, 2017, http://www.scmp.com/news/china/policies-politics/article/2071131/drug-resistant-bacteria-are-rampant-chinas-poultry#comments (accessed March 21, 2017).

68. Jonathan Buttram, in discussion with author, August 2015.

69. Corbo, in discussion with author, February 28, 2017.

70. "The Business of Broilers: Hidden Costs of Putting a Chicken on Every Grill," Pew Charitable Trusts, December 20, 2013, http://www.pewtrusts.org/en/research-and-analysis/reports/2013/12/20/the-business-of-broilers-hidden-costs-of-putting-a-chicken-on-every-grill (accessed February 27, 2017).

71. "Chickens: Last Week Tonight with John Oliver (HBO)," YouTube video, 18:21, posted by "LastWeekTonight" on May 17, 2015, https://www.youtube.com/watch?v=X9wHzt6gBgI (accessed January 5, 2017).

72. Ibid.

73. National Chicken Council, "US Poultry Producers Praise Senate's Call for Reopening Chicken and Turkey Exports to China," press release, July 26, 2017, http://www.national chickencouncil.org/us-poultry-producers-praise-senates-call-reopening-chicken-turkey-exports-china/ (accessed August 5, 2017); National Chicken Council, "NCC Statement on US-China Preliminary Trade Agreement on Beef, Poultry," press release, May 12, 2017, http://www.nationalchickencouncil.org/ncc-statement-us-china-preliminary-trade-agreement-beef-poultry/ (accessed August 5, 2017).

74. *Wikipedia*, s.v. "Thirty-Six Stratagems: Wait at Leisure While the Enemy Labors," last

edited November 17, 2017, https://en.wikipedia.org/wiki/Thirty-Six_Stratagems (accessed February 26, 2017).

75. US Food and Drug Administration, "Mutual Recognition Promises New Framework for Pharmaceutical Inspections for United States and European Union," press release, March 2, 2017, https://www.fda.gov/NewsEvents/Newsroom/PressAnnouncements/ucm544357.htm (accessed March 8, 2017).

76. US Food and Drug Administration, "Mutual Recognition Promises New Framework for Pharmaceutical Inspections for United States and European Union," press release, March 2, 2017. https://www.fda.gov/NewsEvents/Newsroom/PressAnnouncements/ucm544357.htm (accessed December 19, 2017).

CHAPTER 8: TODAY'S GAIN, TOMORROW'S PAIN

1. "World's Largest Container Ship Arrives at the Port of Felixstowe," *Daily Telegraph*, January 7, 2015, http://www.telegraph.co.uk/news/newstopics/howaboutthat/11330264/Worlds-largest-container-ship-set-to-arrive-at-the-Port-of-Felixstowe.html (accessed February 21, 2017).

2. Ibid.

3. "CSCL Globe: Felixstowe Arrival for World's Largest Container Ship," BBC News, January 7, 2015, http://www.bbc.com/news/uk-england-suffolk-30700269 (accessed March 30, 2017).

4. Erica E. Phillips, "Giant Container Ship Unloads at Port of Los Angeles," *Wall Street Journal*, December 30, 2015, http://www.wsj.com/articles/giant-container-ship-unloads-at-port-of-los-angeles-1451513531 (accessed February 21, 2017).

5. Jonathan Bloom, "Largest Container Ship to Ever Visit US Arrives in Bay Area," ABC7 News, December 31, 2015, http://abc7news.com/business/largest-container-ship-to-ever-visit-us-arrives-in-bay-area/1142294/ (accessed February 21, 2017).

6. Associated Press, "Biggest Container Ship to Visit US Barely Clears Golden Gate Bridge," NBC News, December 31, 2015, http://www.nbcnews.com/business/business-news/biggest-container-ship-visit-u-s-barely-clears-golden-gate-n488641(accessed February 21, 2017).

7. CMA CGM, "CMA CGM Deploys the Largest Cargo Vessel Ever to Call at a US Port," press release, December 14, 2015, https://www.cma-cgm.com/news/1023/cma-cgm-deploys-largest-cargo-vessel-ever-to-call-at-a-u-s-port (accessed February 21, 2017).

8. "This Ship Is Too Big for Any American Port," video, CNN, March 9, 2015, http://money.cnn.com/video/news/2015/03/09/worlds-largest-container-ship-msc-oscar.cnnmoney/ (accessed February 21, 2017).

9. Dr. Margaret Hamburg, "Meeting the Challenges of Globalization and Strengthening International Collaboration for Improved Health and Safety" (speech at Peking University,

Beijing China, November 17, 2014), https://wayback.archive-it.org/7993/20170111003408/
http://www.fda.gov/NewsEvents/Speeches/ucm423280.htm (accessed December 22, 2017).

10. Zepol, "Trade View Report" (China, January 1, 2007 to December 31, 2014), 2015, spreadsheet (accessed March 6, 2015). In author's possession.

11. Ibid. See also https://www.drugs.com/otc/104656/walgreens-instant-hand-sanitizer .html (accessed December 19, 2017).

12. Zhaoruixue and Lixiang, "China Factory Well-Suited to Help in Ebola Fight," *China Daily*, October 29, 2014, http://usa.chinadaily.com.cn/business/2014-10/29/ content_18818002.htm (accessed February 21, 2017).

13. *Reliance on Foreign Sourcing in the Healthcare and Public Health Sector* (Washington, DC: US Department of Commerce, December 2011), https://www.bis.doc.gov/index.php/ forms-documents/doc_view/642-department-of-homeland-security-dhs-assessment-impact-of -foreign-sourcing-on-health-related-infra (accessed February 21, 2017).

14. Varun Saxena, "Trade Agreement with China Paves the Way for Reduction in Medical Device Tariffs," FierceBiotech, November 14, 2014, http://www.fiercemedicaldevices.com/ story/agreement-china-over-trade-paves-way-reduction-medical-device-tarrifs/2014-11-14 (accessed February 21, 2017).

15. Ibid.

16. Jon Dobson, in conversation with author, March 2017.

17. US Food and Drug Administration, letter to Jiangsu Magspin Instrument Company, December 22, 2015, https://www.accessdata.fda.gov/cdrh_docs/pdf15/K151074.pdf (accessed March 20, 2017).

18. US Food and Drug Administration, "510(k) Premarket Notification," http://www .accessdata.fda.gov/scripts/cdrh/cfdocs/cfpmn/pmn.cfm?ID=K140202 (accessed March 20, 2017).

19. US Food and Drug Administration, "510(k) Premarket Notification," http://www .accessdata.fda.gov/scripts/cdrh/cfdocs/cfpmn/pmn.cfm?ID=K151591 (accessed March 20, 2017).

20. US Food and Drug Administration, "510(k) Premarket Notification," http://www .accessdata.fda.gov/scripts/cdrh/cfdocs/cfpmn/pmn.cfm?ID=K143160 (accessed March 20, 2017).

21. US Food and Drug Administration, "510(k) Premarket Notification," http://www .accessdata.fda.gov/scripts/cdrh/cfdocs/cfpmn/pmn.cfm?ID=K140202 (accessed March 20, 2017).

22. US Food and Drug Administration, "510(k) Premarket Notification," http://www .accessdata.fda.gov/scripts/cdrh/cfdocs/cfPMN/pmn.cfm?start_search=51&Center=&Panel =&ProductCode=&KNumber=&Applicant=Jiangsu&DeviceName=&Type=&ThirdParty Reviewed=&ClinicalTrials=&Decision=&DecisionDateFrom=&DecisionDateTo=03%2F20 %2F2017&IVDProducts=&Redact510K=&CombinationProducts=&ZNumber=&PAGE NUM=10&SortColumn=dd%5Fdesc (accessed March 20, 2017).

23. US Food and Drug Administration, "510(k) Premarket Notification," http://www .accessdata.fda.gov/scripts/cdrh/cfdocs/cfPMN/pmn.cfm?start_search=11&Center=&Panel

NOTES

=&ProductCode=&KNumber=&Applicant=Jiangsu&DeviceName=&Type=&ThirdParty
Reviewed=&ClinicalTrials=&Decision=&DecisionDateFrom=&DecisionDateTo=03%2F20
%2F2017&IVDProducts=&Redact510K=&CombinationProducts=&ZNumber=&PAGE
NUM=10&SortColumn=dd%5Fdesc (accessed March 20, 2017).

24. US Food and Drug Administration, "510(k) Premarket Notification," http://www
.accessdata.fda.gov/scripts/cdrh/cfdocs/cfPMN/pmn.cfm?start_search=21&Center=&Panel
=&ProductCode=&KNumber=&Applicant=Jiangsu&DeviceName=&Type=&ThirdParty
Reviewed=&ClinicalTrials=&Decision=&DecisionDateFrom=&DecisionDateTo=03%2F20
%2F2017&IVDProducts=&Redact510K=&CombinationProducts=&ZNumber=&PAGE
NUM=10&SortColumn=dd%5Fdesc (accessed March 20, 2017).

25. Hamburg, "Meeting the Challenges of Globalization."

26. "Controlling Supply Costs: Supply Expense Growth Outpacing All Others," Advisory
Board Company, https://www.advisory.com/Technology/Surgical-Profitability-Compass/
Controlling-supply-costs (accessed February 22, 2017).

27. The 13th Five Year Plan for Economic and Social Development of the People's
Republic of China (2016-2020), http://en.ndrc.gov.cn/newsrelease/201612/P02016
1207645765233498.pdf (accessed December 19, 2017).

28. Mihir Torsekar, *US Firms Pursue Opportunities to Supply China's Growing Medical
Device Market* (Washington, DC: US International Trade Commission, August 2013), https://
www.usitc.gov/publications/332/Torsekar_MedicalDeviceExportstoChina_FINAL.pdf
(accessed February 23, 2017).

29. Steven Weisman, "China Stand on Imports Upsets US," *New York Times*, November
16, 2007, http://www.nytimes.com/2007/11/16/business/worldbusiness/16trade.html?_r=0
(accessed March 5, 2017).

30. *Medical Devices and Equipment: Competitive Conditions Affecting US Trade in Japan
and Other Principal Foreign Markets*, publication 3909 (Washington, DC: US International
Trade Commission, March 2007).

31. "Unpacking Made in China 2025 for US Healthcare Cos," AmCham China, January
15, 2016, http://www.amchamchina.org/news/made-in-china-2025-can-help-us-healthcare
-companies (accessed March 6, 2017).

32. Ibid.

33. Torsekar, "US Firms Pursue Opportunities.'"

34. "China," General Electric, http://www.gesustainability.com/where-we-work/china/
(accessed February 24, 2017).

35. Chen Jia and Liu Jie, "GE Healthcare Adding to Staff, Budget for R&D," *China Daily*,
December 21, 2011, http://www.chinadaily.com.cn/cndy/2011-12/21/content_14296397.htm
(accessed February 24, 2017).

36. Medtronic, "Medtronic Signs Agreement to Acquire China Kanghui Holdings,"
press release, September 27, 2012, http://newsroom.medtronic.com/phoenix.zhtml?c
=251324&p=irol-newsArticle&ID=1770621 (accessed February 24, 2017).

37. Brad Perriello, "Medtronic, Lifetech Expand China Pacemaker Deal," MassDevice
.com, July 28, 2014, http://www.massdevice.com/medtronic-lifetech-expand-china-pacemaker
-deal/ (accessed March 20, 2017).

38. "Atrial Septal Defect," Mayo Clinic, March 7, 2017, http://www.mayoclinic.org/
diseases-conditions/atrial-septal-defect/basics/definition/con-20027034 (accessed November
26, 2017).

39. ACN Newswire, "Lifetech Becomes the First Chinese Brand to Enter the Mainstream
Medical Device Market in Western Countries," Yahoo! Finance, November 27, 2014, https://
sg.finance.yahoo.com/news/lifetech-becomes-first-chinese-brand-232800000.html (accessed
February 22, 2017).

40. Ibid.

41. Ibid.

42. US Food and Drug Administration, "Premarket Approvals," Class III Medical Devices,
Lifetech, https://www.accessdata.fda.gov/scripts/cdrh/cfdocs/cfPMA/pma.cfm (accessed
December 20, 2017).

43. US Food and Drug Administration, "510(K) Is a Premarket Submission," http://www
.accessdata.fda.gov/scripts/cdrh/cfdocs/cfPMN/pmn.cfm (accessed December 20, 2017).

44. Robert D. Atkinson, "Chinese Investment in the U.S., Part 2," video, C-SPAN, January
26, 2017, https://www.c-span.org/video/?422783-2/chinese-investment-us-part-2 (accessed
February 26, 2017).

45. US Department of Health and Human Services, Centers for Medicare and Medicaid
Services, "National Health Expenditure Fact Sheet," https://www.cms.gov/research-statistics
-data-and-systems/statistics-trends-and-reports/nationalhealthexpenddata/nhe-fact-sheet.html
(accessed December 19, 2017).

46. Thilo Hanemann and Cassie Gao, "Record Deal Making in 2016 Pushes Cumulative
Chinese FDI in the US Above $100 Billion," Rhodium Group, December 30, 2016, http://rhg
.com/notes/record-deal-making-in-2016-pushes-cumulative-chinese-fdi-in-the-us-above-100
-billion (accessed February 22, 2017).

47. Ibid.

48. Jerry Underwood, "Alabama Officials Welcome Golden Dragon's First US Factory,"
MadeinAlabama.com, May 28, 2014, http://www.madeinalabama.com/2014/05/first-golden
-dragon-copper-tube-u-s-factory/ (accessed February 23, 2017).

49. Bonnie Cao and Ye Yie, "Chinese Build US Factories, Bringing Tensions Along with
Jobs," *Bloomberg*, August 30, 2015, https://www.bloomberg.com/news/articles/2015-08-30/
chinese-build-u-s-factories-bringing-jobs-along-with-tensions (accessed February 23, 2017).

50. Betsy Bourassa, "US and China Breakthrough Announcement on the Bilateral
Investment Treaty Negotiations," *Treasury Notes* (blog), July 15, 2013, https://www.treasury
.gov/connect/blog/Pages/U.S.-and-China-Breakthrough-Announcement-.aspx (accessed
February 21, 2017).

51. Ibid.

52. Lori Wallach, in discussion with author, May 26, 2016.

53. Ibid.

54. Public Citizen, "Proposed US-China Bilateral Investment Treaty Would Expose US Laws to Extrajudicial Attacks by Chinese Corporations Operating Here, Incentivize More Offshoring of American Jobs," press release, July 10, 2014, http://www.citizen.org/documents/ press-release-u.s.-china-bit-july-2014.pdf (accessed February 20, 2017).

55. Nathalie Bernasconi-Osterwalder and Martin Dietrich Brauch, "State of Play in Vattenfall v. Germany II: Leaving the German Public in the Dark," International Institute for Sustainable Development, December 2014, http://www.iisd.org/library/state-play-vattenfall-v -germany-ii-leaving-german-public-dark (accessed February 22, 2017).

56. "Why Vattenfall Is Taking Germany to Court," Vattenfall, December 9, 2014, https:// corporate.vattenfall.com/press-and-media/news/2014/why-vattenfall-is-taking-germany-to -court/ (accessed February 23, 2017).

57. Ibid.

58. Bernasconi-Osterwalder and Brauch, "State of Play in Vattenfall v. Germany II."

59. Benedict Mander, "Uruguay Defeats Philip Morris Test Case Lawsuit," *Financial Times*, July 8, 2016, https://www.ft.com/content/1ae33bc8-454e-11e6-9b66-0712b3873ae1 (accessed February 22, 2017).

60. Malena Castaldi and Anthony Esposito, "Philip Morris Loses Tough-on-Tobacco Lawsuit in Uruguay," Reuters, July 8, 2016, http://www.reuters.com/article/us-pmi-uruguay -lawsuit-idUSKCN0ZO2LZ (accessed February 22, 2017).

61. Mander, "Uruguay Defeats Philip Morris."

62. Gareth Hutchens, "Australian Government Wins Plain Packaging Case against Philip Morris Asia," *Sydney Morning Herald*, December 18, 2015, http://www.smh.com.au/federal -politics/political-news/australian-government-wins-plain-packaging-case-against-philip -morris-20151218-glqo8s.html (accessed December 22, 2017).

63. "The Arbitration Game," *Economist*, October 11, 2014, http://www.economist.com/ news/finance-and-economics/21623756-governments-are-souring-treaties-protect-foreign -investors-arbitration (accessed March 20, 2017).

64. "Fact Sheet: Investor-State Dispute Settlement," Office of the United States Trade Representative, March 2015, https://ustr.gov/about-us/policy-offices/press-office/fact -sheets/2015/march/investor-state-dispute-settlement-isds (accessed February 21, 2017).

65. Ian Talley, "US Treasury Secretary Mnuchin: China Bilateral Investment Treaty 'On Our Agenda,'" *Wall Street Journal,* June 6, 2017, https://www.wsj.com/articles/u-s-treasury -secretary-mnuchin-china-bilateral-investment-treaty-on-our-agenda-1496774628 (accessed December 22, 2017).

66. State of Vermont, "Senator Virginia Lyons Statement on Chinese Objection to Proposed Environmental Legislation in Vermont," press release, August 12, 2008, http://www .citizen.org/documents/VT_LyonsStatement081208.pdf (accessed February 21, 2017). This link works.

67. Senator Virginia Lyons, in discussion with author, September 2015.

68. State of Vermont, "Senator Virginia Lyons Statement."

69. Lyons, in discussion with author.

70. Anne Bartlett, "Pr. Geo.'s Delegate Rankles Chinese Government," *Washington Post*, June 23, 2008, http://voices.washingtonpost.com/annapolis/2008/06/pr_geos_delegate _rankles_chine.html (accessed February 21, 2017).

71. Lyons, in discussion with author.

72. "China," Gallup, Washington, DC, February 2013 to February 2016, http://www .gallup.com/poll/1627/china.aspx (accessed February 21, 2017).

73. Joseph Stiglitz, Free Fall: America, Free Markets, and the Sinking of the World Economy (New York: W.W. Norton, 2010).

74. Joseph Stiglitz, "The Chinese Century," *Vanity Fair*, January 2015, p. 42.

75. Henry Paulson, *Dealing with China: An Insider Unmasks the New Economic Superpower* (New York: Grand Central, 2015).

76. "Full Text of Clinton's Speech on China Trade Bill," *New York Times*, March 9, 2000, http://partners.nytimes.com/library/world/asia/030900clinton-china-text.html (accessed March 4, 2017).

CHAPTER 9: ARE DRUGS FROM CHINA SAFE?

1. Dr. James Duncan, email correspondence with author, March 2, 2017.

2. House Committee on Energy and Commerce, letter to Dr. Robert M. Califf, March 29, 2016, https://energycommerce.house.gov/sites/republicans.energycommerce.house.gov/ files/documents/114/letters/20160329FDA.pdf (accessed March 25, 2017).

3. Ibid.

4. Ibid.

5. Ibid.

6. US Food and Drug Administration, warning letter to Beijing Shunxin Meihua Bio-Technical, September 29, 2014, https://www.fda.gov/ICECI/EnforcementActions/ WarningLetters/2014/ucm418141.htm (accessed March 25, 2017).

7. Ibid.

8. Ibid.

9. Ibid.

10. US Food and Drug Administration, warning letter to Beijing Taiyang Pharmaceutical Industry Company, October 19, 2016, http://www.fda.gov/ICECI/EnforcementActions/ WarningLetters/2016/ucm527005.htm (accessed March 6, 2017).

11. US Food and Drug Administration, "Type II Drug Master Files for APIs for Generic Drug Applications" (Diphenhydramine Hydrochloride), January 20, 2017, www.fda.gov/ downloads/ForIndustry/UserFees/ . . . /UCM332875.pdf (accessed March 6, 2017);

NOTES

"Diphenhydramine Hydrochloride," Beijing Taiyang Pharmaceutical Industry Company, http://
www.pharmacompass.com/us-drug-master-files-dmfs/beijing-taiyang-pharmaceutical-industry
(accessed March 6, 2017).

12. US Food and Drug Administration, warning letter to Suzhou Pharmaceutical
Technology Company, January 6, 2017, http://www.fda.gov/ICECI/EnforcementActions/
WarningLetters/2017/ucm536866.htm (accessed March 6, 2017).

13. Ibid.

14. Suzhou Weather in June, China Highlights, http://www.chinahighlights.com/
suzhou/weather/june.htm (accessed March 6, 2017).

15. US Food and Drug Administration, warning letter to Suzhou Pharmaceutical
Technology Company.

16. US Food and Drug Administration, warning letter to Lumis Global Pharmaceuticals,
March 2, 2017, https://www.fda.gov/ICECI/EnforcementActions/WarningLetters/2017/
ucm545464.htm (accessed March 25, 2017).

17. "Gabapentin," Mayo Clinic, last updated March 1, 2017, http://www.mayoclinic.org/
drugs-supplements/gabapentin-oral-route/description/DRG-20064011 (accessed March 25,
2017).

18. Kevin McNeil, in discussion with author, March 2017.

19. US Food and Drug Administration, "Import Alerts, 66-40," January 22, 2016. Copy in
author's possession.

20. *Hearing on China's Healthcare Sector, Drug Safety, and the US-China Trade in Medical
Products, Before US-China Economic and Security Review Commission*, 113th Cong. (2014)
(statement of Christopher Hickey, PhD, country director for the People's Republic of China
in the Office of International Programs), p. 24, https://www.uscc.gov/sites/default/files/
transcripts/USCC%20Hearing%20Transcript_April%203%2C%202014_0.pdf (accessed
December 31, 2017).

21. *Hearing on China's Healthcare Sector, Drug Safety, and the US-China Trade in Medical
Products, Before US-China Economic and Security Review Commission*, 113th Cong. (2014)
(statement of Dennis C. Shea, chairman of the US-China Economic and Security Review
Commission), p. 25, https://www.uscc.gov/sites/default/files/transcripts/USCC%20
Hearing%20Transcript_April%203%2C%202014_0.pdf (accessed December 31, 2017).

22. *Hearing on China's Healthcare Sector, Drug Safety, and the US-China Trade in
Medical Products, Before US-China Economic and Security Review Commission* (Hickey); *Food
Safety: Additional Actions Needed to Help FDA's Foreign Offices Ensure Safety of Imported Food*
(Washington, DC: US Government Accountability Office, January 2015), p. 33, http://www
.gao.gov/assets/670/668952.pdf (accessed March 6, 2017).

23. *Hearing on China's Healthcare Sector, Drug Safety, and the US-China Trade in Medical
Products, Before US-China Economic and Security Review Commission* (Hickey).

24. Robert Walsh, mail correspondence with author, August 17, 2015.

25. Office of the Vice President, "Fact Sheet on Strengthening US-China Economic

272

Relations," White House, December 5, 2013, http://www.whitehouse.gov/the-press-office/2013/12/05/us-fact-sheet-strengthening-us-china-economic-relations (accessed March 6, 2017).

26. *Hearing on China's Healthcare Sector, Drug Safety, and the US-China Trade in Medical Products, Before US-China Economic and Security Review Commission*, 113th Cong. (2014) (statement of Daniel Slane, commissioner of the US-China Economic and Security Review Commission), https://www.uscc.gov/sites/default/files/transcripts/USCC%20Hearing%20Transcript_April%203%2C%202014_0.pdf (accessed December 31, 20107).

27. *Hearing on China's Healthcare Sector, Drug Safety, and the US-China Trade in Medical Products, Before US-China Economic and Security Review Commission* (Hickey).

28. *Food Safety*, p. 22.

29. Ibid.

30. Sabrina Tavernise, "FDA Optimistic on Visas for China Staff," *New York Times*, November 14, 2014, http://www.nytimes.com/2014/11/15/us/fda-optimistic-on-visas-for-china-staff-.html (accessed March 6, 2017).

31. *Food Safety*, p. 33.

32. US Food and Drug Administration, Form 483, April 13, 2015–April 17, 2015, PharmaCompass, p. 7, http://www.pharmacompass.com/assets/pdf/news/FDA-observe-data-integrity-malpractices-at-Pfizer-pharmaceuticals-1446639284.pdf (accessed March 25, 2017).

33. Ibid.

34. Ibid.

35. Ibid., p. 9.

36. Cheryl Neath, email correspondence with author, March 2017.

37. "FDA Says Chinese Pfizer Plant Hid Failures, Used Old Ingredients," *Bloomberg*, October 30, 2015, https://www.bloomberg.com/news/articles/2015-10-30/fda-says-chinese-pfizer-plant-hid-failures-used-old-ingredients (accessed March 25, 2017).

38. "India's Generic Drug Manufacturers: Poised for Continued Growth," NASDAQ, February 29, 2016, http://www.nasdaq.com/article/indias-generic-drug-manufacturers-poised-for-continued-growth-cm586029 (accessed December 20, 2017).

39. US Food and Drug Administration, Form 483, November 7, 2011–December 2, 2011, https://www.fda.gov/ucm/groups/fdagov-public/@fdagov-afda-orgs/documents/document/ucm282550.pdf (accessed April 10, 2017).

40. Neath, email correspondence with author.

41. "State Council Information Office (SCIO) Briefing on China's Food and Drug Safety," China.org.cn, February 29, 2016, http://china.org.cn/china/2016-03/01/content_37909560_9.htm (accessed March 5, 2017).

42. Ibid.

43. Ibid.

44. "China Requires Generics to Obtain Brand-Name Drug Quality," *Xinhua*, March 6, 2016, http://news.xinhuanet.com/english/2016-03/06/c_135160820.htm (accessed December 20, 2017).

45. Eric Palmer, "Updated: Pfizer Chinese JV Partner Zhejiang Hisun Pharma Has Products Banned by FDA," *FiercePharma*, September 17, 2015, https://www.fiercepharma.com/regulatory/updated-pfizer-chinese-jv-partner-zhejiang-hisun-pharma-has-products-banned-by-fda (accessed December 26, 2017).

46. US Food and Drug Administration, warning letter to Zhejiang Hisun Pharmaceutical, December 31, 2015, http://www.fda.gov/ICECI/EnforcementActions/WarningLetters/2015/ucm480035.htm (accessed March 6, 2017).

47. Ibid.

48. Ibid.

49. Ibid.

50. US Food and Drug Administration, "Import Alert, Zhejiang Hisun Pharmaceutical Company," September 9, 2015. Copy in author's possession.

51. Sheri Fink, "Drug Shortages Forcing Hard Decisions on Rationing," *New York Times*, January 29, 2016, https://www.nytimes.com/2016/01/29/us/drug-shortages-forcing-hard-decisions-on-rationing-treatments.html?_r=0 (accessed March 6, 2017).

52. NSD Bio, "Potential Health and Safety Impacts from Pharmaceuticals and Supplements Containing China-Sourced Raw Ingredients," prepared for the US-China Economic and Security Review Commission, April 2010, p. 10, http://www.uscc.gov/sites/default/files/Research/NSD_BIO_Pharma_Report-Revised_FINAL_for_PDF-14_%20April_2010.pdf (accessed March 6, 2017).

53. Mark Paxton, in discussion with author, July 10, 2017.

54. Pfizer, "Pfizer and Hisun Announce Launch of Hisun-Pfizer Pharmaceuticals Co., Ltd.," press release, September 12, 2012, http://press.pfizer.com/press-release/pfizer-and-hisun-announce-launch-hisun-pfizer-pharmaceuticals-co-ltd (accessed March 10, 2017).

55. Anna Edney, "Facing Cancer Drug Shortage, US Relies on Banned Chinese Plant," *Bloomberg*, July 22, 2016, https://www.bloomberg.com/news/articles/2016-07-22/facing-cancer-drug-shortage-u-s-relies-on-banned-chinese-plant (accessed March 6, 2017).

56. Paul Levy, in discussion with author, March 2017.

57. A health system pharmacist, in conversation with author, March 2016.

58. Edney, "Facing Cancer Drug Shortage."

59. US Food and Drug Administration, warning letter to Zhejiang Hisun Pharmaceutical.

60. Paxton, in discussion with author, July 17, 2017.

61. US Food and Drug Administration, warning letter to Zhejiang Hisun Pharmaceutical.

62. NSD Bio, "Potential Health and Safety Impacts from Pharmaceuticals and Supplements Containing China-Sourced Raw Ingredients," prepared for the US-China Economic and Security Review Commission, April 2010, p. 11, http://www.uscc.gov/sites/default/files/Research/NSD_BIO_Pharma_Report-Revised_FINAL_for_PDF-14_%20April_2010.pdf (accessed March 5, 2017).

63. Ibid.

64. US Food and Drug Administration, "FDA Facts: Implementing Arrangements

with China," December 17, 2014, https://www.fda.gov/downloads/InternationalPrograms/
Agreements/MemorandaofUnderstanding/UCM427309.pdf (accessed December 20, 2017).

65. Peter Saxon, in discussion with author, August 6, 2016.

66. Former FDA official, in conversation with author, October 2015.

67. Barbara Unger, in discussion with author, March 2017.

68. Industry executive, in discussion with author.

69. "Glaxo Whistleblower Lawsuit: Bad Medicine," CBS News, December 29, 2010,
https://www.cbsnews.com/news/glaxo-whistle-blower-lawsuit-bad-medicine/ (accessed
December 20, 2017).

70. Gardiner Harris and Duff Wilson, "Glaxo to Pay $750 Million for Bad Products," *New
York Times*, October 26, 2010, http://www.nytimes.com/2010/10/27/business/27drug
.html?mtrref=www.bing.com&gwh=BCAAFE83456CA2055647C54614CEB26D&gwt=pay
(accessed December 20, 2017).

71. "Glaxo Whistleblower Lawsuit."

72. Harris and Wilson, "Glaxo to Pay $750 Million for Bad Products."

73. US Department of Justice, "GlaxoSmithKline to Plead Guilty & Pay $750 Million
to Resolve Criminal and Civil Liability Regarding Manufacturing Deficiencies at Puerto Rico
Plant," October 26, 2010, https://www.justice.gov/opa/pr/glaxosmithkline-plead-guilty-pay
-750-million-resolve-criminal-and-civil-liability-regarding (accessed December 20, 2017).

74. "Glaxo Whistleblower Lawsuit."

75. McNeil, in discussion with author, February 2017.

76. Pharmaceutical Integrity Coalition, http://www.pharmaceuticalintegritycoalition
.org/ (accessed February 9, 2017).

77. Ibid.

78. Ibid.

79. Susan Winckler, in discussion with author, October 2, 2015.

80. Craig Langdale, in discussion with author, April 2016.

81. Paxton, in discussion with author, July 17, 2017.

82. Neath, email correspondence with author.

83. Paxton, in discussion with author, March 29, 2016.

84. Steve Dickinson, email correspondence with author, August 20, 2015.

85. Saxon, in discussion with author.

86. David Carter, in discussion with author, March 14, 2017.

87. Louis Garguilo, "Amgen Three-Deep with Suppliers; Lilly 'Making Medicine
Together,'" Outsourced Pharma, April 17, 2015, https://www.outsourcedpharma.com/doc/
amgen-three-deep-with-suppliers-lilly-making-medicine-together-0001 (accessed January 5,
2017).

88. Ibid.

89. Dr. Margaret Hamburg, "Meeting the Challenges of Globalization and Strengthening
International Collaboration for Improved Health and Safety" (speech at Peking University,

Beijing China, November 17, 2014), https://wayback.archive-it.org/7993/20170111003408/
http://www.fda.gov/NewsEvents/Speeches/ucm423280.htm (accessed December 20, 2017).

90. Ibid.

91. Dr. Margaret Hamburg, "Food and Drugs: Can Safety Be Ensured in a Time of
Increased Globalization?" transcript, Council on Foreign Relations, January 31, 2011, http://
www.cfr.org/world/food-drugs-can-safety-ensured-time-increased-globalization/p34918
(accessed March 25, 2017).

92. Deborah Autor, "Remarks to the American Association of Exporters and Importers
Biannual Education Meeting" (speech, March 20, 2013). Transcript copy in author's possession.

93. Ibid.

CHAPTER 10: MADE IN CHINA, SUE IN AMERICA? GOOD LUCK

1. Charlisa Allen, in discussion with author, June 2016.

2. Steven Dickinson, email correspondence with author, August 20, 2015.

3. US Food and Drug Administration, "Updated Questions and Answers on Heparin
Sodium Injection (Baxter)," June 18, 2008, https://www.fda.gov/Drugs/DrugSafety/Postmarket
DrugSafetyInformationforPatientsandProviders/ucm112606.htm (accessed December 8, 2017).

4. Dickinson, email correspondence with author.

5. Dan Harris, email correspondence with author, August 21, 2015.

6. Dickinson, email correspondence with author.

7. Ibid.

8. Charlisa Allen, etc. v. American Capital Ltd., et al., No. 1:10HC60098 (N.D. Ohio
2016), http://www.leagle.com/decision/In%20FDCO%2020160518E03/IN%20RE%20
HEPARIN%20PRODUCTS%20LIABILITY%20LITIGATION (accessed March 2, 2017).

9. Charlisa Allen, CaringBridge, February 27, 2008.

10. Charlisa Allen, CaringBridge, February 28, 2008.

11. Allen, CaringBridge, March 2, 2008.

12. Allen, CaringBridge, March 3, 2008.

13. Allen, CaringBridge, March 4, 2008.

14. Allen, CaringBridge, March 6, 2008.

15. Allen, in discussion with author, June 2016.

16. Allen, CaringBridge, March 7, 2008.

17. Allen, in discussion with author, June 2016.

18. Ibid.

19. *Charlisa Allen*, p. 4.

20. Ibid.; "Cardiogenic Shock," National Library of Medicine, last updated November 6,
2017, https://www.nlm.nih.gov/medlineplus/ency/article/000185.htm (accessed November
26, 2017).

21. *Charlisa Allen*, p. 4.

22. The condition is called disseminated intravascular coagulation (DIC). It is a condition where blot clots form in small blood vessels throughout the body. The blood clots block or reduce blood flow through the blood vessels and can damage the body's organs. *PubMed Glossary*, s.v. "Disseminated Intravascular Coagulation (DIC)," https://www.ncbi.nlm.nih.gov/pubmedhealth/PMHT0022062/ (accessed March 2, 2017).

23. Allen, in discussion with author, June 2016.

24. Charlisa Allen, etc. v. American Capital Ltd., et al., No. 1:10HC60098 (N.D. Ohio 2010), complaint.

25. *Charlisa Allen*, p. 5.

26. Allen, in discussion with author, June 2016.

27. *Statistical Analysis of Multidistrict Litigation, Fiscal Year 2015* (Washington, DC: United States Judicial Panel on Multidistrict Litigation, 2015), p. 27, http://www.jpml.uscourts.gov/sites/jpml/files/JPML_Statistical_Analysis_of_Multidistrict_Litigation-FY-2015_0.pdf (accessed March 6, 2017).

28. *Charlisa Allen*, p. 4.

29. Charlisa Allen, etc. v. American Capital Ltd., et al., No. 1:10HC60098 (N.D. Ohio 2011), reply in support of defendants' motion for summary judgment, p. 2.

30. Ibid., p. 3.

31. "Contact Mayo Clinic," Mayo Clinic, http://www.mayoclinic.org/about-mayo-clinic/contact (accessed March 10, 2017); "Mayo Clinic's Campus in Arizona," Mayo Clinic, http://www.mayoclinic.org/patient-visitor-guide/arizona/clinic-hospital-buildings (accessed March 10, 2017).

32. Daniel Lapinski, letter to Judge James Carr in Charlisa Allen, etc. v. American Capital Ltd., et al., No. 1:10HC60098-JGC (N.D. Ohio 2011).

33. Charlisa Allen, etc. v. American Capital Ltd., et al., No. 1:10HC60098 (N.D. Ohio 2011), notice of defendants' withdrawal of their motion of summary judgment.

34. Allen, in discussion with author, June 2016.

35. Barbara Jacobs Rothstein and Catherin Borden, "Managing Multidistrict Litigation in Product Liability Cases: A Pocket Guide for Transferee Judges," p. 40, https://www.americanbar.org/content/dam/aba/administrative/litigation/materials/2012_jointcle_materials1/7_3_Managing_Multidistrict_Litigation_in_Products_Liability_Cases.authcheckdam.pdf (accessed December 20, 2017).

36. Allen, in discussion with author, June 2016.

37. Ibid.

38. Charlisa Allen, in discussion with author, April 2016.

39. Ibid.

40. Ibid.

41. Charlisa Allen, etc. v. American Capital Ltd., et al., No. 1:10HC60098 (N.D. Ohio 2015), motion for summary judgment.

42. Allen, in discussion with author, June 2016.

43. *Charlisa Allen* (2016), p. 11.

44. *Statistical Analysis of Multidistrict Litigation, Fiscal Year 2015*, p. 27.

45. Ibid.

46. Sharon Romito, email correspondence with author, September 8, 2016.

47. Allen, in discussion with author, June 2016.

48. Ibid.

CHAPTER 11: THE PERFECT CRIME

1. David B. Blossom et al., "Outbreak of Adverse Reactions Association with Contaminated Heparin," *New England Journal of Medicine* 359, no. 25 (December 18, 2008), http://www.nejm.org/doi/full/10.1056/NEJMoa0806450#t=article (accessed February 9, 2017).

2. "Public Health Advisory: Important Warnings and Instructions for Heparin Sodium Injection (Baxter)," US Food and Drug Administration, February 28, 2008, https://www.fda.gov/Drugs/DrugSafety/PostmarketDrugSafetyInformationforPatientsandProviders/ucm051133.htm (accessed December 20, 2017).

3. FDA Media Briefing on Heparin, March 19, 2008, https://wayback.archive-it.org/7993/20170112225928/http://www.fda.gov/downloads/NewsEvents/Newsroom/Media Transcripts/UCM169335.pdf (accessed December 31, 2017).

4. Heiko A. Kaiser et al., "Contaminated Heparin and Outcomes after Cardiac Surgery: A Retrospective Propensity-Matched Cohort Study," *PLOS ONE* 9, no. 8 (August 27, 2014), http://journals.plos.org/plosone/article/comments?id=10.1371/journal.pone.0106096 (accessed February 9, 2017).

5. Takashi Kei Kishimoto et al., "Contaminated Heparin Associated with Adverse Clinical Events and Activation of the Contact System," *New England Journal of Medicine* 358 no. 23 (June 5, 2008): 2457, http://www.nejm.org/doi/pdf/10.1056/NEJMoa0803200 (accessed February 18, 2017).

6. Charlisa Allen, in discussion with author, April 2016.

7. Dr. James Duncan, email correspondence with author, March 2, 2017.

8. US Food and Drug Administration, "Information on Adverse Event Reports and Heparin," https://wayback.archive-it.org/7993/20170113124004/http://www.fda.gov/Drugs/DrugSafety/PostmarketDrugSafetyInformationforPatientsandProviders/ucm112669.htm (accessed December 20, 2017).

9. "Questions and Answers on FDA's Adverse Event Reporting System," US Food and Drug Administration, last updated November 14, 2017, https://www.fda.gov/Drugs/GuidanceComplianceRegulatoryInformation/Surveillance/AdverseDrugEffects/default.htm (accessed November 26, 2017).

10. FDA Media Briefing on Heparin.

11. Ibid.

12. Ibid.

13. US Food and Drug Administration, "Information on Adverse Event Reports and Heparin."

14. Lee B. Murdaugh, "Adverse Drug Reaction Reporting," Association of Health-System Pharmacists, http://www.ashp.org/DocLibrary/Bookstore/For-Institutions/ADR-Reporting .pdf (accessed February 17, 2017).

15. Madris Tomes, in discussion with author, January 18, 2017.

16. US Food and Drug Administration, "Information on Adverse Event Reports and Heparin."

17. US Food and Drug Administration, "Drug/Biologic/Human Cell, Tissues and Cellular and Tissue-Based Product Manufacturers, Distributors, and Packers," https://www.fda. gov/Safety/MedWatch/HowToReport/ucm085692.htm (accessed January 15, 2018).

18. Tomes, in discussion with author.

19. Barbara Unger, in discussion with author.

20. Madris Tomes, email correspondence with author, March 10, 2017.

21. Ibid.

22. Ibid.

23. Brian Overstreet, "A Closer Look at FDA's Adverse Event Reporting System," *Patient Safety and Quality Health Care*, January 24, 2012, https://www.psqh.com/analysis/a-closer -look-at-fdas-adverse-event-reporting-system/ (accessed December 20, 2017).

24. Ibid.

25. Ibid.

26. Wade Roush, "Overstreet, Winner in Startup Tax Battle, Gets $2M for Adverse Events," *Xconomy*, April 16, 2014, http://www.xconomy.com/san-francisco/2014/04/16/ overstreet-winner-in-startup-tax-battle-gets-2m-for-adverseevents/ (accessed February 9, 2017).

27. Ibid.

28. Tomes, email correspondence with author.

29. Tomes, in discussion with author.

30. Kevin McNeil, in discussion with author, February 2017.

31. "Facts about the Current Good Manufacturing Practices," US Food and Drug Administration, January 6, 2015, http://www.fda.gov/Drugs/DevelopmentApprovalProcess/ Manufacturing/ucm169105.htm (accessed February 10, 2017).

32. McNeil, in discussion with the author.

33. Terry Graedon, "Patients Vindicated! Generic Wellbutrin Withdrawn," *People's Pharmacy*, September 3, 2012, https://www.peoplespharmacy.com/2012/09/03/generic -wellbutrin-budeprion-xl-300-withdrawn-vindication/ (accessed December 19, 2017).

34. ConsumerLab.com, "Five Years after ConsumerLab.com Reported a Problem, FDA Agrees Generic Version of Wellbutrin XL Is Not Equivalent and Is Pulled Off Market: Important Lessons about Generics," press release, October 4, 2012, https://www.consumerlab

.com/news/Generic_Wellbutrin_XL_Pulled_from_Market/10_4_2012/ (accessed February 10, 2017).

35. "Drug Test: "Wellbutrin v. Generic Bupropion," ConsumerLab.com, October 12, 2007, https://www.consumerlab.com/reviews/Wellbutrin_vs_Generic_Bupropion/Wellbutrin/#whatclfound (accessed February 10, 2017).

36. Ibid.

37. ConsumerLab, "Five Years after ConsumerLab.com Reported a Problem."

38. "Update: Bupropion Hydrochloride Extended-Release 300 mg Bioequivalence Studies," US Food and Drug Administration, October 3, 2012, http://www.fda.gov/Drugs/DrugSafety/PostmarketDrugSafetyInformationforPatientsandProviders/ucm322161.htm (accessed February 10, 2017).

39. ConsumerLab, "Five Years after ConsumerLab.com Reported a Problem."

40. David Carter, in discussion with author, March 14, 2017.

41. Ibid.

42. Anna Edney, "Generic Drug Testing Goes Widespread in US FDA Effort," *Bloomberg*, February 22, 2014, https://www.bloomberg.com/news/articles/2014-02-21/first-u-s-testing-of-generic-drugs-is-unveiled-by-fda (accessed February 13, 2017).

43. Ibid.

44. "Drug Quality Sampling and Testing Programs: Testing Standards and FDA Response to Substandard Outcomes," US Food and Drug Administration, last updated September 22, 2017, https://www.fda.gov/Drugs/ScienceResearch/ucm407277.htm (accessed November 27, 2017).

45. US Food and Drug Administration, warning letter to Medisca Inc., November 25, 2015, http://www.fda.gov/ICECI/EnforcementActions/WarningLetters/2015/ucm474892.htm (accessed February 18, 2017).

46. Ibid.

47. "FY14 Active Pharmaceutical Ingredient Test Results," US Food and Drug Administration, https://www.fda.gov/downloads/Drugs/ScienceResearch/UCM466383.pdf (accessed February 18, 2017).

48. "Drug Quality Sampling and Testing Programs: Post-Market Sampling and Testing Results FY2014," US Food and Drug Administration, http://www.fda.gov/Drugs/ucm407277.htm (accessed February 20, 2017).

49. Customer service representative, in discussion with author, July 2015.

50. "Atorvastatin Calcium Tablet, Film Coated," DailyMed, last updated October 15, 2015,https://dailymed.nlm.nih.gov/dailymed/drugInfo.cfm?setid=865f4e70-ead8-4480-96a4-6ca7b7d8ed69 (accessed November 28, 2017).

51. "Pfizer Lipitor" (label), DailyMed, http://dailymed.nlm.nih.gov/dailymed/image.cfm?type=img&name=lipitor-06.jpg&setid=c6e131fe-e7df-4876-83f7-9156fc4e8228 (accessed February 20, 2017).

52. George Akerlof, "The Market for Lemons: Quality Uncertainty and the Market Mechanism," *Quarterly Journal of Economics* 84, no. 3 (1970): 488–500.

53. "Product Review: Vitamin C Supplements," ConsumerLab.com, last updated April 8, 2017, https://www.consumerlab.com/reviews/vitamin-C_supplement_review/vitaminc/#results (accessed November 28, 2017).

54. Ibid.

55. *Chinese Herbs: Elixir of Health or Pesticide Cocktail?* (Beijing: Greenpeace East Asia, 2013), p. 17, http://www.greenpeace.org/international/Global/eastasia/publications/reports/food-agriculture/2013/chinese-herbs-testing-results.pdf (accessed February 18, 2017).

56. Eric Darier, "Exported: Chinese Herbs Laced with Toxic Pesticides," *Greenpeace* (blog), July 1, 2013, http://www.greenpeace.org/international/en/news/Blogs/makingwaves/exported-chinese-herbs-laced-with-pesticides/blog/45792/ (accessed February 17, 2017).

57. Wang Yi, "Packaging Trove Triggers Sweep on Fake Medicines," *China Daily*, November 23, 2011, http://ipr.chinadaily.com.cn/2011-11/23/content_14146537.htm (accessed February 17, 2017).

58. Ibid.

59. Dr. Stephen Tower, in discussion with author, July 2015.

60. Douglas Van Citters, in discussion with author, September 2015.

61. *The History of Drug Regulation in the United States* (Washington, DC: US Food and Drug Administration, 2006), http://www.fda.gov/AboutFDA/WhatWeDo/History/FOrgsHistory/CDER/CenterforDrugEvaluationandResearchBrochureandChronology/ucm114470.htm (accessed February 20, 2017).

62. Lyman F. Kebler, *Drug Legislation in the United States* (Washington, DC: Government Printing Office, 1909), p. 7.

63. Joseph Winters England and John Eicholtz Kramer, *The First Century of the Philadelphia College of Pharmacy, 1821–1921* (Philadelphia: Philadelphia College of Pharmacy and Science, 1922), p. 131, https://archive.org/details/firstcenturyofph00philrich (accessed February 17, 2017).

64. Kebler, *Drug Legislation in the United States*, p. 61.

65. "*History of Drug Regulation.*"

66. "Part II: 1938, Food, Drug, Cosmetic Act," US Food and Drug Administration, last updated October 5, 2017, https://www.fda.gov/AboutFDA/WhatWeDo/History/Origin/ucm054826.htm (accessed November 28, 2017).

67. McNeil, in discussion with author.

68. Dr. Lucinda Maine, email correspondence with author, April 5, 2017.

69. Teresa L. Stevens v. Boston Scientific Corporation et al., No. 2:16-cv-00265 (S.D.W. Va. 2016).

70. Robert Weisman, "Grand Jury Convened in Probe of Boston Scientific," *Boston Globe*, April 13, 2016, https://www.bostonglobe.com/business/2016/04/13/grand-jury-convened-probe-boston-scientific/v00hHy7djMd3xJfAH5f37J/story.html (accessed February 19, 2017).

71. US Department of Justice, "Medtronic to Pay $4.41 Million to Resolve Allegations It Unlawfully Sold Medical Devices Manufactured Overseas," press release, April 2, 2015, http://

www.justice.gov/opa/pr/medtronic-pay-441-million-resolve-allegations-it-unlawfully-sold
-medical-devices-manufactured (accessed February 19, 2017).

72. United States of America, Plaintiff, *ex rel.* etc. v. Medtronic, Inc., et al., No. 12SC25C2
(D. Minn.), complaint, https://www.manatt.com/uploadedFiles/Content/4_News_and
_Events/Newsletters/Corporate_Investigations_White_Collar_Defense/Medtroniccomplaint
.pdf (accessed December 20, 2017).

73. Ibid.

74. Ibid.

75. Joe Carlson, "Medtronic Pays $4.4 million to Settle Government Lawsuit,"
Minneapolis Star Tribune, April 2, 2015, http://www.startribune.com/medtronic-pays-4-4
-million-to-settle-government-lawsuit/298535011/ (accessed December 20, 2017).

76. *Food and Drug Administration, Justification of Estimates for Appropriations Committees*
(Washington, DC: US Department of Health and Human Services, 2014), p. 4, http://
www.fda.gov/downloads/AboutFDA/ReportsManualsForms/Reports/BudgetReports/
UCM347422.pdf (accessed February 19, 2017).

77. Ibid., p. 4.

78. Ibid.

CHAPTER 12: WHERE DOES THE SECRETARY OF DEFENSE PROCURE HIS MEDICINE?

1. Associated Press, "US Admiral in Disputed South China Sea: 'We Will Be Here,'"
Military Times, March 3, 2017, http://www.military.com/daily-news/2017/03/03/us-admiral
-disputed-south-china-sea-we-will-be-here.html (accessed April 13, 2017).

2. Guy Villax, in discussion with author, April 5, 2016.

3. Hovione, "Hovione's Antibiotic Doxycycline Joints Fight against Anthrax," press
release, November 5, 2001, http://www.hovione.com/press-room/press-release/hoviones
-antibiotic-doxycycline-joins-fight-against-anthrax (accessed February 1, 2017). See also
https://www.pharmacompass.com/pdf-document/other-inspection/Hovione-other
-inspection-1443597776.pdf (accessed December 26, 2017).

4. Ibid.

5. John Adams, "Remaking American Security: Supply Chain Vulnerabilities and
National Security Risks Across the US Defense Industrial Base," 2013, http://s3-us-west-2
.amazonaws.com/aamweb/uploads/research-pdf/RemakingAmericanSecurityMay2013_2.pdf
(accessed December 26, 2017).

6. Ibid.

7. Ibid.

8. Ibid.

9. John Adams, in discussion with author, March 2017.

10. Major Ben Sakrisson, email correspondence with author, March 24, 2016.

11. Ibid.

12. Soma Das, "India Relies on China for 90 Percent of Drug Raw Materials," *Economic Times*, October 29, 2014, http://economictimes.indiatimes.com/industry/healthcare/biotech/pharmaceuticals/india-relies-on-china-for-90-per-cent-of-drug-raw-materials/articleshow/44965918.cms?intenttarget=no (accessed February 20, 2017).

13. "Novartis' Plant Shut Down Creates Urgency to Find Alternatives to Chinese APIs: Chinese APIs Are Already a Security Threat for India," PharmaCompass, July 30, 2015, http://www.pharmacompass.com/radio-compass-blog/novartis-plant-shut-down-creates-urgency-to-find-alternatives-to-chinese-apis (accessed February 3, 2017).

14. Coalition for Government Procurement, http://thecgp.org/about-us (accessed February 20, 2017).

15. Donna Lee Yesner, "Trade Agreements Act Limitations on Procurement of Pharmaceuticals and Potential VA Solutions," http://thecgp.org/images/TAA.pdf (accessed February 20, 2017).

16. Coalition for Government Procurement.

17. Ibid.

18. "Office of Acquisition and Logistics: Trade Agreements Act," US Department of Veterans Affairs, last updated July 17, 2017, https://www.va.gov/oal/business/fss/taa.asp (accessed November 28 28, 2017).

19. Ndidi Mojay, email correspondence with author, March 27, 2017.

20. P. R. Bienkowski, C. H. Byers, and D. D. Lee, *Expedient Antibiotics Production Final Report* (Oak Ridge, TN: Oak Ridge National Laboratory, 1988), https://www.osti.gov/scitech/servlets/purl/6917476 (accessed November 28, 2017).

21. Christopher Nelson, Anna Bruse, et al., *Reliance on Foreign Sourcing in the Healthcare and Public Health Sector* (Washington, DC: US Department of Commerce, December 2011), p. 30, https://www.bis.doc.gov/index.php/forms-documents/doc_view/642-department-of-homeland-security-dhs-assessment-impact-of-foreign-sourcing-on-health-related-infra (accessed January 15, 2017).

22. Ibid., p. 69.

23. Ibid., p. 65.

24. Ibid., p. 70.

25. Ibid., p. 75.

26. Ibid.

27. Ted Kirk, in discussion with author, March 2016.

28. Villax, in discussion with author.

29. Ibid.

30. Dr. Janet Woodcock, "Introduction of Proposal for Reintroduction of Bovine Heparin in the US Market" (presentation, US Food and Drug Administration, June 4, 2014), slide 9.

31. US Food and Drug Administration, transcript of the Science Board Meeting, June 4,

2014, p. 229, https://wayback.archive-it.org/7993/20170406193307/https://www.fda.gov/downloads/AdvisoryCommittees/CommitteesMeetingMaterials/ScienceBoardtotheFoodandDrugAdministration/UCM405670.pdf (accessed December 26, 2017).

32. Ibid., p. 229–30.

33. Clare Stroud et al., eds., *Prepositioning Antibiotics for Anthrax* (Washington, DC: National Academy of Sciences, 2012), p. 71, http://www.nap.edu/read/13218/chapter/5#71 (accessed January 15, 2017).

34. *Testimony on Influenza: Perspective on Current Season and Update on Preparedness, Before Subcommittee on Oversight and Investigations, Committee on Energy and Commerce, US House of Representatives*, 113 Cong. (2013) (statement of Dr. Jesse L. Goodman, chief scientist at the Food and Drug Administration), http://docs.house.gov/meetings/IF/IF02/20130213/100255/HHRG-113-IF02-Wstate-GoodmanJ-20130213.pdf (accessed December 26, 2017).

35. Jesse Goodman, "The Safety of Prescription Drugs Made Outside the US," interview by Diane Rehm, Diane Rehm Show, February 20, 2014, https://thedianerehmshow.org/shows/2014-02-20/safety-prescription-drugs-made-outside-us (accessed February 15, 2017).

36. Paul Levy, in discussion with author, April 14, 2016.

37. Ibid.

38. Joe Gould, "US-Made Sneakers May Be Afoot for Military Recruits," *USA Today*, September 1, 2014, https://www.usatoday.com/story/news/nation/2014/09/01/new-balance-sneaker-prototype-boot-camp/14940075/ (accessed December 26, 2017).

39. National Defense Authorization Act for Fiscal Year 2017, p. 273, https://www.congress.gov/114/bills/s2943/BILLS-114s2943enr.pdf (accessed March 23, 2017).

40. Gould, "US-Made Sneakers."

41. "Master Sgt. Says No to Chinese-Made Boots," *Military Times*, March 28, 2013, http://www.militarytimes.com/story/military/archives/2013/03/28/master-sgt-says-no-to-chinese-made-boots/78536634/ (accessed March 23, 2017).

42. Ibid.

43. Senator Sherrod Brown, "Brown Urges Defense Department to Buy Uniforms and Boots Made in America, Not China, for Military Servicemembers," press release, October 18, 2012, https://www.brown.senate.gov/newsroom/press/release/brown-urges-defense-department-to-buy-uniforms-and-boots-made-in-americanot-chinafor-military-servicemembers (accessed March 23, 2017).

44. Dan Stone, "Is Your Country Food Independent?" *National Geographic*, April 13, 2014, http://onward.nationalgeographic.com/2014/04/13/is-your-country-food-independent/ (accessed February 8, 2017).

45. Flavius Vegetius Renatus, *De Re Militari*, trans. John Clarke (390 AD; 1767, copyright expired), p. 5, https://www.usna.edu/Users/history/abels/hh381/vegetius.html (accessed March 23, 2017).

46. Dr. Gary Sheffield, "The Battle of the Atlantic: The U-Boat Peril," BBC, March 30,

2011, http://www.bbc.co.uk/history/worldwars/wwtwo/battle_atlantic_01.shtml (accessed February 8, 2017).

47. J. F. C. Fuller, *The Conduct of War, 1789–1961* (London: Eyre & Spottiswoode, 1961), p. 178.

48. *Annual Energy Outlook 2017 with Projections to 2050* (Washington, DC: US Energy Information Administration, January 5, 2017), http://www.eia.gov/outlooks/aeo/pdf/0383(2017).pdf (accessed February 8, 2017).

49. Paul Hesse, email correspondence with author, February 8, 2017.

50. Adams, in discussion with author.

51. Lee Levkowitz, Nathan Beauchamp-Mustafaga, "China's Rare Earths Industry and Its Role in the International Market," US-China Economic and Security Review Commission, November 3, 2010, https://china.usc.edu/sites/default/files/legacy/AppImages/uscc-2010 -china-rare-earths.pdf (accessed December 26, 2017).

52. Keith Bradsher, "China Said to Widen Its Embargo of Metals," *New York Times,* October 19, 2010, http://www.nytimes.com/2010/10/20/business/global/20rare.html?_r=0 (accessed March 5, 2017).

53. Lee Levkowitz and Nathan Beauchamp-Mustafaga, "China's Rare Earths Industry and Its Role in the International Market," US-China Economic and Security Review Commission, November 3, 2010, https://china.usc.edu/sites/default/files/legacy/AppImages/uscc-2010 -china-rare-earths.pdf (accessed December 26, 2017).

54. Ibid.

55. Ibid.

56. Ibid.

57. Keith Bradsher, "China Said to Widen Its Embargo of Metals," *New York Times,* October 19, 2010, http://www.nytimes.com/2010/10/20/business/global/20rare.html?_r=0 (accessed March 5, 2017).

58. Ibid.

59. "Staph Infections," Mayo Clinic, last updated June 20, 2017, http://www.mayoclinic .org/diseases-conditions/staph-infections/basics/treatment/con-20031418 (accessed November 28, 2017).

60. Gareth McDonald, "Pfizer Vancomycin Supplier Zhejiang Medicine Warned by US FDA," *in-PharmaTechnologist.com,* August 17, 2016, http://www.in-pharmatechnologist .com/Ingredients/Pfizer-vancomycin-supplier-Zhejiang-Medicine-warned-by-US-FDA?utm _source=copyright&utm_medium=OnSite&utm_campaign=copyright (accessed February 15, 2017); US Food and Drug Administration, warning letter to Zhejiang Medicine Company, August 4, 2016,http://www.fda.gov/ICECI/EnforcementActions/WarningLetters/2016/ ucm516163.htm (accessed February 1, 2017).

61. McDonald, "Pfizer Vancomycin Supplier."

62. US FDA, warning letter to Zhejiang Medicine.

63. McDonald, "Pfizer Vancomycin Supplier."

64. Ibid.

65. *DR-TB Drugs under the Microscope, Sources and Prices for Drug-Resistant Tuberculosis Medicines*, 3rd ed. (Geneva; Paris: Medecins San Frontieres; International Union Against Tuberculosis and Lung Disease, 2013), p. 16, http://www.msfaccess.org/sites/default/files/ MSF_TB_Report_UTM3rdEdition-2013.pdf (accessed March 6, 2017); Anna Nicholson et al., *Developing and Strengthening the Global Supply Chain for Second-Line Drugs for Multi-Drug Resistant Tuberculosis* (workshop summary; Washington, DC: National Academy of Sciences, 2013), p. 56, http://www.ncbi.nlm.nih.gov/books/NBK115060/pdf/TOC.pdf (accessed February 20, 2017).

66. *Tuberculosis Medicines: Technology and Market Landscape* (Geneva: UNITAID, October 2014), p. 48, http://ajanweb.org/resourcecentrenewsletter/pdfs/UNITAID-TB _Medicines_Landscape-2nd_edition.pdf (accessed December 13, 2016).

67. "Import Alerts," US Food and Drug Administration, http://www.accessdata.fda.gov/ cms_ia/importalert_189.html (accessed January 22, 2016).

68. "Anthrax: The Threat," Centers for Disease Control and Prevention, last updated August 1, 2014, http://www.cdc.gov/anthrax/bioterrorism/threat.html (accessed February 20, 2017).

69. Kirk, in discussion with author.

70. Industry member, in email correspondence with author.

71. Villax, in discussion with author.

72. Industry official, in conversation with author.

73. Bharat Mehta, in conversation with author, February 2016.

74. Adams, in discussion with author.

75. Mark Hansen, in conversation with author, September 18, 2015.

CHAPTER 13: CHINA BASHING? TAKE A LOOK AT THIS

1. *Hearing on Chinese Investment in the United States: Impacts and Issues for Policy Makers, Before US-China Economic and Security Review Commission* (2017) (statement of Jeffrey Z. Johnson, president and CEO of SquirrelWerkz), http://www.uscc.gov/sites/default/files/ Johnson_USCC%20Hearing%20Testimony012617_0.pdf (accessed February 15, 2017).

2. Ibid.

3. Shanghai Disney Resort, https://www.shanghaidisneyresort.com.cn/en/about (accessed March 25, 2017); Christopher Palmeri and Alexandra Ho, "Disney Unveils Tomorrowland for Chinese in $5.5 Billion Park," *Bloomberg*, July 15, 2015, http://www .bloomberg.com/news/articles/2015-07-15/disney-unveils-tomorrowland-for-5-5-billion -shanghai-theme-park (accessed March 25, 2017).

4. Sophia Yan, "Billionaire Vows to Crush Disney in China," CNN, May 24, 2016,

http://money.cnn.com/2016/05/24/news/china-wang-jianlin-disney-shanghai-resort/index
.html?iid=EL (accessed March 5, 2017).

5. Ibid.

6. Jethro Mullen, "Disney Characters Seen at Chinese Tycoon's Theme Park," CNN, May 31, 2016, http://money.cnn.com/2016/05/31/media/china-wanda-disney-wang-jianlin/index
.html (accessed April 10, 2017).

7. Ibid.

8. Jeffrey Johnson, "Forum Focuses Chinese Investment," video, January 26, 2017, C-SPAN, Part I, https://www.c-span.org/video/?422783-1/forum-focuses-chinese
-investment-us (accessed March 6, 2017).

9. Ibid.

10. David Drummond, "A New Approach to China," Google (blog), January 12, 2010, https://
googleblog.blogspot.com/2010/01/new-approach-to-china.html?m=1 (accessed March 5, 2017).

11. Jim Finkle, "Google China Hackers Stole Source Code," Reuters, March 3, 2010, http://mobile.reuters.com/article/idUSN0325873820100303 (accessed March 25, 2017).

12. Mike Elgan, "Fake Google Search Engine Emerges in China," ITWorld, January 28, 2010, http://www.itworld.com/article/2759917/networking-hardware/fake-google-search
-engine-emerges-in-china.html (accessed March 5, 2017).

13. David Drummond, "A New Approach to China: An Update," Google (blog), March 22, 2010, https://googleblog.blogspot.com/2010/03/new-approach-to-china-update.html (accessed March 30, 2017).

14. Ibid.

15. Ibid.

16. Brad Stone and Bruce Einhorn, "How Baidu Won China," *Bloomberg*, November 22, 2010, https://www.bloomberg.com/news/articles/2010-11-11/how-baidu-won-china (accessed December 26, 2017).

17. James McGregor, *China's Drive for Indigenous Innovation: A Web of Industrial Policies* (Washington, DC: US Chamber of Commerce, July 20, 2010), https://www.uschamber.com/
sites/default/files/legacy/reports/100728chinareport_0.pdf (accessed March 28, 2017).

18. "On the Rails Worldwide, High-Speed Projects from Siemens," Siemens, http://www
.siemens.com/press/pool/de/events/industry/mobility/2010-04-velaro-d/whitepaper_siemens
_velaro_projekte_en.pdf (accessed March 30, 2017).

19. McGregor, China's Drive for 'Indigenous Innovation.

20. Jack Purcher, "Beijing Court Rules That Apple's iPhone 6 Models Violate Chinese Design Patent and May Be Banned," Patently Apple, June 17, 2016, http://www.patentlyapple
.com/patently-apple/2016/06/beijing-court-rules-that-apples-iphone-6-models-violate-chinese
-design-patent-and-may-be-banned.html (accessed April 5, 2017).

21. Ben Lovejoy, "Bizarre Beijing Ruling Says iPhone 6 Copies Chinese Phone, Apple Must Halt Sales," 9to5mac.com, June 10, 2016, https://9to5mac.com/2016/06/17/iphone
-copies-chinese-phone-beijing/ (accessed April 5, 2017).

22. Jack Purcher, "A Beijing Court Overturns Ruling That the iPhone 6 Design Infringed the Design of a 'Shenzhen Baili' Smartphone," Patently Apple, March 25, 2017, http://www.patentlyapple.com/patently-apple/2017/03/a-beijing-court-overturns-ruling-that-the-iphone-6-design-infringed-the-design-of-a-shenzhen-bali-smartphone.html (accessed April 7, 2017).

23. Roger Fingas, "Apple Loses Exclusive Rights to 'iPhone' Trademark for Non-Smartphone Products in China," AppleInsider.com, May 3, 2016, http://appleinsider.com/articles/16/05/03/apple-loses-exclusive-rights-to-iphone-trademark-for-non-smartphone-products-in-china (accessed April 5, 2017).

24. Mikey Campbell, "Apples iTunes Movies, iBooks Store Go Dark in China 6 Months after Launch," AppleInsider.com, April 14, 2016, http://appleinsider.com/articles/16/04/15/apples-itunes-movies-ibooks-goes-dark-in-china-6-months-after-launch (accessed April 5, 2017).

25. Patrick Seitz, "Apple iPhone Loses No. 1 Position in China Smartphone Market," *Investor's Business Daily*, January 27, 2017, http://www.investors.com/news/technology/click/apple-iphone-loses-no-1-position-in-china-smartphone-market/ (accessed April 5, 2017). Sales defined as total smartphone units shipped.

26. Patrick Seitz, "Apple iPhone Loses No. 1 Position in China Smartphone Market," *Investor's Business Daily*, January 27, 2017, http://www.investors.com/news/technology/click/apple-iphone-loses-no-1-position-in-china-smartphone-market/ (accessed April 5, 2017).

27. Jacob Pramuk, "Icahn: We're out of Apple, and It's China's Fault," CNBC, April 28, 2016, http://www.cnbc.com/2016/04/28/icahn-we-no-longer-have-a-position-in-apple.html (accessed April 5, 2017).

28. "J&J to Fight China Loss of Diabetes-Test Trademark," *Wall Street Journal*, January 9, 2014, https://www.wsj.com/articles/jampj-to-fight-china-loss-of-diabetestest-trademark-1389272885 (accessed April 10, 2017).

29. "J&J Will Appeal China Ruling to Revoke Diabetes-Strip Trademark," *Bloomberg*, January 9, 2014, https://www.bloomberg.com/news/articles/2014-01-09/j-j-will-appeal-china-ruling-to-revoke-diabetes-strip-trademark (accessed April 10, 2017).

30. Liu Zhihua, "Johnson & Johnson Trademark Revoked in China," *China Daily*, January 8, 2014, http://usa.chinadaily.com.cn/business/2014-01-08/content_17225923.htm (accessed March 25, 2017).

31. Johnson & Johnson customer service in China, email correspondence with author, April 23, 2017.

32. Robert D. Atkinson, "Chinese Investment in the U.S., Part 2," video, C-SPAN, January 26, 2017, https://www.c-span.org/video/?422783-2/chinese-investment-us-part-2 (accessed February 26, 2017).

33. Patrick Jenevein, "Chinese Investment in the U.S., Part 2," video, C-SPAN, January 26, 2017, https://www.c-span.org/video/?422783-2/chinese-investment-us-part-2 (accessed February 26, 2017).

34. Ibid.

35. Ibid.

36. Ibid.

37. Ibid.

38. Ibid.

39. Ibid.

40. Ibid.

41. Howard Kurtz, "Ex-CBSer Rips Network," *Washington Post*, January 24, 2005, http://www.washingtonpost.com/archive/business/technology/2005/01/24/ex-cbser-rips-network/858ce373-6969-4aea-a2b1-467af09d50cb/ (accessed March 5, 2017).

42. Ibid.

43. Howard French, "Bloomberg's Folly," *Columbia Journalism Review*, May–June 2014, http://www.cjr.org/feature/bloombergs_folly.php (accessed March 5, 2017).

44. Ibid.

45. J. William Carpenter, "Top 5 Companies Owned by Disney," Investopedia, October 29, 2015, http://www.investopedia.com/articles/markets/102915/top-5-companies-owned-disney.asp (accessed April 5, 2017).

46. "About CBS Corporation," CBS Corporation, 2017, https://www.cbscorporation.com/about-cbs/ (accessed April 5, 2017); Joseph Milord, "The World's 10 Largest Media Conglomerates," Elite Daily, July 2, 2013, http://elitedaily.com/money/the-worlds-10-largest-media-conglomerates/ (accessed March 5, 2017).

47. CBS Interactive, 2017, http://www.cbsinteractive.com/about (accessed April, 5, 2017).

48. Julie Makinen, "Universal Studios to Open Beijing Theme Park in 2019," *Los Angeles Times*, October 13, 2014, http://www.latimes.com/business/la-fi-universal-studios-beijing-20141012-story.html (accessed April 5, 2017).

49. "CDER Alert: FDA Warns of Potential Contamination of Drug Shipments from Explosions in Tianjin City," US Food and Drug Administration, last updated December 22, 2015, http://www.fda.gov/Drugs/DrugSafety/ucm478170.htm (accessed March 6, 2017).

50. Ibid.

51. "Prednisone," Mayo Clinic, last updated March 1, 2017, http://www.mayoclinic.org/drugs-supplements/prednisone-oral-route/description/DRG-20075269 (accessed March 25, 2017). "Tianjin Tianyao Pharmaceuticals," PharmaCompass, 2017, http://www.pharmacompass.com/us-drug-master-files-dmfs/tianjin-tianyao-pharmaceuticals-co-ltd (accessed March 25, 2017).

52. Josh Rudolph, "Minitrue: Don't Hype Tainted Tianjin Pharma Products," *China Digital Times*, December 24, 2015, http://chinadigitaltimes.net/2015/12/minitrue-cyanide-in-tianjin-pharma-products/ (accessed March 16, 2017).

53. *China Digital Times*, http://chinadigitaltimes.net/about/ (accessed March 16, 2017).

54. Rudolph, "Minitrue."

55. Sarah Kotler, email correspondence with author, February 5, 2016.

56. *Annual Reporting Conditions Survey* (Beijing: Foreign Correspondents' Club of China, 2014), https://cpj.org/blog/fccc_report_may_2014.pdf (accessed April 10, 2017).

57. Ibid., p. 5.

58. Ibid.

59. Ibid.

60. "Watch What You Say, Even at Home," *Economist*, March 31, 2014, http://www .economist.com/node/21599931/print (accessed April 5, 2017).

61. Ambrose Evans-Pritchard, "China Losing Control as Stocks Crash Despite Emergency Measures," *Daily Telegraph*, July 27, 2015, http://www.telegraph.co.uk/finance/china-business/ 11766449/China-losing-control-as-stocks-crash-despite-emergency-measures.html (accessed March 25, 2017).

62. Kristie Lu Stout, Twitter, March 30, 2014, 11:17 p.m., https://twitter.com/klustout/ status/450517256494006272 (accessed November 28, 2017).

63. John Adams, speech at the Boston Massacre Trials, December 1770, available online at http://www.bostonmassacre.net/trial/acct-adams3.htm (accessed February 21, 2017).

64. Mike Boehm, "Hillary Clinton Will Give Five Artists Medals for Embassy Art," *Los Angeles Times*, November 30, 2012, http://articles.latimes.com/2012/nov/30/entertainment/ la-et-cm-hillary-clinton-will-give-five-artists-medals-for-embassy-art-20121129 (accessed March 30, 2017).

65. Leah Binkowitz, "What a Blast: Artist Cai Guo-Qiang Sets off Explosions on the Mall," *Smithsonian*, November 30, 2012, http://www.smithsonianmag.com/smithsonian -institution/video-what-a-blast-artist-cai-guo-qiang-sets-off-explosions-on-the-mall -149904639/ (accessed March 20, 2017).

66. Ibid.

67. "Raw: Cai Guo-Qiang Lights up Christmas Tree at Freer Gallery," video, *Washington Post*, November 30, 2012, http://www.washingtonpost.com/lifestyle/style/christmas-tree -explosion-in-dc/2012/11/30/f445324e-3b2b-11e2-a263-f0ebffed2f15_video.html (accessed March 20, 2017).

CHAPTER 14: A TEN-STEP PLAN TO BRING IT HOME

1. "Locations," Community Health Systems, 2015, http://www.chs.net/serving -communities/locations/#USMap (accessed March 17, 2017).

2. Dave Barkholz, "CHS' Largest Investor Turns Activist," *Modern Health Care*, March 13, 2017, http://www.modernhealthcare.com/article/20170313/NEWS/170319984 (accessed March 15, 2017); Community Health Systems, "Schedule 13D," Securities and Exchange Commission, March 8, 2017, https://www.sec.gov/Archives/edgar/data/1108109/ 000119312517079434/d361876dsc13d.htm (accessed December 26, 2017).

3. Ted Kirk, in discussion with author, March 2016.

4. Thomson Reuters, "Newport Premium (for Generics)," https://www.scribd.com/ document/274292111/Newport-Premium-for-Generics-Cfs-En (accessed January 14, 2018).

5. Kirk, in discussion with author.

6. Rensselaer Polytechnic Institute, "Synthetic Version of Heparin Created for Use in Kidney Patients," *Science Daily*, February 23, 2014, https://www.sciencedaily.com/releases/2014/02/140223215103.htm (accessed April 5, 2017).

7. Craig Langdale, in discussion with author, March 2016.

8. Peter Saxon, in discussion with author, August 6, 2016.

9. Jordan Rau, "Medicare Reveals How Much It Spends on Prescription Drugs for Americans," PBS, May 1, 2015, http://www.pbs.org/newshour/rundown/medicare-reveals-much-spends-prescription-drugs-americans/ (accessed March 25, 2017).

10. US House of Representatives, Committee on Energy and Commerce, 21st Century Cures Act, November 28, 2016, https://energycommerce.house.gov/sites/republicans.energycommerce.house.gov/files/documents/114/analysis/20161128%20Cures%20Fact%20Sheet.pdf (accessed March 20, 2017).

11. Steve Arnoff, "Generic Drugs Continue to Deliver Billions in Savings to the US Healthcare System, New Report Finds," Generic Pharmaceutical Association, October 19, 2016, http://www.gphaonline.org/gpha-media/press/generic-drugs-continue-to-deliver-billions-in-savings-to-the-u-s-healthcare-system-new-report-finds/ (accessed August 2, 2017).

12. Gardiner Harris, "US Identifies Tainted Heparin in Eleven Countries," *New York Times*, April 22, 2008, http://www.nytimes.com/2008/04/22/health/policy/22fda.html (accessed March 6, 2017).

13. US Food and Drug Administration, "Mutual Recognition Promises New Framework for Pharmaceutical Inspections for United States and European Union" (press release, March 2, 2017), https://www.fda.gov/NewsEvents/Newsroom/PressAnnouncements/ucm544357.htm (accessed March 8, 2017).

14. Langdale, in discussion with author.

APPENDIX: HOW TO FIND OUT WHERE YOUR MEDICINES ARE MADE

1. "About DailyMed," DailyMed, National Institutes of Health, National Library of Medicine, https://dailymed.nlm.nih.gov/dailymed/about-dailymed.cfm (accessed March 2, 2017).

2. "Wellbutrin XL," Drugs.com, https://www.drugs.com/availability/generic-wellbutrin-sr.html (accessed March 10, 2017).

3. "Losartan Potassium," GoodRx, http://www.goodrx.com/losartan/images?filter-dosage=25mg&filter-brand=Losartan+Potassium (accessed April 1, 2017); "Losartan Potassium," DailyMed, last updated October 1, 2015, http://dailymed.nlm.nih.gov/dailymed/drugInfo.cfm?setid=3d6a61cd-77c4-4f52-b826-c030df979270 (accessed April 1, 2017).

4. Bob Kennedy, "China Increases Its Activity in Regulated Markets," Thomson Reuters, 2012, https://www.slideshare.net/BobKennedy15/chinaincreasesactivity regulatedmarkets-62276973 (accessed December 28, 2017); Pack Pharmaceuticals, http://risingpharma.com/about-rising/history (accessed December 28, 2017).

5. "WellPatch Capsaicin Pain Relief Pads, Large, 4-Count Boxes (Pack of 3)," Amazon, http://www.amazon.com/WellPatch-Capsaicin-Relief-Large-4-Count/dp/B0024NLF8M (accessed March 5, 2017).

6. Ibid.

7. Mentholatum customer service representative, in discussion with author.

8. "Mentholatum," DailyMed, last updated November 8, 2017, http://dailymed.nlm .nih.gov/dailymed/drugInfo.cfm?setid=c4cd6323-320b-4a0b-af78-63be4cda23ba (accessed November 28, 2017).

INDEX

acetaminophen
  China as dominant producer
    of active ingredient in, 35
  closure of last European manu-
    facturing plant, 35
active pharmaceutical ingredient
  centralization of global supply,
    33, 195, 198
  China as largest global sup-
    plier of, 9
  as commodities, 56
  defined, 32
  estimated unsafe products in
    Europe, 55
  importation from unregulated
    plants, 53–54
  shift in global manufacturing
    of, 33
Adams, John, 190–91, 200, 204
Advanced Persistent Threat
  groups, 96–97
adverse event reporting to FDA
  consumer reporting, 233
  difficulty of reporting, 175
  inadequate use of reports,
    176–77
  MedWatch, 175
  requirements to report, 175

Akerlof, George, 181
Allen, Bob, 17, 24, 46, 163, 175
Allen, Charlisa, 17–21, 24, 26, 38,
  161–70, 173, 175
American Chamber of Commerce
  in China, 93–95, 97, 123–24
American Chemical Society, 83
American Society of Health-
  System Pharmacists, 81
amlodipine besylate, 30
Andre, Philippe, 44–45
anthrax
  antidotes
    Cipro, 203
    ciprofloxacin, 10, 192,
      203–204
    doxycycline, 27, 31, 37,
      80–81, 189–90, 204
  attacks, 203–204
Apple (company)
  market share in China, 210
  trademark challenges, 209
arbitrage and medicines, 49
arbitration in bilateral investment
  treaties
    Philip Morris, 129–30
    Tang Energy, 211–12
    Vattenfall, 129

Aricept, 29
ascorbic acid
    cartel, 71–72
    China as dominant global producer, 70
    shift in global suppliers, 70
    US Court of Appeals cartel ruling, 72–73
    US government cartel prosecution, 71
aspirin
    acetylsalicylic acid, active ingredient in, 34
    closure of last manufacturing plant in United States, 36
    International Trade Commission dumping decision, 36
    Rhodia, 35, 120
    St. Joseph, 34
    US manufacturing history, 34–35
Atkinson, Robert, 96, 126, 211
Autor, Deborah, 160

Bain & Company, 94
Biden, Joseph, 143
Boehringer Ingelheim (pharmaceutical company), 145
Boston Consulting Group
    Chinese consumer affluence, 91
    India dependence on China, 34, 192

Boston Scientific (manufacturing company), 186
Breckenridge Pharmaceutical, 29
Bristol-Myers Squibb (pharmaceutical company), 75
Brown, Sherrod
    American-made military clothing, 199
    country-of-origin drug labeling, 36
Budeprion XL 300
    ConsumerLab.com testing of, 178
    FDA non-equivalence determination, 179
Buttram, Jonathan, 106, 113

cancer drug shortage, 145–46, 149
capreomycin, 203
Cargill (company), 108, 112–13
Carr, James, 167–69
cartels
    ascorbic acid, 120
    China's strategic use of, 205
    impact on drug shortages, 79, 225
    impunity for, 81
    penicillin, 120
    risks of, 223
    unequal treatment of, 81
    US Court of Appeals decision, 72–73

Carter, David, 158, 179
censorship
    after Tianjin explosions, 218
    impact on US medicines, 214
    of journalists in China,
        216–17
Centers for Disease Control and
    Prevention
    medicine stockpiles, 196
    tracing heparin contamina-
        tion, 22, 167
centralization of global supply
    of active ingredients. *See under*
    active pharmaceutical ingredient
cephalosporins, 38
Changzhou SPL (company)
    Baxter decision not to inspect
        before buying heparin, 47
    Baxter inspection post-hep-
        arin, 46
    as Baxter supplier, 25
    differences in US and China
        plant, 47
    FDA decision not to inspect,
        44
    FDA inspection after heparin
        contamination, 24–26
chicken imports from China,
    approval of, 103, 115
China
    cyber-economic campaigns,
        205–207

    dominant producer of active
        ingredients, 35, 37
    favoring domestic companies,
        93, 123, 133
    labor cost difference in, 90
    response to heparin contami-
        nation, 26
    13th Five-Year Plan, 123
    trends in consumer affluence,
        91
    US security implications of
        dependence on, 33, 195,
        198, 221
China Digital Times (web news),
    215
China Food and Drug Adminis-
    tration, 147, 151, 157
China lobby, 59, 116
China price, 158, 163
Christmas tree explosion, 217
Cleveland Clinic, 149
clindamycin, 31
Clinton, Bill, 58, 133–34, 217
Coalition for Common Sense Pro-
    curement, 192–93
commodities, medicines as, 56,
    102, 223, 226
consumer attitudes
    on China as economic threat,
        132
    on drugs made in China, 38
ConsumerLab.com, 182

INDEX

Cooperman, Todd, 178
Corbo, Tony, 106–107, 109, 111–13
country-of-origin labeling
    customs law, 35–36
    FDA requirements, 36
cyber-economic campaigns,
    205–207

DailyMed (website), 28–31, 118,
    232
defense industrial base, 190
Defense Logistics Agency, 191
DeLauro, Rosa, 64, 103
Department of Agriculture, 10,
    102, 108, 113, 223
Department of Commerce, 194
Department of Defense, 191
Department of Homeland Secu-
    rity, 194
Department of Veterans Affairs,
    10, 121, 154, 186
dependence on China
    for active ingredients, 33,
        37–39, 147, 194
    for heparin, 11, 34
    US security implications of,
        39, 88, 196
Dickinson, Steven, 158, 162–63
diethylene glycol, in toothpaste,
    63
DiLoreto, John, 68
Dingell, John, 42, 50

Disney resort in China, 206
Doctors Without Borders, 203
donepezil, 29, 191
doxycycline
    as anthrax antidote, 27, 37,
        189, 191, 203–204
    Guy Villax, 189
    high cost of, 80
    Hovione, 189
    in Operation Desert Storm,
        190
    price-fixing allegations, 81
Drug Price Competition and
    Patent Term Restoration Act, 55
drug shortages
    American Society of Health-
        System Pharmacists, 81
    FDA monitoring of, 79
Duncan, James, 137, 174

Ebola, 121, 191
Eckard, Cheryl, 153–54
Electric Boat. See General
    Dynamics Electric Boat
Eli Lilly (pharmaceutical
    company), 95–96, 180, 194
Elward, Alexis, 22–23
erythromycin, 119, 191
ethical drug manufacturing
    corporate responsibility,
        155–56
    due diligence and, 47

example of, 156
organizational culture, 147
European Active Pharmaceutical
  Ingredients Committee, 55
European Medicines Agency
  manufacturing challenges for,
    151, 155
  mutual recognition agreement
    with FDA, 228

FireEye (cybersecurity), 96–97
Food and Drug Administration
  (FDA)
  budget compared with Mont-
    gomery County, Maryland,
    62
  concern over US dependence
    on China for heparin, 50,
    196
  exempting Hisun products
    from import ban, 149, 203,
    228
  forced closure of Guangzhou
    and Shanghai offices, 66, 143
  funding for, 187
  global standard for public pro-
    tection, 185
  import alerts, 54–55, 67, 139,
    142, 145–46, 149, 157
  increase in foreign inspections,
    67
  Science Board, 196

testing of drug products,
  179–80, 182, 228
transfer of agency intellectual
  property to China, 98
visas for FDA staff in China
  delayed, 64, 142–43
Food and Water Watch (organization), 106, 111, 113, 115
Foreign Correspondents' Club of
  China, 216
foreign suppliers of pharmaceutical and other medical products, study of, 194
Fricke, Fred, 53

Gallup (company), 132
gemcitabine, 32
General Dynamics Electric Boat
  (company), 197
General Electric (company)
  CT scanner manufacturing in
    China, 124
  prefabricated factories, 91
GlaxoSmithKline (pharmaceutical
  company)
  commitment to discovery in
    China, 93
  Puerto Rico plant woes,
    153–54
globalization, as deregulation, 11
goji berries, 182
Goldman, Lynn, 196

INDEX

Goldman Sachs (company)
    investment in heparin
      company, 78
    ownership in Shuanghui, 76
Goodman, Jesse, 97
Google, exit from China market,
    207–208
Gorsky, Alex, 85
Graedon, Joe, 57, 178
Graedon, Terry, 178
Greenpeace East Asia, 182
Greenstone (pharmaceutical
    company), 31
Groton, Connecticut
    economic impact of layoffs,
      88–90
    penicillin manufacturing site, 74
    Pfizer building demolition, 87

Hamburg, Margaret
    Council on Foreign Relations,
      159
    Peking University speech, 98,
      119, 123, 159
    US trade deficit with China in
      pharmaceuticals, 119
Harris, Dan, 162
Hatch-Waxman Act, 55
heparin
    contamination
      Baxter recalls of heparin, 23
      blue ear disease in pigs, 25

countries affected by, 26
    import bans on suppliers,
      66–67
    inspection of Changzhou
      SPL, 24, 26
    oversulfated chondroitin
      sulfate, 25
    product liability litigation,
      167
    reports of deaths associ-
      ated with, 174
    "show" factories selling
      heparin, 66
    St. Louis Children's Hos-
      pital, 21, 23, 137, 174,
      229
    stockpiled and recycled in
      China, 138
    dependence on China for, 50
    shortages of, 196
    Smithfield Foods sale and,
      77–78
    synthetic manufacture, pros-
      pects for, 224
    ubiquitous use in hospitals,
      196
Hickey, Christopher, 68, 142–43
hospital drug purchasing, 150
Hovione (pharmaceutical
    company), 9, 27, 46, 189, 196
Hubbard, William, 26, 49, 61, 63,
    66

hydrogen cyanide contamination, 214

Icahn, Carl, 210
import alerts, 54–55, 67, 139, 142, 145–46, 149, 157
India
    anti-dumping duties on paracetamol, 35
    national security risks of dependence on China, 34
    penicillin fermentation, 34
intellectual property theft, 93, 95–99, 124, 206–207, 209
international comity, 73
International Trade Commission, 35, 123–24
ivermectin, 37

Janssen (pharmaceutical company), 32
Jenevein, Patrick, 211–12
Johnson & Johnson (pharmaceutical company)
    Doxil manufacturing issues, 145
    layoffs in United States, 85
    trademark challenges in China, 210

Kessler, David, 53
Kirk, Ted, 33, 75, 195, 203, 223

Kramss, Rich, 83–84
Krieger, Steve, 87, 90

labor cost difference in China. *See under* China
Langdale, Craig, 156, 225
lawfare, 211
Layoff Project, 84
Leavitt, Michael, 66
level playing field, 146
levetiracetam, 31
Levonest, 28–29
Levy, Paul, 150, 198
Lonngren, Thomas, 55
losartan potassium, 30, 39, 232
Lyons, Virginia, 131–32

Maine, Lucinda, 74, 186
McDonald's (food chain), 76, 110, 186
McKesson (healthcare company), 63, 150
McNeil, Kevin, 142, 154–55, 177–78, 185
medical devices
    China as largest exporter to United States, 123
    products imported from China, 122
    trade deficit with China in, 122
medicines as strategic asset, 222–23

Medtronic (company)
  business dealings in China,
    124–25
  whistleblower lawsuit against,
    186–87
MedWatch (online reporting
  program), 175
Mehta, Bharat, 10, 79, 204
melamine, 38, 64–66, 103
Melancon, Charles, 46
Mentholatum (pharmaceutical
  company), 233
Merck (pharmaceutical company),
  70, 74, 85, 92, 95
Mitchell, Jack, 56, 60
Mnuchin, Steven, 131

National Conference of State Legislatures, 132
national security, 10, 34, 188, 191,
  195–97, 200
Neath, Cheryl, 157
Nelson, David, 44, 46–47, 54
nevirapine, 29
New England Journal of Medicine,
  25, 173
Nielsen, Carl, 53
Northstar Rx (pharmaceutical
  company), 28–29
Novartis (pharmaceutical
  company), 37–38, 84
Novo Nordisk (pharmaceutical
  company), 93

Oakridge National Laboratory,
  193
Obrey, Lian, 89
Office of the US Trade Representative, 104, 130, 132, 201
Oldenhof, Chris, 45–46, 55
Overstreet, Brian, 176–77
oversulfated chondroitin sulfate,
  25–26, 139

Parkinson, Robert, 43–44, 46–47
patent protection, 56
Paulson, Henry, 133
Paxton, Mark, 149, 151, 157
penicillin
  availability in World War II,
    74, 221
  Bristol-Myers Squibb plant
    closure, 75
  Chinese cartel, 74–75
  pollution from manufacturing
    of, 75
People's Pharmacy (website), 57,
  178
permanent normal trade relations,
  58–59, 133–34
Pfizer (pharmaceutical company)
  antibiotic research program,
    86
  building 118 demolition, 87
  doxycycline country of origin,
    27

economic impact of layoffs, 85–86, 89

FDA inspection of Dalian plant, 144

history in Groton, Connecticut, 86

joint venture with Zhejiang Hisun, 92, 149

Lipitor loses patent protection, 88

penicillin supplier in World War II, 74

research investments in China, 86–87

Pharmaceutical Integrity Coalition, 142, 154–55, 177, 185

PharmaCompass (database), 10, 79, 192, 204

Philip Morris Asia (company), 130

Philip Morris International (company), 129–30

Pope, Larry, 76–77

Public Citizen (nonprofit group), 127, 129

rare earth elements, 10, 190, 201

Reagan, Ronald, 55

recycled cooking oil, 35

Remaking American Security (Adams), 190

Rhodia (company)
    aspirin manufacture in United States before plant closure, 35
    paracetamol plant in Europe before closure, 35

risperidone, 29

Sagent Pharmaceuticals, 30

Sanders, Bernie, 59

Sandoz (pharmaceutical company), 30, 56, 181

Sanofi (pharmaceutical company), 95

Saxon, Peter, 90, 152, 158, 226

Scott, John, 74, 89

Shea, Dennis, 142

Shlaes, David, 86

Shuanghui International (food company), 76–77, 129

Siemens (company), 207–208

Simpson, Tony, 89

60 Minutes (news program), 154

Slane, Daniel, 76

Smithfield Foods, 76–78, 129

South China Sea, 10, 189, 216

Stiglitz, Joseph, 133

St. Joseph aspirin, 34

St. Louis Children's Hospital, 21–23, 137, 174, 229

Strunce, David, 43, 47

Stupak, Bart, 43, 46–47, 49

superbugs, 86, 112, 202

supply chain complexity, 159

Tang Energy (company), 211–12
Taylor, John, 41, 60, 62
Teva Pharmaceutical Industries, 56, 150, 178–79, 192
Thayer School of Engineering at Dartmouth, 183
Thomson Reuters (company), 28, 30, 80, 92, 223
Tianjin, China, explosions in, 214–15
Tomes, Madris, 175, 177
toothpaste contamination, 63–64, 120
Tower, Stephen, 183
Trade Agreements Act, 191–93
trade deficit
    with China in medical devices, 121
    with China in pharmaceuticals, 119
    cumulative US with China, 133
tuberculosis medicines, 203

Unger, Barbara, 152, 175
Upjohn (pharmaceutical company), 54, 194
US Chamber of Commerce, 93–95, 109, 123, 208

US-China Bilateral Investment Treaty, 127, 212
US-China Economic and Security Review Commission, 76, 97, 108, 110, 126, 142, 149, 151, 205, 211
US-China Trade Relations Act of 2000, 60, 120

vancomycin, 33, 202, 223
Vattenfall (company), 129
Villax, Guy, 9, 37, 46, 189–90, 196

Wallach, Lori, 127–28
Wellbutrin XL 300, 178, 232
whistleblowers, 154–55, 186
Winckler, Susan, 156
Woodcock, Janet, 25, 41, 42, 48–50, 78, 174–75, 196
World Health Organization, 182–83
Wyeth (pharmaceutical company), 44

Zhejiang Hisun (pharmaceutical company), 92, 147–51, 203, 228